Beyond the Wall

Beyond the Wall

Memoirs of an East and West German Spy

WERNER STILLER

With Jefferson Adams

BRASSEY'S (US), INC.

A Division of Maxwell Macmillan, Inc.

Washington • New York • London • Oxford
Beijing • Frankfurt • São Paulo • Sydney • Tokyo • Toronto

Original title of the German edition—*Im Zentrum der Spionage.*
Copyright © 1986 v. Hase & Koehler Verlag, Mainz

English-language edition © 1992 Brassey's (US), Inc.
Edited and translated by Jefferson Adams.

Brassey's (US), Inc.

Editorial Offices
Brassey's (US), Inc.
8000 Westpark Drive
First Floor
McLean, Virginia 22102

Order Department
Brassey's Book Orders
c/o Macmillan Publishing Co.
100 Front Street, Box 500
Riverside, New Jersey 08075

Stiller, Werner, date.
  [Im Zentrum der Spionage, English]
  Beyond the wall: memoirs of an East and West German spy / Werner
Stiller with Jefferson Adams.
      p.   cm.—(Intelligence and national security series)
  Translation of: Im Zentrum der Spionage.
  Includes index.
  ISBN 0-02-881007-4
  1. Germany (East). Ministerium für Staatssicherheit.
2. Espionage, West German—Germany (East) 3. Intelligence service—
Germany (East) 4. Internal security—Germany (East) 5. Secret
service—Germany (East) 6. Stiller, Werner, date. I. Adams,
Jefferson. II. Title. III. Series: Pergamon-Brassey's intelligence
& national security library.
UB271.G352S7513   1992   91-39629
327.1′2′09431—dc20   CIP

10 9 8 7 6 5 4 3 2 1

PRINTED IN THE UNITED STATES OF AMERICA

Contents

Foreword by Roy Godson   vii

Preface to English Edition by Jefferson
    Adams   ix

Introduction   xv

Abbreviations   xvii

Organizational Charts   xviii

1 Prologue   1

2 A Youth in the "New Germany"   8

3 My Path to State Security   16

4 The Years of Apprenticeship   41

5 The Daily Grind   75

6 A Tour de Force   101

7 My New Goal   119

8 Face to Face with the BND   160

9 The People from Pullach   177

10 On the Powder Keg   200

11 The Final Escape   218

12 Epilogue   232

Index   235

Foreword

Brassey's Intelligence & National Security Library is intended to provide students, scholars, and national security experts with a select set of books on intelligence that make a unique or significant contribution to its study. Individual volumes are reviewed by an editorial advisory board consisting of scholars in the field and former senior intelligence officials from North America and Western Europe to ensure that the Library's selections are serious and important works.

However, with the Cold War over, why another book on intelligence by a former officer of a secret service that no longer exists? There are several good reasons.

First, it is a valuable exercise in stretching what might be called the democratic imagination. As de Tocqueville noted more than a century and a half ago, liberal democracies typically have a poor sense of history and, as a result, are inclined to see world events and international affairs through the lens of their current, more benign domestic political state.

From Werner Stiller's account and other materials that have come to light since the Berlin Wall fell, it is clear that the espionage and counterespionage efforts of the East Germans were not only sophisticated but massive in scale. *Beyond the Wall* is the first detailed insider account in English of East German operations at home and abroad. Publishing Stiller's memoirs is a useful reminder of what in fact is possible when a state and its leaders are determined to see everyone, including its own people, as potential enemies.

Second, *Beyond the Wall* is an excellent account of the reality and complexities of recruiting and handling *human* agents. For those interested in understanding the ways and basic elements of intelligence, Stiller's memoirs, like *Mole* by former CIA operative William Hood, serve as an outstanding primer on the topic of human intelligence collection.

Third, *Beyond the Wall* is a valuable resource for the student and scholar of intelligence. For too long, the subject of intelligence was dominated by writings partisan or exposé-like in nature. For those interested in a balanced and objective assessment of the role of intelligence in the statecraft of nations, the material from which one could reliably draw was thin. Gradually, progressively, this is changing. And Stiller's account of his recruitment, training and experiences as an officer—a successful officer— of the Ministry of State Security, or MfS, is a substantial addition to the list of titles and archival material that has made the serious study of intelligence possible.

More exactly, this book offers those interested in the subject of intelligence a solid, comparative perspective to review the inner workings of one of history's more successful secret services. An integral part of a totalitarian state, the MfS, as Stiller shows, was also (perhaps surprisingly so) bound up and governed to a large extent by the rules and mores typical of a large bureaucratic organization. Sorting out what was unique about the secret service of the late East Germany from what it shared with its rival intelligence organization in the West is no small step in advancing the field of intelligence studies.

Finally, Stiller's account of his life as an intelligence officer is also a very good read—indeed, it was a best seller when it was first published in Germany. *Beyond the Wall,* updated since the reunification of Germany, is a book to be learned from, and enjoyed.

ROY GODSON

General Editor
Brassey's Intelligence & National Security Library

Preface to English Edition

For forty years after the Second World War, Germany existed as a divided country. A democratic government—the Federal Republic of Germany (FRG)—had been established in the West, whereas communist control of the East had resulted in the founding of the German Democratic Republic (GDR). In nearly all fields, the policies pursued by these two governments differed in major respects. Yet it was in matters of intelligence and state security that many of the most striking contrasts emerged. In the FRG, as in other Western democracies, the responsibility for domestic surveillance and foreign intelligence fell to two separate institutions and remained subject to ultimate parliamentary control. The GDR, on the other hand, followed the model of the Soviet KGB and created a monolithic system of espionage and internal control under the direction of a ruling party elite.

The Ministry of State Security (MfS) was established four months after the GDR's founding in October 1949. Although the precise duties and jurisdiction of the MfS were never spelled out in any public document, no one ever doubted its prime function as the "sword and shield" of the ruling Socialist Unity Party (SED). When the MfS was dissolved in the fall of 1989, it included over 85,000 full-time personnel and more than 500,000 part-time agents and informers. For a state with a total population of approximately 17 million persons, that meant an internal web of extraordinary density. In addition, because of the overwhelming presence of agents recruited and placed by the MfS, the FRG counted as one of the most heavily penetrated Western countries.

The intense hatred felt for these state security officials—or "Stasis" as they were commonly nicknamed—became dramatically evident during the events leading to the collapse of the GDR. In the fall of 1989, as hundreds of thousands of demonstrators marched through the streets of Leipzig, Dresden, and other cities and towns, no louder or more fervent chants could be heard than "Stasis out" and "Put the Stasis to work." Indeed, when various citizens' groups decided to seize control of local MfS offices, this "peaceful" revolution nearly lost its nonviolent character. At one point, an angry crowd even stormed the heavily fortified headquarters complex in East Berlin and managed to inflict considerable damage.

Yet prior to these unprecedented occurrences, few persons outside the two Germanys knew of the MfS's existence. Journalists rarely dealt with the subject, while most academics, despite a burgeoning interest in the GDR, gave the topic a wide berth. Occasionally a fictional work took up the theme, but in the most famous instance—*The Spy Who Came in from the Cold* by John le Carré—the author's antipathy toward his former employer, the British secret service, largely obscured the actual workings of its East German counterpart. (Kim Philby called the whole plot "basically implausible" to anyone with a real knowledge of the business.) In the meantime, once German unification was accomplished in 1990, an emotionally charged debate began concerning former GDR citizens and officials suspected of MfS complicity. As a result, some new misconceptions about the nature of the organization started to circulate.

Fortunately, Werner Stiller has given us an exceptionally insightful and absorbing account of his experiences as an MfS case officer. Born in a small village in Saxony, he had become a party enthusiast during his early school years. After later enrolling as a physics student at the University of Leipzig and joining the SED, Stiller responded favorably to his initial approach by the MfS. His subsequent rise in the organization was rapid. He first worked as a part-time agent at the university before being assigned to the staff of the GDR Physics Society in East Berlin. A year later, in August 1972, the real breakthrough in his career occurred—a position in the Chief Intelligence Directorate (*Hauptverwaltung Aufklärung;* HVA) or foreign intelligence branch of the MfS. Specifically, he was given the rank of lieutenant and assigned to the nuclear physics department within the so-called Sector of Science and Technology.

Stiller performed brilliantly in this capacity. Besides creating a domestic network of roughly thirty persons, he succeeded in placing several important agents in the West. This was well above the norm of his colleagues and helped him gain the special confidence of his superiors. On this basis alone, his account merits attention. Yet this is also the story of his gradual disillusionment with the ruling communist regime and decision to work clandestinely for the Federal Intelligence Service (*Bundesnachrichtendienst;* BND) of West Germany. Seeing how Stiller then managed to function as a double agent in the GDR not only heightens the suspense of his narrative but vividly juxtaposes the aims and operational procedures of the two intelligence organizations.

Stiller's career corresponded to a critical period in the history of the MfS. When the Berlin Wall was erected in 1961—much to the displeasure of the HVA—new ways to dispatch agents over the West German border had to be found. During the 1970s, however, the HVA was confronted by an even more serious setback. With the outbreak of terrorist activity in the FRG, West German authorities began to exercise far greater vigilance at all border crossings. For the HVA, that meant abandoning every route leading directly into the FRG and relying on more costly and cumbersome procedures involving a third country. To compound matters further, this was also the era of détente, as symbolized by the Basic Treaty of 1972 between the GDR and the FRG. Such a relaxation of tensions greatly increased the possibilities for new Western recruitments, yet the HVA often found itself hamstrung by the revised travel restrictions. Nevertheless, as Stiller's experiences show, the pressure from above produce results only intensified.

Ostensibly, Stiller was working in foreign intelligence operations and hoping to be stationed in the West. From the very outset, however, his duties were inextricably tied to the domestic scene of the GDR. By maintaining regular contact with local MfS officials, he sought to build a solid home base, which would then be utilized for activities abroad. Significantly, the greatest achievement for an HVA officer consisted not in the recruitment of a Western citizen but rather in the resettlement of a childless married couple who had been previously trained in the GDR. In addition, as Stiller points out, Erich Mielke, the long-serving chief of the MfS, viewed the personnel of the HVA with a pronounced suspicion. In part, it derived from a personal mistrust of its renowned head, Markus Wolf, but equally important was Mielke's fear that a dangerous elitism would develop without a constant reminder of the "realities" of the GDR. Foreign operations, in other words, only added to the already dense layers of domestic surveillance.

What, then, are the larger lessons to be drawn from this book? Personal ambitions and bureaucratic rivalries are bound to arise in any large organization. Yet as Stiller makes very clear, the massive and relentless infusion of communist ideology into nearly all aspects of the MfS only exacerbated these tendencies. Contrary to a widespread impression, the organization operated with severe handicaps. Besides the glaring hypocrisy between word and deed, there were excessive internal regulations and a bloated administrative apparatus. Like most totalitarian institutions, it could never be held to Western standards of efficient management.

At the same time, however, it would be an error to minimize the many remarkable successes scored by the MfS. Indeed, with the unification of Germany came revelations indicating an even greater high-level penetration of the FRG than previously believed. In light of West Germany's key strategic position in Europe, one can easily understand why the KGB prized the espionage skills of the MfS. Nor were East German efforts confined merely to Europe. By overseeing the development of the security forces in such states as Angola, Mozambique, Libya, Ethiopia, and Nicaragua, the MfS had established a very prominent role in the non-Western world.

What ultimately made the MfS such an imposing adversary was its full-scale utilization of human intelligence. From the very beginning, no task had a higher priority than assembling personal dossiers on both GDR citizens and Western visitors. Once assigned a particular individual, an intelligence officer would carefully sift through the collected information in order to find a psychological opening and then apply the appropriate stratagem from a vast catalogue of developed techniques. That Stiller—a specialist in nuclear physics—had to rely primarily on a correct assessment of human motivations to fulfill his assignments only underscores the fundamental nature of his work. Certainly for anyone interested in the fascinating, multidimensional world of human intelligence, a more instructive volume would be difficult to find.

A few remarks should also be made about this edition. When the book first appeared in 1986, Stiller was addressing a predominantly German audience. As editor, I have adapted his account for a non-German public. That meant not only deleting those specific references that seemed superfluous to the story but also adding an occasional word or phrase to clarify a situation that would have been self-evident to a German. Stiller followed the East German practice of distinguishing between West Berlin and Berlin (the capital of the GDR); I have used the Western designation of East Berlin whenever appropriate. In another instance, since the city's original name of Chemnitz was not restored until after the GDR's collapse, all references to Karl-Marx-Stadt have been retained.

The problems of translation presented many more difficult decisions. Without resorting to a series of contrived American colloquialisms, I have attempted to convey the flavor of the original dialogue as accurately as possible. I have also tried to render the GDR's ponderous official terminology in a lucid manner. If asked to name the decision made with greatest reluctance, I would unhesitatingly answer the translation of "konspirative Wohnung," or "KW," as safe house. This phrase—literally "conspiratorial dwelling"—was the standard term employed by the MfS and conveys its aggressive intentions with particular succinctness. Yet for the sake of clarity, it seemed better to stay with what is generally considered its English equivalent.

As a further guide to understanding the labyrinthine structure of the MfS and the HVA, two organizational charts have been included. They are based on information that became available after the dissolution of the GDR.

JEFFERSON ADAMS

Professor of History
Sarah Lawrence College
Bronxville, New York

Introduction

The idea of recording my experiences as an MfS officer first occurred to me while still living in the GDR. Once I had defected to the FRG in 1979, numerous persons expressed their words of encouragement for this project.

In the following pages, I have avoided a detailed account of my own painful disillusionment with the East German communist regime. Also, I have not felt compelled to make any individual accusations. Rather my purpose is to help the Western reader better understand the main aims and operational methods of this vast state security system. Especially in the later years of détente with the West, the GDR leadership prized the efforts of the MfS more than ever. As Erich Honecker himself phrased it, "dispatching socialist scouts into the enemy camp" formed "a dangerous but important element of party work at the very front line of the class struggle."

I should also point out the stark contrast between the intelligence organizations of the two Germanys—the communist East and the democratic West. During my seven-year career, I saw how the MfS, like the KGB, never hesitated to exploit a human weakness whenever its interest was at stake. The BND, on the other hand, always insisted that in a tight situation my personal safety take precedence over any operational success.

Throughout this book, I have endeavored to stay as faithful to actual occurrences as possible. Occasionally certain details had to be withheld for reasons of governmental security. To protect those persons still close to me, I have also had to alter a few of the geographic locations as well as several real names and codenames. In any event, such instances are rare, and everything took place essentially as described. Since a number of these cases eventually came to trial in the FRG, anyone seeking further corroboration can consult the court transcripts.

Abbreviations

BND   (Bundesnachrichtendienst)—Federal Intelligence Service

CDU   (Christlich-Demokratische Union)—Christian Democratic Union

GDR   (Deutsche Demokratische Republik)—German Democratic Republic

DKP   (Deutsche Kommunistische Partei)—German Communist Party

FDJ   (Freie Deutsche Jugend)—Free German Youth

FRG   (Bundesrepublik Deutschland)—Federal Republic of Germany

GST   (Gesellschaft für Sport und Technik)—Society for Sport and Technology

HVA   (Hauptverwaltung Aufklärung)—Chief Intelligence Directorate

MfS   (Ministerium für Staatssicherheit)—Ministry of State Security

NVA   (Nationale Volksarmee)—National People's Army

OVW   (Objektverwaltung Wismut)—Wismut Installation Authority

SED   (Sozialistische Einheitspartei Deutschlands)—Socialist Unity Party

MINISTRY OF STATE SECURITY (MfS) (1989)

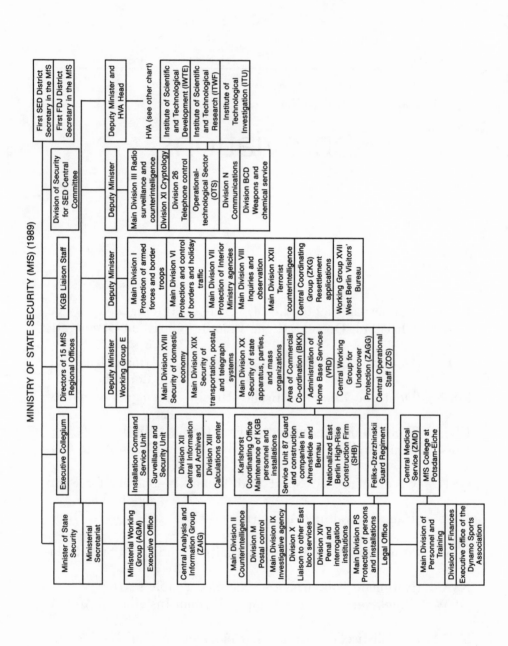

CHIEF INTELLIGENCE DIRECTORATE (HVA)
(1989)

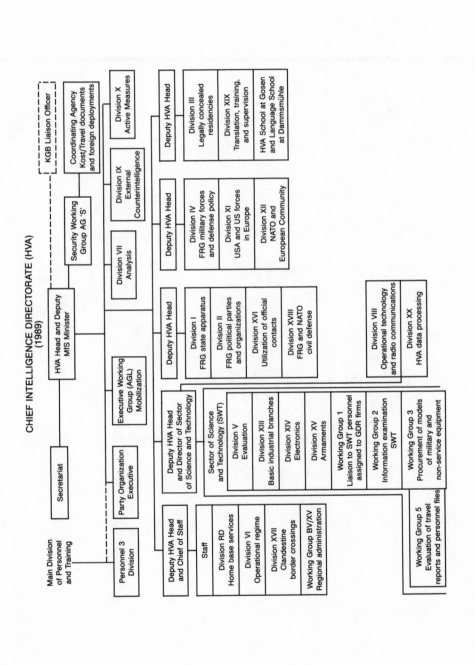

Beyond the Wall

1

Prologue

1

It was a final farewell. In the early morning of January 18, 1979, I left the drab East Berlin apartment house that had been home for me and my family for the past four years.

Some light snow had fallen during the night. Under the harsh neon lights, the fresh crystals glistened on the banks of old snow that lay on the sides of the street. It was bitter cold. As the door closed behind me, I tried to suppress all thoughts about my family and the unlikelyhood of ever being reunited. Despite my longstanding alienation from them, it was not easy.

As the snow crunched underfoot, I recalled the urgent words of warning addressed to me the previous September in Helsinki: "You are in great danger! You must get out now!" In truth, I had expected my first meeting with the West German Federal Intelligence Service (BND) in a neutral country to have turned out somewhat differently. By then, having already conveyed a wealth of valuable information taken from the East German Ministry of State Security (MfS), I knew my authenticity was no longer in doubt. Indeed, my intention had been to acquire some additional material.

Nevertheless the BND official had remained adamant. "Since your cover could be blown at any moment, we can't take the risk anymore and must bring you out. That's definite."

For a long time, I had merely ignored the fact that this moment would eventually come. Now, despite the comfortably warm hotel room, I felt shivers run down my spine. "When?" I asked apprehensively.

"If you were the only one involved, we could do it right now. But since there are others, it will take some planning. We think that 'Day X' will occur in mid-December, but you must avoid taking any more risks."

Nevertheless, a mishap had occurred in the meantime, necessitating a further postponement. Although the next four weeks had seen some added complications, the day of escape had finally arrived, and I was resolved to go. In spite of my last instructions from the BND advising me to think only of my own safety, I was equally determined to take along as much confidential MfS material as possible.

The brisk morning air helped to lessen my apprehension. Both of my cars—a recently acquired Lada 1300, the status symbol of the East German upper middle class, and a brand-new Wartburg, which was used for official duties—stood in the parking lot. The lock of the Wartburg was frozen, but the failure of my earlier escape attempt had taught me to allow extra time for unexpected occurrences. After using my cigarette lighter to release the lock, I got in the car and turned the ignition several times to bring the two-stroke engine to life.

I then paused to check whether anything essential had been forgotten. My official identity card was bound as always by a leather band to the left inside pocket of my jacket. Easily the most cherished possession of an MfS employee, this small rectangular card bearing a photograph and a signature could instantly open nearly any door in the GDR. My other pocket contained the official papers vital for the last stage of my escape. Specifically, they permitted Comrade First Lieutenant Werner Stiller to be operationally active in the regions of Halle and Dresden on January 18 and 19.

I next took the heavy, loaded pistol from under my left shoulder and placed it in my briefcase. Known in the MfS as the "dispatcher," this Hungarian-made type AP9 would be my last resort in an emergency situation. Already in my briefcase were two items that had been prepared by the BND experts: a key to the safe of my divisional head and, most important of all, a standard blue-covered GDR passport.

As everything seemed in order, I put the car in gear and proceeded past the MfS apartment block for the last time. Only a single light was burning; probably one of my neighbors assigned to a border checkpoint had an early shift again. Since I did not want to be in Halle until the following morning, there was no need to rush. Besides having grown up in the region, I had often returned to Halle because of meetings with several of my domestic agents. What I now needed, however, were two items crucial for my escape: a train ticket to Hanover and a yellow entry-and-exit permit that had to accompany my passport.

2

Until only recently, I had possessed the ideal document for crossing the border to the West. A red diplomatic passport, which required no supplementary papers, had been issued in my name just prior to the Finland trip. By stressing the "omnipresence of state enemies" abroad and the need for a better cover, I had secured the approval of the deputy head of my division, First Lieutenant Christian Streubel. After the trip, I ignored the rule stipulating its prompt return to my departmental head, Peter Bertag, and kept it hidden in a desk drawer. In my pessimistic moods, there was a feeling of reassurance merely in knowing that it had been stamped "multiple exits permitted until December 31, 1979" and "valid for all countries." I would have encountered no difficulty making a trip to West Berlin, Munich, or Vienna.

In late December 1978, as I was routinely preparing for the next MfS party conference, Bertag unexpectedly knocked at my office door. Approaching my desk and raising his eyebrows, predictably an ominous sign, he asked, sounding somewhat astonished: "Since when have you been making secret trips to West Berlin?"

Fortunately my recent promotion to first divisional party secretary allowed me to remain seated, for otherwise he would have surely detected the sudden weakness in my knees. With no line of retreat available to me, I imagined that my darkest fears of a military tribunal and death by firing squad would soon be realized. Yet strangely the utter bleakness of my predicament helped me regain a more assertive stance.

"Why?" I replied. "Would you like to come?"

"Not really, but where is your diplomatic passport?"

I had long anticipated this question. "Naturally, with the divisional head."

"But it isn't there!"

"It must be there." Then, as if to verify my statement, I started leafing through the bulky files in my desk. Careful that my search was neither too brief to be obvious nor too extensive to make Bertag impatient, I found the missing passport in some of my papers. Bertag accepted my feigned embarrassment and apology as genuine, and all I received was a disapproving look. Following an appropriate pause, I found some pretext to approach my divisional head, whose good mood and lack of suspicion helped dispel my lingering anxiety. As I was leaving, Bertag entered to present the passport to my divisional head. "Such sloppy behavior," he called out to me, but the normally friendly tone had returned to his voice.

After breathing a sigh of relief, I suddenly realized that my escape plan was endangered. Although a fall-back variation had been devised, I lacked the entry-and-exit permit required at the GDR border crossing. A forged permit had been prepared by the BND for the original escape, but the date had expired and the time was too short to obtain another one. In addition, since the disaster of "Day X," my contact with the BND had become much less frequent, thus leaving me to my own devices. This explained why I was now on my way to Halle.

3

Despite icy and foggy weather, I arrived in the city punctually at 8:00 A.M. En route, I had reviewed my plan in detail, and all the pieces seemed to fit together perfectly. Nevertheless, when I went to the main train station and requested a second-class ticket to Hamburg via Magdeburg and Hanover, the elderly female clerk looked at me so suspiciously that my normal self-confidence as a feared MfS officer suddenly vanished. Realizing my mistake, I quickly added, "A round trip ticket."

"What else would it be?" she answered.

I forced a smile at this feeble joke. "Are you traveling on official business?" she asked.

"Yes."

"Where is your foreign currency authorization receipt?"

How, I thought to myself, could I have forgotten that the GDR railroad issued tickets to the West only upon presentation of this paper. In fact, the BND had forged one for my use, but it lay behind in my East Berlin safe house.

"Where then do you work?" she inquired.

"At the Academy of Sciences."

When she insisted that this authorization form must have been issued, I tried to play innocent. "Nobody ever told me that."

Her request to see my passport further diminished my chances of obtaining a ticket. I also did not want to have my cover blown. "Since my trip received a late authorization, I won't be getting it until this afternoon." My answer only contributed to her growing mistrust.

To my added misfortune, I noticed a railroad policeman stationed at the door separating the ticket booth from the waiting room. Luckily an impatient West German standing directly behind me saved the day. "Hurry up," he said, "my train's about to leave!" I muttered something about "collect" and "come back" and beat a hasty retreat.

Without either a ticket or a complete set of papers, I was now in a real quandary. On the way back to the car, however, a new sign—"Travel Agency of the German Democratic Republic"—caught my eye. Glancing over several placards in the window promoting skiing holidays in the High Tatra, I spotted a special counter for international train tickets. On duty was a quite young, well-dressed, but not very attractive woman. Yet the expression on her face left no doubt at all that she wanted to be noticed. Approaching the ticket counter somewhat absentmindedly, I pretended to be abruptly startled by her presence. I then gazed deeply into her eyes and gave her a pleasant smile.

"A second-class round trip ticket to Hamburg via Magdeburg and Hanover," I said calmly, placing my passport on the counter.

Completely disconcerted by my rapt attention, she ignored the passport and reached for the ticket book. With her pen nervously shaking in her hand, she replied, "Ninety-seven marks and sixty pfennige."

"I'll be back later for the seat reservation." At least I had recovered a measure of self-confidence, and the necessary ticket was in my possession.

Halle itself, the regional capital of East Germany's main industrial area, has few sights worth seeing. One landmark, according to GDR standards, is the so-called Hochstrasse. Beginning among the small dirty courtyards in the center of town, this long thoroughfare flanks the old Francke Foundation, which then housed a complex of university institutes. After crossing the Saale River, once beloved by poets but now a severely polluted industrial waterway, the street finally terminated in the socialist housing development called "Halle New Town." This product of the GDR's much heralded "residential culture" further added to the dreariness of the landscape. In fact, according to the reports of local MfS officials, these huge buildings intended for the benefit of the working class had proved to be a breeding ground for divorces, suicides, and criminal activities.

Since the mentality of the MfS employees in Halle was well known to me as a native of the region, I had specifically chosen this office as part of my plan. By relying on their goodwill and not appearing as a representative of the almighty East Berlin headquarters, I also knew that my chances of success would be much greater. Despite recognizing me from many previous visits, the smartly uniformed sergeant at the door examined my identity card and official papers in his unfailingly punctilious manner.

Comrade First Lieutenant Klaus Tietz, who oversaw the infiltration of the West German security forces, was the reason for my visit. As fellow classmates at the HVA school in Belzig, Tietz and I had pledged one evening during a drinking session to help one another whenever possible. Because we were both due to return to Belzig the following week for some additional training, this seemed an opportune moment to enlist his assistance in obtaining the vital entry-and-exit permit.

As if by design, when the elevator unexpectedly stopped at the second floor, it was Tietz who opened the door. He could not have known my great relief at having found him on duty and not out sick or away on vacation.

After we had cordially greeted one another, I began my story. "Klaus, you must help me. Just imagine, I wanted to send an agent over to the West today, but the stupid guy used his real name on the exit permit. He's supposed to meet his informant tomorrow, and I don't know how to get him to Bonn. I need a new exit permit."

It was easier than I had anticipated. Still feeling proud about his recent promotion to departmental head, Tietz was anxious to demonstrate his new authority. We first had a coffee together and talked about old times. He then approved the issuance of a blank permit without even checking with East Berlin. To my knowledge, once the news of my defection became known, Tietz did not suffer any severe repercussions for his action. There were simply too many other officials in the main headquarters more strongly implicated.

With the train ticket and exit permit now in my pocket, it was merely a matter of waiting until 7:00 P.M., when the real adventure would begin. I decided to take advantage of the extra time to have a substantial lunch in a special HO restaurant* in Halle. Although the image of a condemned man eating a hearty last meal flashed in my mind, I had the stronger feeling that a higher power would ultimately determine my fate.

That, however, did not deter me from taking the precaution of returning to East Berlin via a different route. To be seen by a colleague in a place contrary to my official orders could well have been fatal. In the late afternoon, I arrived at my safe house in the Marienburger Strasse. This studio apartment—known officially under the codename "fortress"—had originally served as the place to meet my MfS agents. Over the last two years, however, it had turned into a fortress of a quite different sort. My proposal to use this apartment as the base for my BND activities had been rejected at first by the West German officials. Nevertheless, I eventually overcame their objections to what was an obvious breach of rules, and the apartment became a repository for my technical equipment and for photographs of important MfS documents. It was also here that I had received radio messages from Pullach† and met with my BND contact man.

As the final hour approached, I no longer felt any fear or excitement. In fact, simply for amusement, I had taken the short-wave radio from its hiding place above the kitchen ceiling and turned the dial automatically to the BND frequency. Precisely at 5:00 P.M., the familiar rise and fall of the Pullach signal came over the air, followed by the routine announcement of messages. To my complete surprise, I heard my own secret number being called out. Barely retrieving pencil and paper in time, I began to write down the coded message.

What, I wondered, was happening now? With mounting tension, I managed to decipher the message without relying on the usual magnifying glass and codestrip. The first words told me all I needed to know: Pullach felt worried and was therefore sending new exit papers dated for the following Monday. Unfortunately, I was in no position to wait for these

---

* The Commercial Organization (*Handelsorganisation*, or HO) was a series of state-owned enterprises including restaurants, grocery stores, and retail shops. All transactions required Western currency.
† A village five miles south of Munich, Pullach has been the headquarters site of the BND since its establishment in 1956.

skillfully forged documents to arrive. Not only had I solved the problem myself today in Halle, but to delay any further would jeopardize the whole plan. In any event, given the dangers that still lay ahead, I appreciated the expression of good luck at the end of the message.

I had one hour left. Since the safe house would be immediately searched afterward by the MfS, I placed everything that might reveal the scope of my activities for the BND in the burning stove. After making another cup of coffee, I sat down and contemplated my next set of moves. My plan, I concluded, would just have to work.

Then, without any conscious effort on my part, I started thinking about my own past and its connection to the present moment. How could a once totally committed official of the Free German Youth (FDJ) have ended up as a Western agent? When did this gradual process begin that had brought me ultimately to the other side?

2

A Youth in the "New Germany"

I spent my early childhood in the small village of Wessmar, about twenty miles west of Leipzig. My mother, a Silesian immigrant and a divorcée, faced considerable difficulty feeding me and my two older sisters during the postwar years. Since I had known nothing else, this hardship did not seem unusual. An elderly neighbor told me about better times in the past that had ended in catastrophe, but her stories sounded just like the fairy tales I had been reading.

After my mother got a job in the nearby Leuna Works,* our standard of living gradually improved. I was sent to the factory kindergarten, where I received my first "negative" political lesson. After overhearing the teachers talk about the Soviet occupation forces and utter what seemed to be unfavorable references to "Ivan," I began to make an automatic association of the name with the nationality. An embarrassing incident happened the following year in my Russian class when I unhesitatingly translated the

---

* A leading chemical concern before the war, the Leuna Works had been nationalized by the GDR as a "publicly owned enterprise." At this time, it employed approximately 28,000 persons.

name Ivan as "the Russian." By contrast, my first knowledge of the West occurred at the age of five when a Christmas parcel came containing things I had never known existed: bananas, chocolate, and chewing gum.

One summer day at noon, my mother suddenly arrived on a borrowed bicycle to take me home from kindergarten. Large crowds, even more numerous than during the previous month, had gathered in front of the Leuna Works. Although I had twice been allowed to join these demonstrations, this time—to my puzzlement—my mother rushed me by as quickly as possible. Besides ignoring my request to have a closer look, she then made a wide detour to avoid the Russian tanks stationed in the streets of Merseburg. Once back home, she treated all my questions in a nonresponsive or evasive manner. That was my experience of the famous uprising of June 17, 1953.*

We moved to Leuna when I started school. Even though all first-year pupils were required to join the Communist youth group called the "Young Pioneers," it had very little effect on our lives, which were still devoted primarily to play. The following year, however, my decision to take part in religious instruction met with the clear disapproval of my Pioneer leader. When I was later expelled from the religion class for having kissed a girl, my leader mistakenly interpreted the incident as an ideological action on my part. After praising me effusively, she even appointed me chairman of the group council.

My actual interest in sociopolitical activities began a short while later under her successor, whose well-developed feminine charm played a not inconsiderable role. Indeed, my eagerness extended to participation in various "progressive" activities such as collecting used items for resale, group socializing in the afternoon, and mocking the few remaining churchgoers. Of particular significance was a "friendship meeting" arranged with a group of Soviet Pioneers. Besides my avid interest in the Soviet space program ever since the launching of "Sputnik" in the fall of 1957, I had been deeply impressed by various books that recounted how heroic Russian soldiers selflessly prevailed over "White Guard intruders," "fascist mercenaries," and American spies.   •

Nothing, it seemed, could shake my faith in the inevitable triumph of socialism, not even the defections to the West by an occasional fellow pupil or by the Pioneer leader whom I had so worshiped from afar. By my final year, I had become vice chairman of the "Friendship Council," the second-highest Pioneer rank in the elementary school. In this capacity, I felt determined to make a very serious occasion out of the routine

---

* The June 17, 1953, uprising marked the first full-scale revolt against Soviet rule in Eastern Europe. Because of the failure of the GDR's own security forces, armed Soviet troops were used to subdue the protesters.

"Dedication to Youth" ceremony, roughly the atheistic equivalent of confirmation. When I announced that anyone not taking part in the ceremony would be shot, a great uproar ensued involving worried parents, disgruntled teachers, and even the town clergyman. A letter from the school to my mother arrived a week after my act of revolutionary commitment. "Your teacher has had enough of you," she simply told me. "He is sending you on to high school."

The following fall I began to attend the Polytechnic High School in nearby Merseburg. To mark the opening of the year, all the students from the ninth to twelfth grades formed a square around the flagpole in the center of the school courtyard. After several introductions, the flag of the Free German Youth (FDJ)* was raised and a speech made about learning for the sake of socialism. While the returning students were allowed to proceed to their classes, the new ones were introduced to Arthur Schmidt, the party secretary who also taught civics. The fact that his authority superseded that of all other school officials was only added evidence of the party's dominant role and the suppression of the institution's earlier humanistic tradition.

It was not just Schmidt's somber appearance but, as I later discovered, also his character that made him seem so well suited for a medieval court of inquisition. In fact, before his appointment at the school, he had been a warden at the notorious "Red Ox" prison in Halle. Still nostalgic about his tenure there, he kept a sharp lookout for the "enemy in our midst" with his hooded hawk's eyes. We called him "Jailhouse Schmidt."

Otherwise we regarded our teachers very highly and tended to believe all their observations about world affairs. My class had a special affection for our own teacher, who managed to make not only mathematics and physics but also the FDJ afternoons and the "pre-military training" quite palatable. For me he also figured as an undisputed political authority and provided the impetus to examine the teachings of Marx, Engels, and Lenin. Soon known as an expert on their works, I was appointed FDJ class secretary and later propaganda secretary for the entire school.

In addition to meeting the requirements of a normal high school diploma, we also had to complete a course of studies in vocational training. Although my daily activities in this area could hardly be called "training" or "work," it did give me an interesting opportunity to converse with factory workers about current political issues. Immediately after breakfast, my foreman would normally ask me to talk about a subject of my choosing. While the two of us pretended to work by moving various tools from one hand to the

* Although established in the immediate postwar period as a nonpartisan, non-sectarian youth movement, the Free German Youth soon came under the strict control of the SED. Membership in the FDJ was designed for young persons between the ages of fourteen and twenty-five.

other, he would listen to my discourse on such subjects as the role of unions in the proletarian revolution, the question of power in a dictatorship of the proletariat, and the position of the worker in West Germany. Next he would pose some shrewd and insightful questions drawing upon his own practical experience and sound understanding of people. Often he involved the entire workshop in these rambling discussions. Yet, despite the fact that I had received a more honest firsthand picture of the East German working class, my own opinions remained steadfast.

Considering ourselves "old hands" at the beginning of the tenth year, we began to scrutinize the girls in the entering class. Heading my candidate list were Christina, the pretty but reactionary daughter of a bankrupt liquor manufacturer, and Ilona, a strapping FDJ member whose father was an honest and upright factory foreman. My official duties made it easy to approach both of them in the following weeks.

That I eventually chose the "progressive" Ilona was due solely to a series of logical calculations. After discovering that love was fun, we realized that the weekend FDJ seminars held at youth hostels offered many opportunities for love and were therefore fun. Since these seminars were organized by the FDJ, the party, and the state, those were fun as well.

As I approached the end of my eleventh year of school, the choice of a career became a pressing matter. A long talk with my class teacher helped me decide on the field of pure science. Convinced that Leipzig was the only place worth considering, I had no difficulty gaining acceptance to Karl-Marx University. Nevertheless, I first had to face a medical examination for active military duty. Rumors were then circulating that many high school graduates would soon be donning the uniform of the National People's Army (NVA) for an eighteen-month stint, making me feel quite apprehensive. However ardent my devotion to the "socialist homeland," the mere thought of drumbeating and goosestepping had always been repugnant. Fortunately, the combination of a planned major in theoretical physics and my own mechanical ineptitude convinced the draft board to give me a deferment until the conclusion of my university studies. By that time, however, it seemed beside the point, for I was firmly in the employment of the MfS.

2

In late August 1966, I joined approximately 2,000 other new students for the opening ceremonies. After the university rector gave a short and dignified speech, the first secretary of the local SED made a bombastic appeal and specifically invoked Walter Ulbricht as the greatest living German revolutionary. With those words, a gleam of approval seemed to appear on the huge photograph of the GDR leader in the background. When the student next to me began to yawn irreverently, I could not help grinning at him in return.

We agreed to meet afterward for a beer and were soon joined by several other students from the physics faculty. To mark my first university convocation, my mother had sent me money to buy a new FDJ blue shirt, but I was easily persuaded by my comrades that the funds were better spent on another round or two of beer. Despite being the only person with a well-developed "GDR-consciousness," I found the group congenial and joined in the merriment.

Afterward, my new friend from the opening ceremony accompanied me back to the railway station. A native Leipziger, he pointed out the former brothel where Walter Ulbricht had reputedly lived before the war. In fact, not long after Ulbricht's death, a high-ranking MfS officer personally confirmed the fact that the East German leader had lived in this establishment for a considerable period during the early 1930s.

A brief exposure to the political outlook of my fellow students made me understand why I had been immediately appointed FDJ secretary of my entering physics class. In truth, I gained no real pleasure from this office and could see the malicious smirk that it provoked on the faces of my colleagues. Later, I discovered that their attitude merely reflected the negative feelings toward the political system held by East German students in general. In our seminar group, the most enthusiastic activist turned out to be the one non-FDJ member. In reality, only by pretending to be a loyal GDR citizen—masterfully in this case—could he pursue his studies unhindered and then later immigrate to West Germany.

As was customary, the first three weeks of the fall semester were concerned with agriculture rather than physics. Yet upon hearing that we were to be sent to the countryside to help the farmers' cooperatives with the potato harvest, most of us suddenly developed acute symptoms of illness. A few students even found clever ways to become physically incapacitated. The next required program, intended as an introduction to university life, was an intensive five-day-long "red-light therapy." It amounted to a series of mediocre political lectures that reiterated everything that we had already heard in our high school civics classes.

In July 1967, I submitted my formal membership application to the SED. Beforehand my fellow students had argued with me at length, contending that this step should be taken only as a last resort. Besides, they said, a new party member almost automatically became an informer for the MfS. Since I was determined to realize a long-cherished dream, their arguments had no real effect on me. I felt completely convinced that the party was doing the right thing for the people, albeit not always in the most skillful manner.

In addition, my ranking FDJ position made me vulnerable to the pressure of the party secretary of the Physics Institute. "We have to win the power struggle this year at the university," he told me. "You're a worker's son. You belong to us." My resolve to join the SED merely increased.

At my first meeting as a party member, I was impressed by the candid and constructive airing of various problems at the institute. Moreover, a genuine proletarian democracy seemed to prevail as well. A porter, for example, was not only sitting next to a professor, but conversing with him on a first-name basis. Indeed, to hear a comment of mine acknowledged by the director of the institute made me feel even more convinced of the wisdom of my choice.

Only much later did I realize that this candor was merely a facade and that nothing had been left to chance. The catchphrases of the party were repeatedly used to spin complex webs of intrigue and to further personal ambitions. When a senior assistant eulogized the policies of the SED, his sole purpose was to help secure his promotion to assistant professor. When a full professor sought the approval of a particular research topic, his aim in most cases was to obtain permission for official travel to the West. In many other instances, seemingly objective arguments were used merely to further one's own career by raising doubts about a rival's political trustworthiness.

Shortly afterward, I met a chemistry student named Irma who provided the first serious challenge to my strong party loyalty. The daughter of an important SED official, she not only had her own room but could recount many complicated political machinations, replete with spicy details. Needless to say, few party officials emerged in a favorable light. While no erotic relationship existed between us—her own preference was Oriental guest students—we had full and open discussions. In her room, I could also read *Der Spiegel* on a regular basis. It too caused me to look at many of my "absolute truths" with much greater ambivalence.

One day Irma intimated that several comrades had paid a visit and asked that she put her desire for Orientals in the service of the state. A refusal, she was warned, would result in the termination of her studies at the university. Realizing that the MfS probably stood behind this request, I decided to avoid seeing her for the time being. When our relationship eventually resumed, it was never quite the same, for, as I later discovered, she had indeed placed her strong sexual drive at the disposal of the Stasis.

At the beginning of my second year, we faced not the relatively harmless prospect of another potato harvest but rather ten days of pre-military training at a camp in Thuringia belonging to the "Society for Sport and Technology" (GST).* Despite my deep aversion, I sought no exemption and submitted to the strident commands, the unison marching, and the childish military exercises.

This course was to culminate in a sort of joint maneuver. After an all-day trek, two parties were to advance to a designated battleground via different

---

* Founded in 1952, the Society for Sport and Technology was intended to develop the pre-military skills of GDR youth. It gained special importance a decade later with the introduction of compulsory military service.

routes. My group had been assigned the defense of a hill codenamed "Height 607." In a driving rain we managed to sleep only briefly under a canvas sheet before the battle began early the next morning. To repulse the advance of the enemy forces, we were armed with practice explosive devices and smoke grenades. Yet as soon as our opponents emerged from a dripping wet spruce preserve, all of us rose at once and yelled together, "Idiocy!" From the other side came an immediate and identical response.

Someone in our class had devised this scheme, which had been passed by word of mouth, and all five hundred students had agreed to participate. Our leaders were naturally furious. Nevertheless, despite threats of harsh disciplinary action and close questioning of everyone involved, the culprit was never found. That such a large body of students could act as one to sabotage the "pre-military" war games and then never reveal the instigator was a heated topic at many later FDJ and party meetings.

3

In 1968, the fresh winds of the "Prague Spring" could also be felt in Leipzig and other parts of the GDR. For us, it seemed extraordinary that the party leaders of a Warsaw Pact state could speak so emphatically about freedom and democratization and rally the whole population behind them. Fueled by the sudden release and rehabilitation of many old prisoners as well as the peaceful direction of events, discussions raged seemingly without end. Despite our many experiences and natural intractability, very few of us felt ready to criticize socialism itself. Even many skeptics, myself included, found the events in Prague proof that a more idealistic form of democratic socialism was worth pursuing. It thus came as a keen disappointment to observe how the top Soviet and GDR leaders remained completely silent about the Czechoslovakian crisis and, when that was no longer possible, ascribed it to manipulations by the West.

The subsequent party meetings made me realize how thin the veneer of our intraparty democracy was. Besides determining the policies for the masses to follow, a small elite even felt empowered to order what they should be thinking. We were clearly warned that any sympathy shown for the "activities of the counter-revolutionary forces in Czechoslovakia" would inevitably result in expulsion. To be sure, authorities quickly moved to suppress any form of spontaneous behavior, and disciplinary actions against students became a daily occurrence.

An uneasy peace soon resulted. Even though news bulletins became sparser, many of us continued to believe that an agreement between the Kremlin leaders and the Prague reformers could be found. Moreover, we wondered why similar experiments could not be attempted in the East bloc as long as the foundation of socialism was respected. The answer to our question came in the early morning of August 21, 1968. Interrupting the regular radio broadcast, the voice of the announcer had an unfamiliar tone. "Responding to a request from our comrades there, troops of the Warsaw Pact United Strike Forces have entered Czechoslovakian territory to safeguard the peace, to protect the achievements of socialism, and to defend against a threatened imperialistic attack."

Only after hearing the announcement repeated several times could I believe my ears. To make certain that its "colony" stayed "within the empire," the Soviet Union was now in the process of suppressing the Czechoslovakian people. It was only thirty years before that Hitler had similarly placed Bohemia and Moravia under the "protection" of the Third Reich, and once again German troops were on the scene. Infuriated by the official lies of an imperialistic threat and a "call for help" from Prague, I jumped onto my motor scooter to join a friend. Soon a whole group of us had gathered, all feeling simultaneously outraged and impotent.

Even though I was later taught how to analyze political events critically and to understand why certain measures had to be taken, the events of 1968 left an enduring impression. At the time, some of us thought that an uprising might break out in the GDR and that the real perpetrators of this crime would receive their just punishment. But the Kremlin had planned well. The indignant protests of the West soon disappeared, and a deathly quiet came to prevail in the East. Under the iron control of the official state apparatus, we students feared too much for our own lives to undertake any bold action. And since we considered ourselves to be the most engaged and enlightened segment of society, it was impossible to imagine anyone else willing to challenge the party's verdict.

The excitement had subsided by the beginning of my third year. Working as a waiter at the Leipzig trade fair had helped me achieve a degree of financial independence. Upon beginning my dissertation, I also gave up my small student's room in Leipzig. That meant living with my mother in Leuna two days a week and spending the remaining three in the physics laboratory doing the required experiments around the clock. On weekends I earned extra money by working at the Riesa Steelworks. It was an orderly if not strenuous existence.

3

My Path to State Security

1

It hardly came as a surprise when I was told by a neighbor in Leuna that a well-dressed, middle-aged man had been making inquiries about me. In reality, I had been expecting a visit from the MfS for some time. Nothing presumably was wrong, as I had exercised great discretion since receiving my thesis topic and was still considered reliable by the party organization. Rather, as was common knowledge at the university, all students, and particularly future physicists, were considered targets for recruitment by the MfS. One colleague of mine, having gained a knowledge of radio communications while serving in the East German army, had been approached by the plainclothes officials of the KGB for many years. Now it was my turn.

This strong interest in students arises from the very nature of a communist regime. As opposed to Western democracies, which wisely separate the functions of domestic security and foreign intelligence and maintain the primacy of individual rights through oversight provisions, a communist state security system inevitably forms an imposing monolithic structure. Rather than protecting the community, it essentially exists to secure the power of those in command and to increase communist influence abroad. In this imperialist expansion, nearly all means are permissible—from industrial

16

and political espionage to internal subversion and destabilization. At that time, however, unaware of any other way, we thought the interest shown in us to be perfectly natural.

The MfS relied on young academics in a multiplicity of ways. Students were employed as spies and informers to keep a watchful eye on both their colleagues and the teaching faculty. They were further used to recruit other students, to convey instructions to agents stationed in the FRG, and to assist with the infiltration of double agents into Western intelligence organizations. Also placed within the FDJ, they sought to exploit connections with Western and Third World youth organizations. If successful, they often became full-time MfS employees themselves.

At the same time, students often posed enormous problems for the security forces. Critical by nature, the majority of East German students felt little support for SED policies. Sometimes this opposition was cautiously voiced within trusted circles. In other instances, it took more overt forms—distributing anti-government pamphlets, participating in church groups, and forming underground resistance movements. Although loosely organized, a genuine opposition continued to exist during these years, as shown by the counter-demonstrations mounted in East Berlin during the GDR anniversary celebrations of 1977 and 1978.

Nevertheless, the SED leadership could count on a certain number of dedicated supporters. Anyone who possessed a home-instilled loyalty to the GDR and a reasonable intelligence had been allowed to study. The mostly corrupted children of leading party and state bureaucrats—the "successor" generation—had naturally received guaranteed spaces. In addition, many of the most professionally ambitious had made their compromises with the system. The remaining students—the politically indifferent middle-of-the-roaders—attracted the attention of the MfS only as a reservoir of potential opposition.

The MfS further realized that students enjoy a greater independence and social mobility than other groups and often have a wider network of friends and acquaintances. These traits made students all the more appealing to the MfS but also a potentially more dangerous threat to the regime. Similarly, just as their young personalities might be molded in service to the state, so too were they highly susceptible to the appeals of opposition groups. In short, it is little wonder that students remained so intensely scrutinized by the MfS.

Many different recruitment methods were available, and a specific choice rested on such considerations as the ultimate objective, the subject area of the department, and the personalities and abilities of the MfS employees involved. Each year, suitable candidates in nearly every conceivable field were systematically sought, often from the same lists, by departments with the most varied specializations. The ponderous, multilayered MfS bureaucracy along with the strict official regulations only compounded the difficulties of the search. Not uncommonly a student responded to a recruitment attempt by saying: "Someone else was here first. I'm already taken!"

All students belonging to the SED automatically received an MfS screening and, barring any character defect, would be approached later. For this purpose, a special unit operating under the jurisdiction of the regional MfS office had been assigned to each institution of higher learning. Whereas a two- or three-person staff would oversee a small vocational college, a large university frequently required up to twenty officers. I later had many dealings myself with the so-called "installation authority" at the Dresden Technical University. Working primarily through agents and informers, these units were responsible for the internal security of the institution. Although all academic disciplines came under their purview, those considered to be "ideologically vulnerable"—medicine, cultural studies, natural sciences, theology, and particularly the social sciences—received the most thorough attention.

In contrast to a potential foreign intelligence officer, a student selected for domestic surveillance faced a much less stringent set of criteria. In fact, by utilizing persons known to be enemies of the state, the MfS could more effectively infiltrate opposition groups. First, however, the resistance of the person had to be broken, since someone hostile to the regime usually found the MfS the most detestable part of the entire state apparatus. Many years of experience had produced special techniques for overcoming resistance. If an initial attempt proved unsuccessful, the recruiter often resorted to stronger pressure, including blackmail. Sometimes the mere thought of losing one's place at the university or facing an uncertain professional future was enough of an incentive to sign an agreement. Indeed, more than once a student who had been found distributing illegal pamphlets or telling a caustic political joke left the interrogation room having concluded a pact with the MfS. Similarly, if an attractive female student was known to have responded to the advances of a Western businessman at the Leipzig trade fair, she would then be compelled to seduce future visiting capitalists on a regular basis.

Naturally it was preferable for no pressure to be necessary. Most students knew that if they overcame their initial reluctance, cooperation with the MfS brought many concrete advantages. Only in rare instances was money offered. The most common and desirable reward involved assistance with one's career—a higher examination grade, for instance, or an important promotion later on. Sometimes simply knowing that one would be immune from an unfavorable investigation could produce an agreement.

Then, too, a desire for adventure could be a prime motivation. One well-known case involved the East German student Tamara Bunke. In 1966, several years after Fidel Castro's consolidation of power in Cuba, the Soviet Union learned that one of his followers, Che Guevara, had left to spread revolution throughout South America. Fearful that his activity might provoke a strong response from the United States and thereby imperil the newly won Cuban bastion, the Kremlin wanted to see Che stopped. Enlisted by the Soviets, the MfS found a fluent Spanish interpreter named Tamara Bunke. Che was invited to East Berlin, and she was assigned a role as an agent of influence to divert him from his revolutionary goals. Instead, she became a convert to his movement and returned with him to Bolivia, where they were both killed. Needless to say, this was not what the MfS had intended.

2

The MfS recruiter did not return to my neighborhood for several days. Certain that he was bound to reappear, I started contemplating how best to respond to his offer. Given my strong FDJ and party involvement, it would be impossible to appear totally aloof and unapproachable. I also did not want to put my approaching diploma examination in jeopardy. Yet the idea of spying on my friends and fellow students was a repellent one. I therefore decided to wait and see what was expected of me.

When he knocked at our door, my mother quickly surmised his MfS affiliation. Introducing himself as "Haustein," he proceeded to ask her a barrage of questions, and then left a sealed envelope for me. Upon returning home, I found my mother very upset by his visit. I nervously opened his message, which requested a meeting the following morning in Leipzig. The possibility of a compromise now appeared more remote than ever. I knew all too well that once ensnared a person could never voluntarily sever a relationship with MfS.

Feeling very apprehensive, I arrived at the designated spot in Leipzig and saw a stocky forty-year-old man of average height. As he pointed in my direction and gave me a nod, I winked at him in confirmation. He then came toward me with his arms open wide and gripped me by the shoulders.

"Thank goodness I've finally found you," he exclaimed. "I was just about to give up." His jovial tone seemed genuine. He furtively took me aside to reveal an official identity card hanging from a leather band on the inside pocket of his suit coat.

"My name is Leo. Let's go inside the hotel and have our talk over breakfast."

Judging from his order—a ham platter, coffee, and French cognac—Leo obviously considered himself a man of the world. He also enjoyed taking a patronizing role toward me. When he asked me to talk about myself, I told him that my neighbors had doubtlessly revealed everything already.

"Well, yes." He paused. "But it would interest me to know, for example, how you came to join the party. Also what kind of a future do you envision for yourself, and what are your immediate plans?"

I answered at length, having learned from various party activities how to give the expected answer at the opportune moment. I noted how my mother had raised me in accordance with our modest social station. I stressed my deep need to belong to the party of the working class, as well as my distress about the ideological slackness of so many students. As far as the future was concerned, I said simply: "I will go where the party sends me."

Apparently delighted with my response, he then launched into a lecture about the subversive machinations of the class enemy and the crucial role of the MfS in guarding socialism from both domestic and foreign adversaries. To my surprise, however, he said nothing about monitoring my fellow students but proceeded to recount some of his complicated and dangerous missions, including several in the FRG. He also made quite clear that his base of operations was in East Berlin rather than Leipzig.

After his fifth cognac, he finally showed his trump card. "It's my job to beat the class enemy on his own territory. You're a clever lad. If you make an effort and cooperate with us, you won't need to look for a job when your studies are finished. After some training, you'll be sent over the border as a scout."

Receiving such an offer after two hours together only added to my confusion. It seemed best to remain vague and uncertain. Still, I agreed to submit a detailed résumé and a complete list of my relatives, and also to keep our conversation a secret. Our next meeting was scheduled at the Restaurant Kiev in two weeks' time. When he started an effusive farewell, I remarked with some embarrassment that an important appointment with my diploma advisor was pressing. He offered to give me a lift to an area near the institute in his red Volkswagen.

When I made a comment about his five cognacs, he replied, "Who do you think I am? Do you think the police will bother me?"

Quite by chance, one of my most closest friends spotted me getting out of the car. After Leo had driven away, he smiled at me understandingly and commented merely, "Aha!" At my coaxing, he admitted having discussed me earlier with Leo, but insisted that his remarks were highly favorable. Knowing him to be a party loyalist, I gave the matter no more thought.

What preoccupied me was my exemption from having to serve as an informer. Moreover, if what Leo said was true, I would be able to go to the West and possibly remain permanently. Admittedly, I had no real concept of what life was like there, and would not have otherwise pursued this goal. It was rather the temptation of leaving the GDR temporarily, and perhaps for good, that persuaded me in the end to accept Leo's offer.

When I arrived at the appointed time, Leo rushed over and gave me a warm greeting. Knowing that the restaurant had an excellent selection of Ukrainian specialties, I rapidly accepted his invitation to a noontime meal. After looking at my carefully prepared résumé and list of relatives, he noted that much hard work was required, including the detection of "enemies in our midst," before obtaining the "award" of service in the FRG. To my relief, he explained that this phase was merely a routine formality in my case and could be expedited very quickly.

Nevertheless, in order not to spoil my long-term prospects with the MfS, I had to somehow satisfy this preliminary request. Without naming any names, I told Leo in general terms about the bad ideological situation at the Physics Institute, stating that even some party members had shown signs of laxity. Although my observations were to be submitted in writing, he warned me that my report should not be prepared until immediately before our next meeting. Further, I was not to be seen en route nor show any change in my outward behavior.

Two weeks passed before our next luncheon meeting. If any specific individuals were incriminated in my full report, I had made certain that they were the more stubborn and dogmatic party members. In addition, I gave Leo the names and addresses of two attractive and easily "approacha-ble" women—one a hairdresser, the other a student in the college of education. His face beamed as he carefully noted all their particulars. Evidently anxious to start work right away, he even dispensed with the obligatory political talk.

My next task was to compile profiles of students who appeared to me as potential contacts for the MfS. I was also instructed to sign all future reports with my newly assigned codename, "Iron Man."

Soon my "working lunches" with Leo became regular affairs. One day, however, he remarked that his superior wanted to meet me at the next one. Describing the man as somewhat peculiar in certain matters, Leo thought it best to prepare me through a series of possible questions and appropriate responses. The political dimension, having diminished in our relationship, now assumed a renewed importance. Leo also stressed that under no conditions should my future position be mentioned, admitting with some embarrassment that it should never have been revealed in the first place.

Sitting next to Leo at our next meeting was an elegantly dressed man in his early forties. With graying blond hair combed straight back, he had a friendly expression, yet strikingly alert eyes. Introduced as "Werner," he quickly took control of the conversation as if we were old acquaintances and relegated Leo to the background. Posing one question after another and revealing practically nothing about himself, he was clearly a quite different type of personality.

From his detailed knowledge of me, Werner chose to probe the so-called "weak points" in my development. Why was I no longer an FDJ secretary? Why was my trial period for party membership overextended? What did I think about the events in Czechoslovakia two years ago? Why was I friendly with a student who had been temporarily placed in a labor camp because of his politically aberrant behavior?

Strenuously I sought answers that would satisfy him. My FDJ commit-ment had been reduced because of the extra demands of my university diploma. My trial period had been extended because of the summer vacation. My thoughts about the Czechoslovakian invasion were positive, since it was essential to protect socialism. My friend had indeed wandered astray but was now returning to the party with my assistance.

Apparently content, Werner turned next to the questions that Leo had given me in advance, and I answered in the prescribed way. After that hurdle was cleared, Werner's tone became more affable. If my work continued to develop in the same satisfactory manner, he assured me, then a promising future lay ahead.

"Have you any serious marriage plans?" he asked bluntly.

I could not dodge his question. While working as a waiter at the Leipzig trade fair, I had fallen in love with a Hungarian girl. A translator with a visiting delegation, she returned home afterward, but because of my extra jobs, I had earned enough to visit her frequently in Budapest. When I announced that we were already engaged, Werner and Leo exchanged a look that was not immediately clear to me. Later I discovered that this relationship had disqualified me from any mission to West Germany.

Upon parting, however, Werner confidently stated that we would be meeting again soon. My marriage followed in the summer of 1970, although some emigration technicalities temporarily delayed Ilona's departure from Hungary.

3

While my meetings with Leo became less frequent, I began to receive more extensive assignments. The sheer number of the various reports, assessments, and political evaluations required of me was starting to take its toll. Leo, however, informed me of a meeting in East Berlin scheduled for early December that I was to attend. Its purpose was to discuss my future, and also present would be Werner's immediate superior. Advising me that this man should be treated with even greater caution, Leo once again laid out a set of questions, which I completely mastered.

When I boarded the train on the designated day, I felt confident that this meeting was merely proof of my progress and that a posting in the West would eventually follow. Without difficulty I found the East Berlin address, an ugly four-story building dating from the turn of the century and containing at least three rear courtyards. After ringing the bell next to the name "Haustein," I was met by Werner at the door. A musty-smelling kitchen was on one side of the corridor, on the other a half-living room, half-office outfitted with modern furniture.

Sitting in an armchair was a man roughly thirty-five years old. The vulturelike, furtive look on his face reminded me instantly of "Jailhouse Schmidt" from my schoolboy days. Werner introduced him as Christian, and as he greeted me, I noticed a gold tooth in his upper jaw. This man, I thought to myself, is indeed dangerous and probably has the mental power to see through any of my statements.

After requesting another recitation of my complete résumé, Christian quickly fired away at me. "What did Leo tell you? Did he prepare you for our talk as he usually does?"

Knowing that a lie would never work, I acknowledged the rehearsed set of questions and answers as well as the prospect of a position in the West. The two men exchanged glances.

"Forget all that rubbish. Leo is a windbag!" Christian said. "We're here to put our relationship on a firm footing. All we can promise now is a lot of work and effort." By that time, I had noticed that he had a slight squint and lisp.

What followed was the standard lecture about the GDR's position in the world and the sinister threat posed by the class enemy. After making some vitriolic remarks about Washington and Bonn, Christian stressed the need for support of the MfS by all loyal citizens of East Germany. "Are you unconditionally prepared to fulfill all assignments we give you?" he asked.

I felt just like a mouse trapped by the cat. All my calculations vanished, and I agreed to his demand.

My oral assent, however, was not enough, as Werner then produced a specimen copy of an MfS written agreement for me to review and to add any amendments of my own. I was given pen and paper, and started to work. The final result read as follows:

"Statement of Commitment—I, Werner Friedhelm Stiller, born in Wessmar on August 24, 1947; student at the Karl-Marx University in Leipzig; and resident at 23 Friedrich-Ebert Strasse in 422 Leuna, herewith voluntarily agree to cooperate with the Ministry of State Security of the German Democratic Republic and am prepared to fulfill all assignments given me in an honest, conscientious, and diligent manner. I realize that I am thereby assuming the citizen's noble task of defending and strengthening the German Democratic Republic. At the time of this declaration, I was informed that all the working methods, persons, technical equipment, et al. that become known to me during my training period must remain completely secret. I therefore cannot divulge any of this information—including my employment by the MfS—to any person, including relatives, acquaintances, and other social and governmental bodies. To protect my own person as well as my unofficial activity I choose the codename 'Iron Man' and will continue to use this name for the duration of my MfS employment. I am also aware that a violation of this commitment would severely damage the interests of the GDR and that I can be held directly accountable under the existing laws of the GDR.

Berlin, December 6, 1970, Werner Stiller."

Laying down the pen, I realized all too clearly that my own political views could not be reconciled with this commitment. In fact, it would not have been surprising had Christian detected my inner misgivings and found me guilty of deception. But he silently took the document from me, rechecked each word, and placed the folded paper in his coat pocket.

Both men then rose from their seats to congratulate me on having joined the important frontline struggle against domestic and foreign enemies. I was even presented with a bouquet of flowers. Our glasses filled with an expensive French cognac, we proceeded to toast my future work with the MfS. My contact with Leo was presumably over, and to my relief, Werner, rather than Christian, would be my new case officer. I was also given the East Berlin telephone number where the two men could be reached.

As the conversation turned from politics to physics, I found that they possessed no more than a good overview of the field. That they seemed best informed about nuclear physics made me correctly suspect that foreign espionage in this area was their real speciality. The level of the cognac bottle rapidly fell, and Christian began to show signs of slight inebriation. As I left, he said with a heavy lisp that my first task was to start learning conspiratorial work from scratch and that my training as a physicist would become advantageous later.

On the train trip back to Leuna, I was filled with mixed emotions. While their real plans for me seemed as mysterious as before, I did know one thing for certain. With his stealthy gaze and keen intellect, Christian would pose a genuine danger for me. As it turned out, nothing occurred during the next eight years to change this original assessment.

4

The following January I received my first message in the mail from Werner. Lacking a return address, it merely summoned me to a meeting in Leipzig.

To my surprise, we drove together in his Wartburg to a district well known to me. In fact, he stopped the car directly in front of the building where my former friend Irma had lived. It occurred to me that perhaps out of convenience the MfS maintained several apartments in the same building. Possibly, too, all her relationships with Oriental students had been initiated and maintained by the MfS, but on second thought that seemed too farfetched to be true.

We proceeded to a door marked "Hoffmann Engineering." Inside was an exact replica of the apartment in East Berlin, and like all the safe houses I was later to see, it exuded an unmistakable atmosphere. Following coffee and cognac, my formal intelligence training commenced with a lesson about the MfS's role as the "upholder of law" in East Germany. As ludicrous as the notion seemed, I pretended to be sympathetic. Two years later, I learned from Werner himself how, as a young MfS employee, he had dragged citizens from their beds before dawn, "softened them up" with a beating, and then, regardless of the actual evidence, locked them up until a charge could be fabricated. I tried to maintain the same outward reaction.

For now, Werner was mostly concerned that I grasp the main rule of conspiratorial work. "You must realize," he repeatedly stated, "that a person should know only enough to carry out his task!"

When the mood of the training session began to lighten, I decided to ask the question uppermost in my mind. "Tell me, what are my chances of getting the kind of assignment that Leo had indicated?"

Reaching for his cognac, Werner gave me an oblique look and said, slightly annoyed, "Even if that fool had considered it possible, do you really believe after your marriage to a Hungarian that we could let you move to the West? You can get that idea out of your head and show us now what you can do!"

That meant not only the end of my dream but the beginning of a hated career as a Stasi informer. Even though I tried to hide my disappointment, Werner seemed to notice the shift in my mood. "Forget that I ever mentioned it," he added in a casual but firm manner, "but we also need young people at the main headquarters."

I felt relieved. Working in East Berlin would doubtlessly offer a variety of opportunities, and my dedication might pay off after all. I would now have to redouble my efforts in order to pass the battery of examinations that were bound to be required.

Things seemed back on track, and we agreed on the date of the next meeting. I was also asked to prepare two "positive individual reports." As Werner explained to me, these so-called "tips" identified those GDR citizens whose political convictions, personal characteristics, and potential operative abilities made them attractive prospects for MfS collaboration.

Before closing the door, however, I noticed that Werner was reaching for the coffee tin again, presumably in expectation of another visitor. Curious about who that person might be, I quickly left the building and found a seat at a nearby café that allowed me to observe the entrance of Hoffmann Engineering. Werner's car also remained parked in the same spot.

A few minutes later I was astonished to see Klaus Hübner, the ex-FDJ secretary of our institute, enter the door to the safe house. I recalled that Klaus had been partially aware of my ideological doubts during the Czechoslovakian crisis. Had he conveyed this information to Werner, I would certainly have been considered unreliable and never recruited. On the other hand, I might well have been one of his own "tips" for the MfS, or perhaps he was never asked about me in the first place.

At any rate, I was now determined to land a position in the MfS headquarters in East Berlin. It seemed wise to start by strengthening the perception of my political reliability at the institute. At the next party meeting, I sat next to Klaus as if by coincidence and engaged him in a lengthy conversation. As the Ulbricht era was nearing an end and the GDR faced a change in leadership, there was no lack of issues to be discussed. Apparently impressed with my ability to raise questions and express viewpoints in accordance with party guidelines, Klaus invited me for a beer afterward. We were soon joined by several other party members, and I took advantage of the opportunity to advance my political image even more. The results were soon apparent, and my prestige at the institute started to grow.

After a three-week interval, I arrived punctually and well prepared for the next meeting at Werner's safe house. Not seeing his Wartburg in front of the building, I was surprised to find him inside. Werner explained that a car should always be parked some distance away but that he had been in a hurry the last time. Naturally I kept to myself his other, far more serious mistake of holding consecutive meetings in the same locale with two agents who knew one another.

I then gave him the two requested "tips," which had taken a great deal of time and effort to prepare. The first one concerned Klaus Roth, my own thesis advisor; the second, Klaus Hübner. Even though Werner showed self-control and registered no change in expression, he committed an error by looking immediately and intensely at the second dossier and giving the first one only a cursory glance. I drew the conclusion that Roth was probably not working for the MfS, at least not under Werner. Incidentally, my report on his agent Hübner was decidedly positive.

Evidently very satisfied with my work, Werner decided to skip the topic "assessment of individuals" and move directly to the critical matter of devising plausible cover stories. To be sure, the quality of a deception based on the background of an agent, an action, or a complete institution can easily determine the success or failure of an intelligence operation. After a theoretical exposition illustrated by both real and hypothetical examples, Werner asked me to prepare some possible cover stories dealing with a variety of situations. The obligatory political discussion took place this time at the end of the meeting, but I had devised a new tactic in advance. By posing many political questions myself and spontaneously expounding on current events, I was able to score many points in my favor.

The next meeting was to occur in four weeks' time and would examine the topic "investigation of individuals." In the interim, I was to gather as much information as possible about two families, one in Halle, the other just north of East Berlin in Zepernick.

With only a few supporting details related by Werner, I first went to Halle on my motor scooter. From a distance, it was easy enough to determine that two elderly, quite well-off persons lived in the house. Devising a plausible reason to approach them proved more difficult, until I recalled that a national census had recently taken place. I returned to Leipzig and, despite some difficulty, obtained one of the detailed personal questionnaries.

Posing as an official of the Central Office of Statistics, I felt slightly nervous ringing the bell of the house in Halle. The man who answered the door seemed surprised to find a stranger at his door. Taking great care to be polite, I explained that an oversight on my part had rendered several census questionnaires useless, including the one from his household. Moreover, since my superior was a very strict taskmaster, I faced an inevitable punishment unless those forms could be filled out anew. By stressing my embarrassment for asking such a favor, I succeeded in gaining entry into the house.

Sympathetically, the man asked me to take a seat in the living room while he fetched the compulsory "house book."* In his absence, I quickly looked around, noting that the contents of the bookcase reflected intellectual interests and a liberal political attitude. From the mail on the desk, I wrote down the addresses of family relatives in the West. Besides the house book, a few specific questions supplied me with the remaining information needed for this project. I felt genuinely grateful and thanked the man effusively. The final report contained nearly twenty single-spaced pages.

With greater self-confidence, I began my second assignment in Zepernick. In this case, drawing on my prior knowledge that the couple in question was religious and had seven children, I presented myself as a theology student working for a charity devoted to large families. To obtain the required information, I explained that a scientific study was under way comparing the position of similar families in the parish. Admittedly not the most admirable of methods, it nevertheless achieved its purpose, and I was even given a family picture at the end of my visit.

After reviewing my two reports, Werner reimbursed my expenses and gave me a fifty-mark bonus. As I thanked him and put the money in my pocket, it seemed that my objective of working in East Berlin had grown much nearer.

5

At our next meeting, Werner noted that the upcoming spring trade fair in Leipzig would offer an excellent opportunity to further my training. Since working there as a waiter had always provided my best source of extra income, the idea was less appealing to me. In addition, because of my marriage and my degree work, I had stopped working weekends at the Riesa Steelworks.

Werner insisted, however, and instructed me to initiate two contacts. I was also to prepare complete personality profiles so that these relationships

---

* Every residence or apartment house in the GDR was required to maintain a house book, which listed not just births, deaths, and marriages but also personal information about all visitors.

could later be consolidated. Although working as a waiter had brought me into contact with many West Germans, Werner wanted me to appear in a different guise with a watertight cover story. That, thanks to my diploma project, was relatively simple. I knew that the electron spin resonance spectrometers made in the GDR could not match the quality of those produced by two Western companies, one in Karlsrube, the other in Zurich. Moreover, representatives from both firms were to be in Leipzig. For my cover, I chose a branch of the Academy of Sciences that utilized these spectrometers and decided on the name "Schilling," which was also to be used frequently in my future work.

Proceeding first to the Swiss firm's booth, I examined the instrument in a knowing manner. That prompted the appearance of a respectable-looking man in his early thirties. As we began to talk shop, I hinted at the possibility of our institute approving the purchase of a Western-made spectrometer, and he became noticeably friendlier. A bit later, glancing at my watch, I pretended to be late for an urgent appointment. Reacting as I had hoped, he regretted having to break off our conversation and expressed his desire to continue it at another time. He also mentioned that he had plenty of free time at his disposal, and we agreed to meet for a beer the next evening. It was important that he extend the invitation, for Werner had instructed me that one should avoid being the host whenever possible.

My next stop was the nearby booth of the Karlsruhe firm. Since nobody came forward to assist me, there was time to scrutinize the exhibit before a voice behind me asked whether I knew anything about electron spin resonance. After responding with the prepared cover story, I noticed that my diploma adviser had just appeared at the same booth. Because GDR citizens must first clear a hurdle of official forms and regulations to attend the trade fair, we both felt quite surprised at seeing one another. Fortunately, this encounter was equally inconvenient for him, and he quickly left before the Karlsruhe representative noticed anything. Using the same tactics as before, I secured an invitation for two nights later.

When I reported back to Werner at a so-called "walking meeting" in Clara-Zetkin Park, he expressed little interest in the Zurich representative. "Drink a beer with him, but he has no long-range potential for us." The man from Karlsruhe, on the other hand, seemed of greater importance. After taking his business card, Werner said we would meet again soon for another short session.

At that meeting he confirmed my assignment: "We are very interested in the Karlsruhe man, and you should keep your appointment with him by all means. Get all the personal details you can, especially any family connections in the GDR. Here are two admission tickets for a nightclub."

When I told the man about the nightclub, he seemed somewhat surprised, no doubt aware that such tickets are in short supply during the trade fairs, but agreed to come. I first had to meet the Swiss representative as arranged. Respectable, honest, and naive—the very characteristics that frustrate all espionage agents—he proved to be completely unproductive. At the same time, his unmistakable pride in his Swiss nationality gave me my first impression of what it means to be a free citizen of a free nation.

The Karlsruhe representative arrived punctually at the "Eden" bar the following evening. Having never been to a nightclub before, I chose to wear a dark, conservative suit, which had often been my attire at various university social activities, and tried to affect a confident, worldly air. As the evening continues to evoke uncomfortable memories, I wonder whether the man noticed how nervous I really was.

We proceeded to the table for four indicated by the admission tickets. A young couple was already seated there. In the course of the evening, however, I sensed something peculiar about their behavior. Not only did they wear unmatched wedding rings,* but they hardly spoke to each other, appearing reluctant to show even the most common forms of intimacy. As I discovered a year later, they were indeed part of a cleverly devised testing operation for me.

My attempts to take the offensive role toward my companion soon foundered. An adroit conversationalist, he easily outmaneuvered me, especially when the topic turned to politics, for the views he expressed were actually those that I had gradually come to believe myself. Despite my thoroughly prepared cover story about the institute, he questioned me so intensely that my answers began to appear very thin. By the end of our meeting, it was clear that I had been talking much more than listening. Although the other couple seemed to catch little of our conversation and the man agreed to continue our discussion at the next trade fair, I was anxious to bring this inglorious evening to an end. It then took some considerable embellishment to make my report sound fairly successful.

In any event, Werner appeared most satisfied at our next meeting. Then, in a dramatic tone of voice, he told me that the MfS had identified a member of a spy ring actively plotting against the state. My next assignment was to observe this man as closely as possible, recording even the smallest detail, since the GDR's very existence was purportedly at stake. According to Werner, he was to meet one of his accomplices the following day at 3:00 P.M. at the entrance gate to a house on the Sachsenplatz, and would probably be carrying a folding umbrella. I should wait for him and then stay on his trail. At 4:00 P.M. I would be relieved by another MfS agent. Losing him, I was warned, would have dire national consequences.

Already harboring a certain suspicion because of the couple in the bar, I decided to be at the Sachsenplatz half an hour before the designated time.

---

* It is a common German custom that the two marriage partners wear matching wedding rings.

Fifteen minutes after I arrived, a man fitting the description Werner had given me got out of a taxi and entered the building. He had no umbrella, but then it was a bright sunny day. Another twenty minutes passed, and he emerged again. For the next hour, acting as if pursued by the hounds of hell, he followed a highly circuitous route through the center of town. At one point, he appeared to have noticed me and made several complicated loops. Thinking that I had been thrown off the track, he slowed his pace and went directly to the Leipzig lost-and-found bureau to report the loss of his umbrella. After stating that it had been left behind in a taxi, he gave a telephone number where he could be reached. I immediately recognized it, for it was the number Werner used during the trade fairs. In reality, this secret agent was a first lieutenant in the MfS and later proved to be a good-natured colleague.

I knew from this experience that my reliability and operational skills were still being tested before I would receive any headquarters posting. It also meant many sleepless nights trying to determine how much about my private contacts should be reported to Werner. When I accidentally happened to see Irma again and hinted at my next assignment at the trade fair, she listened but made no comment. That I was actually planning to cultivate Western contacts beyond my stated instructions seemed best left unsaid to her and to Werner.

In this regard, my aim was not merely to acquire all the information possible about new instruments in the physics field but also to use each conversation with company representatives to learn more about their mentality and manner of argumentation. After my ignominious experience in the nightclub, I wanted to be much better prepared for future meetings.

At one of the booths, I was approached by a man who introduced himself as a representative of a West German steel concern. Very handsome, well educated, and well traveled, he was evidently a man of the world and radiated self-confidence. At the time, it seemed our meeting was purely a matter of chance, although I later believed him to be a business associate of the exhibitor. Apparently finding pleasure in our conversation, he invited me to dinner that evening.

"Küster" showed an especially keen interest in the social and political conditions in the GDR. His appealing manner removed many of my inhibitions, and a very candid conversation ensued—perhaps too candid, as I realized at the end of the evening. After paying the bill, he asked whether this meeting would have any unpleasant repercussions for me at the institute, as close contacts between East German citizens and Western trade fair visitors were generally discouraged. I replied simply that it would remain unreported to my superiors. Having already violated one of the main rules of conspiracy by using my real name, I had decided not to tell Werner about this contact, and say instead that no one of interest had surfaced that evening.

Indeed, I found my new West German acquaintance most sympathetic and immediately agreed to his suggestion that we exchange addresses in order to remain in contact. Nevertheless, he thought it better not to start a written correspondence and to wait until he returned to the next trade fair. Only much later did I realize that—in addition to Küster's genuine liking for me—our paths had not crossed as coincidentally as it seemed.

6

Several weeks after the trade fair, Werner arrived at our meeting in a state of alarm. Apparently an accident had eliminated the use of a particular courier, and as a result, some important messages could not be relayed from West Berlin. Although I was still a relative novice in the business, Werner felt I probably possessed enough courage to go to the other side of the "Anti-Fascist Protective Wall" and collect the contents of a dead-letter drop. As he stressed that a certain danger was involved, it seemed yet another test of my skill and reliability. Nevertheless, I repeated my solemn pledge to carry out any assignment of the party, and Werner looked relieved. Before dismissing me, he also told me to be ready on a moment's notice.

A week later, I received a phone call at the institute instructing me to be at the Schönefeld train station in East Berlin the following evening and to wear dark, inconspicuous clothes. When Werner arrived as planned, we got into his Wartburg, and I received my final instructions while riding through the environs of the city. As the buildings began to give way to a dark, forested area, I completely lost my bearings.

Stopping the car, Werner stated that we were approaching the border crossing and told me to lie on the backseat covered with a blanket. I did as he requested. After he drove a short distance on what seemed to be a dirt road, the car stopped again, and light appeared through the blanket as if at a checkpoint. When we resumed the trip, the roughness of the road became even more pronounced, and I was very relieved to get out of the car the next time Werner came to a halt.

He whispered to me to follow him. After making our way through a thicket of spruce trees for about 500 yards, we arrived at a barbed-wire fence with a white sign marked "Halt! Border! No trespassing in this zone!" Werner pulled the loosely fastened wire off the post, thus allowing me to crawl through, and wished me luck.

Following his directions, I walked along a path for about 200 yards, and found myself in a large clearing. My goal was a towering, isolated tree perfectly silhouetted against the clear night sky. Seeing no one in sight, I proceeded as instructed and found the deep crevice among the roots containing a packet wrapped in plastic, about the size of an audio cassette.

Everything went according to plan. When I returned, Werner praised me highly for such a speedy execution. That I never really believed we had left East Berlin seemed best kept to myself. (As it turned out, I later organized similar sham assignments for my agents, albeit in a more realistic manner. On one occasion, a unit of the GDR Border Patrol even agreed to imitate the West German police, thereby surprising but not rattling my examinee.)

Having cleared the last hurdle for a headquarters appointment, I finally had several undisturbed weeks to devote to my degree work. The next message that came—typewritten as usual and bearing no return address— advised me of a meeting at the East Berlin safe house, which I now knew under its codename "office."

Upon arriving, I noticed that the nameplate "Haustein" had been replaced by one marked "Helbig." Both Werner and Christian were waiting for me inside. After a few introductory remarks, Christian delivered an ideological harangue so intense that the listener could only feel self-contempt because of his meager sacrifice for the socialist cause. Besides experiencing this type of lecture many times subsequently, I also learned how to use it with my own agents.

When Christian asked the seemingly innocent question of how I viewed the future on the eve of my graduation, I answered automatically, "Comrades, I will go where the party directs me." Then I added, "If it should have no use for me, then I will seek a job that enables me to serve socialism to the fullest extent."

Recognizing my reply as one of the stock responses tutored by Leo, Werner smiled discreetly. His face changed, however, when he saw Christian's sullen expression and heard his next question.

"Are you willing to take on duties as a party worker?"

I agreed.

"Under any conditions?"

"Yes, under any conditions."

Even though I continued to answer in the same mechanical manner, my responses were apparently convincing enough. Christian closed the discussion of my future with a short but telling remark. "If you continue to prove your worth, a place for you in our ranks will be found in due course."

Christian left the meeting at this point. Opening his briefcase, Werner removed an official MfS questionnaire of about thirty pages, and the two of us set to work. Never had I answered so many personal questions, ranging from every address, even when on vacation, to every social function ever attended, and every childhood illness ever experienced. Those questions I could not answer from memory were noted, and I was required to obtain the missing information as soon as possible. Werner also requested that I prepare yet another complete résumé.

When I returned to the safe house a week later, only Werner was present.

"Do you know the GDR Physics Society?" he asked.

"No."

"Well, that's where you'll be working as soon as you receive your diploma this summer."

Somewhat stunned, I asked, "I thought I was going to work for you . . ."

"Once you've proved your worth," he answered.

"But what if the Physics Society doesn't accept me?"

"Of course it will. Just don't ask so many questions. At ten A.M. on July first you are to introduce yourself to Comrade Reinhard Linke, the secretary of the society, and say that you've heard about a vacancy."

"Who is Linke?"

"A colossal ass!"

Werner's reply left me baffled. "And where shall I live in East Berlin?" I asked.

He told me to follow him. From the apartment, we crossed the Prenzlauer Allee and turned into Immanuelkirchstrasse. The block was filled with dingy apartment buildings dating from the late nineteenth century, with only a single toilet for each floor. We entered one of the buildings, which became darker and more sinister with each step.

When Werner opened a door of the ground-floor apartment marked "Hüther," I expected another safe house. It exuded a dank, bone-chilling, musty air. To my surprise, however, the large two-room apartment was nicely furnished and even included a bathroom. It was also clear that the last residents had vacated so quickly that most of their belongings had been left behind. In any event, this would be not only my family's new home, but also the scene of the few happy years of my marriage.

7

In late June 1971, I passed my diploma examinations and had a final drink with my fellow students. As I boarded the train to East Berlin a week later, my thoughts revolved around my new position at the Physics Society. I began to wonder whether my contract with the MfS had been a mistake; not only was my own scientific research now at an end, but a foreign intelligence assignment seemed a very remote possibility. I also questioned my ultimate intention of migrating to the West and finding suitable employment. Besides, I was young, still happily married, and the proud father of a baby daughter. The MfS could hardly permit my family to leave as well.

Moreover, I was beginning to view my Stasi involvement in a new light. Despite feeling estranged from East Germany and the SED, I had actually enjoyed carrying out my last MfS assignments. The sense of power that came from operating with a cover story and knowing that a gigantic security apparatus stood behind me had a strangely stimulating effect. Curious as well, I now had a good chance of finally learning how this mysterious object of much speculation functioned in reality.

When I got off the East Berlin streetcar at the Alexanderplatz station, some extra time remained before my meeting with Linke. I took a stroll past the Marienkirche and across the Spree River to a public garden filled with a small forest of chestnut trees. As I came to the Physics Society, I was astonished to see that it was a handsome, middle-sized building. It also had a plaque stating that Gustav Magnus had founded the first German physics institute on this site more than 150 years ago. At least the physical setting of my first job would give no cause for complaint.

The doorman checked my identity card and told me to proceed to the second floor. To my surprise, Linke's secretary indicated I was expected. His office was filled with the penetrating smell of Karos, a cheap brand of cigarettes that I had smoked myself as a student. Sitting behind a massive desk, Linke was wearing an ill-fitting, creased polyester suit and a faintly stained tie. He evidently placed little importance on his outward appearance.

As he ponderously rose to greet me, I was struck by his sheer size and the puffiness of his face—a result, I later learned, of his excessive drinking. In an obvious falsehood, Linke noted that Dr. Roth had informed him of my desire to work for the society. Since I had been instructed to inform my thesis advisor only the night before, it seemed clear that Werner had contacted Linke. That meant that Linke probably worked for the MfS and that I should exercise even more caution. I agreed with Linke's assertion, adding that the prospect of living in East Berlin was appealing and that a modest apartment for my family had already been located.

Linke spent the next hour discussing the role of the Physics Society in the GDR. In addition to organizing various scientific meetings and projects and cooperating with groups in other countries, the society handled inquiries from its members and published a quarterly journal. Linke was overcome several times by intense bouts of smoker's cough, which caused his face to turn scarlet. After describing the party and trade union work of the society, he made some concluding personal observations about the small permanent staff.

When an opportunity finally came for me to ask about my own responsibilities, Linke replied that I would assist him with various administrative tasks and receive a monthly salary of 810 marks. Although I would have preferred more purely scientific work, I heeded Werner's advice and accepted the offer. Linke then introduced me to the other staff members, and gave me a questionnaire to be completed the same day.

I returned to the safe house where Werner was waiting. After expressing satisfaction with my report, he told me that the position would definitely last no longer than a year and that the time should be utilized for further intelligence training. Henceforth, we would meet fortnightly to examine such topics as the initiation of personal contacts, surveillance techniques, and the use of dead-letter drops. Already the technical content of our meetings had begun to increase, while the political component seemed a mere formality. Surprisingly, my relationship to Werner also became quite frank and open. When I told him about the pungent clouds of smoke in Linke's office, he could not suppress a smile, noting that the man had been puffing Karos for the last twenty years. Still, I made no mention of my suspicion about Linke's MfS connection.

In spite of numerous revelations and several personal disappointments, my tenure with the society was generally agreeable. The organization still retained a certain independence and was, at least in principle, governed by its own statutes. The board of directors, which included the GDR's most renowned physicists, met once every three months and discussed issues in an easy, informal manner.

The chairman of this group, Professor Robert Rompe, was introduced to me shortly after my official duties had begun. As a member of the SED Central Committee and the GDR's leading physicist, he was the highest-ranking official I had thus far encountered. Yet like many leading scholars, he seemed completely indifferent to his personal appearance. In fact, this frail seventy-year-old man was so shabbily attired that even Linke would have bested him in a men's fashion competition.

When Rompe commented that he had heard about me from Comrade Willi, I was completely baffled. Although I had already learned that first names were invariably used in MfS undercover work, the name Willi rang no bell at all. It seemed better, however, to conceal my puzzlement and let the remark pass. Still, I wondered whether the MfS was indeed so omnipresent and able to maintain contacts even in the SED Central Committee. It would take another year for my suspicion to be confirmed.

8

My first work was to help prepare for an international congress on Mössbauer spectrometry in Dresden. These administrative tasks quickly gave me a comprehensive overview of all GDR physicists, including their fields of expertise and their political leanings. All this knowledge was to prove highly useful in my later activities. Because I also tried to stay as up-to-date as possible, my MfS co-workers came to call me the "information department."

I also learned about the other, less scientific function of the Physics Society and its international meetings. Attached to every participant from a non-communist country was a GDR "colleague," whose assignment followed established state security procedures. One copy of his final report went to Linke, the other to the international relations division of the Academy of Sciences. While the latter copy was automatically forwarded to counterintelligence for evaluation, the other remained in the extensive MfS files on the Physics Society.

Every Western scientist who ever visited the GDR for professional reasons can be certain of having an MfS dossier. Besides personal and professional information, a character profile that attempted to identify habits and weaknesses as well as political attitudes would be included. Since nearly all Westerners were viewed by the MfS as either declared, disguised, or potential enemies of the GDR, this systematic inquiry was termed a "preventive countermeasure."

One evening during the Dresden congress, Linke drank more than he could handle, and I helped him to his room. When he collapsed on the bed and immediately fell into a deep sleep, I took the opportunity to inspect his briefcase. It contained not only an envelope addressed to Christian but also a social security card indicating that his employer had been the Ministry of the Interior between 1958 and 1969. Since I knew that this ministry was often used as a cover by MfS employees, there remained no doubt in my mind concerning Linke's tie to state security. As a result, I redoubled my efforts to impress him with my political reliability. His evaluation of my performance, Werner later told me, was very favorable.

After the congress, there were very few official duties to perform, particularly since Linke preferred to do as much as possible himself. That allowed me to further my own scientific education, consulting the Max-Planck Library in our building as well as reading scientific periodicals from the West. I also saw Gustav Hertz occasionally in the library. As the only Nobel-prize-winning physicist living in the GDR at the time, he gave me some appreciation of the older humanistic tradition of great German scientists.

Most evenings and weekends, however, were consumed by the extensive training program that Werner had prepared. It was now certain that my future speciality would be espionage against the West. I was instructed to gather "entry information," which meant scrutinizing those East Germans who had received visits from Western friends or relatives and determining whether those contacts could be useful to the MfS. This, as I later learned, was an integral operation of the security apparatus.

Although Werner usually found my reports satisfactory, I occasionally faced the very difficult task of reinvestigating a case. Through the years of communist rule, most East Germans had come to draw a clear dividing line between their family and the outside world. Because of the regime's intense demands for social conformity, the desire to shield one's family from external influences had grown all the stronger. To be sure, since the state regulated nearly all personal contacts, a stranger at the door was regarded with utmost suspicion.

Not surprisingly, the most accessible group was pensioners, who often lived alone and relished some variety in their lives. Still, I had to be careful of those party veterans whose own undercover work before and during the war made them wary of my approach. It was also necessary to change my cover story frequently, appearing sometimes as a student undertaking a sociological survey or as a radio reporter preparing a news report.

On several occasions a homemade identity card managed the trick. Since GDR citizens had become accustomed to all sorts of official documents and were required to identify themselves in the most varied circumstances, these cards came to acquire a life of their own. Put simply, it was through this piece of paper that an individual became a person. I later discovered this phenomenon to be even more widespread in the Soviet Union, where the number of official stamps determined the value of the card. The most impressive example I ever saw consisted of three lines of writing and eighteen different stamps—round, triangular, and hexagonal as well as single- and multicolored—which permitted a member of a North Pole expedition to enter the Chukchi Peninsula by the Bering Strait.

In 1971, I received an unexpected visit from Küster, the West German steel manager whom I had met at the Leipzig trade fair. He said that he was in the area on business and had thought of stopping by my apartment. As both my wife and daughter happened to be out, I wondered whether the timing was mere coincidence. Nevertheless, it was once again a relief to be able to voice my feelings about many depressing aspects of life in the GDR. At the same time, despite his pleasant manner, I wondered how he had discovered my address and whether he might actually be working for a Western intelligence organization. It still seemed worth the risk to continue the relationship, but only with extreme caution. When he asked whether this visit would have any unpleasant repercussions, I fudged the truth and replied negatively.

9

I continued to lead my double life, working days at the Physics Society and spending evenings executing Werner's assignments. I was also required to participate in the unit of the "Combat Groups of the Working Class" at the Academy of Sciences. This was a paramilitary force formed after the workers' uprising of June 17, 1953, and designed to quell any new disturbances, thus eliminating the need for Soviet tanks. It had also played an important role in the construction of the Berlin Wall. Although membership in the academy did not extend to the working class, there were numerous intellectuals committed to the party and seeking to advance their careers. This ambition was exploited by the SED, which had made participation in the combat groups mandatory for academy members. In order to keep up the appearance of a loyal party member, I had no choice but to join when approached by the recruiting officers.

Shortly before the next spring trade fair in Leipzig, I received another visit from Küster, who hoped to see me at the event and also to introduce a close acquaintance of his. Considering my heavy work load at the academy, it seemed dubious whether permission to go would be granted. Nevertheless, feeling determined to attend, I decided to use my earlier contact with the Karlsruhe businessman as a pretext.

Christian responded enthusiastically to my proposal. When I mentioned how much work Linke had been giving me recently, Christian told me not to worry. "Besides the fact that you've been with him longer than anyone else, Linke is one of our officers and will do as I say."

This remark startled me. Although Linke's earlier ties to state security had been quite clear, it was hard to reconcile his present position as secretary of the Physics Society with active MfS duty. Christian replied brusquely to my puzzlement. "How do you think our far-reaching missions for the protection of the republic can be carried out unless we have our people in important positions?" The tone of his voice invited no further discussion.

When I returned to Linke and told him of my Leipzig assignment, his eyes suddenly narrowed. "What do those idiots think they're up to?" he said, venting his anger. "Have they lost my phone number? Why do they always make a decision and never consult me beforehand? That you remain in such a subordinate role has already caused suspicion among the others, and now your absence will raise even more questions. Headquarters has absolutely no idea about the practical side of things."

Eventually, however, Linke yielded. "If I have problems with Mond because of your absence, then I'll just have to talk my own way out of this mess." Mond, who had recently been appointed coordinator of the various scientific branches of the academy, was a personal enemy of Linke and kept a vigilant eye on everything that transpired.

In Leipzig, Küster found me without difficulty and introduced me to his associate, who seemed basically the same agreeable type of person. Küster further assured me that he enjoyed his fullest confidence. We arranged to have dinner that evening, but when I arrived at the restaurant, only the associate was there. His explanation that Küster had to return to the FRG on urgent business left me unimpressed, but I kept my displeasure to myself.

Our conversation soon took a surprising turn. Claiming a full and detailed knowledge of me, Küster's friend began to list things that could have come only from a confidential personal file. Not only did he know that three people had voted against my acceptance into the SED, but he told me what my first duties as a state security officer would be. Feeling suddenly flushed, I tried to find a way to respond to what seemed a deliberate MfS provocation. My companion, however, sensed my panic and managed to convince me that this was not a setup.

While it seemed increasingly probable that Küster and his associate were BND contacts, I had received no explicit confirmation from either man. I also found it hard to believe that a Western intelligence agency could possess such detailed knowledge about me. Moreover, no overt attempt was made to recruit me. Küster's associate merely predicted that I would rise rapidly in the MfS and that my career would be followed with great interest. Presumably that was encouragement to continue following the strategy I had already chosen.

During a short walk after the meal, some of my lingering doubts were dispelled when Küster's associate gave me what he called a "totem." It was the upper half of a broken porcelain medallion with the chain still attached. He told me to carry this object as unobtrusively as possible, at all times. Should I ever encounter someone possessing the other half, even in the distant future, that person could be trusted.

This surprising and quite confusing meeting remained my only contact with the BND for many years. The following morning, however, I again began to suspect a trap when Werner summoned me to an important discussion with two other comrades. Before their arrival, Werner explained that they belonged to the "cadre" or personnel department of the MfS. Presumably they merely wanted to get their own impressions before my acceptance became official.

"These blasted pen-pushers haven't a clue!" he continued. "All you have to do is answer their routine questions along the party lines. If they ask whether you will carry out every mission demanded by the SED, tell them yes, that you're even prepared to sacrifice your own life. That's what they want to hear. In a real crunch, though, I'll bet that not one of them would risk his own neck."

Despite its monolithic appearance, the MfS was teeming with departmental resentments. Just as Linke had no use for anyone not working at his grass-roots level, so the main headquarters officers arrogantly considered themselves to be key strategists. Of course, their attitude overlooked the fact that the placement of their own agents necessarily involved working closely with people like Linke. Nearly everyone disliked the personnel department, which was exclusively bureaucratic in composition and totally isolated from actual operations. Responding to my puzzlement about not holding this meeting in our regular safe house, Werner said, "They simply can't keep their big mouths shut. It's better never to reveal any of my secret locales to them."

The two cadre officials turned out to be relatively young—in their early thirties at most—and properly dressed. After introducing themselves as Karl-Heinz and Günter, they began to ask questions so formulated as to show their close reading of my résumé. They then delivered the long standard lecture about the party in general and the specific role played by the MfS, stressing its hard and selfless defense of the GDR against the forces of imperialism on the "invisible front." Finally came the question of whether I would carry out every SED assignment, regardless of the circumstances. Remembering Werner's instructions, I gave a lengthy, emotionally charged reply that reaffirmed my complete party devotion.

My performance seemed convincing enough to the two men, although I was glad that Werner had not been present to witness this embarrassing display of spurious passion. After a short discussion of Marxist-Leninist theory, our conversation became more informal. Emphasizing the heavy demands of MfS work, they noted how most of their evenings and weekends were involved as well. For added proof, they continued, I needed only to look at the rigorous schedule my own case officer followed. I noticed, however, that they used the name Werner Hengst to refer to the man known to me as Werner Helbig.

Once they had left, I felt confident enough to query Werner directly about this discrepancy. Reacting angrily, he cursed the two officials for having divulged his real name. But he seemed relieved that my interview had gone well. "All too often," he remarked, "those idiots have messed up my candidates with their stupid questions."

Even though Leo had warned me that money was something not openly discussed in the MfS, I decided to broach the subject of remuneration. With a deep breath, Werner replied, "Thank heavens you didn't mention that to those fools from the personnel department. You would have been grilled for hours about ideology and then classified as excessively materialistic in your recruitment file. Our top man especially frowns on such people. Besides, I don't even know myself what your salary will be. In any case, since the party will never let its best fighters starve, you won't have any cause for complaint."

That afternoon I returned to my office in the Magnushaus to reflect on the last few days and to reexamine my decision to join the MfS. Having been surrounded at the Physics Society mostly by calculating careerists as opposed to ardent communists, I was fully aware of the deep hypocrisy of the regime. At the same time, my original idea of making a break to the West seemed even hazier. Not only had no definite agreement been reached with the other side, but I felt opposed to putting my family at risk.

What, then, was the point of joining the MfS? For a moment, I considered obtaining a civilian job to reconcile my inner conflicts, but the mere thought of being a single insignificant physicist was totally repellent to me. By contrast, espionage held an increasing attraction, provided my knowledge of the regime it served could be suppressed. In this regard, Werner proved a positive influence. Apart from the friendly, almost apolitical nature of our relationship, he had himself stated some criticisms of conditions in the GDR. Moreover, by this stage, it would have been extremely difficult to find a plausible reason for refusing to join the MfS. I therefore decided to continue on this path. No matter how absorbing my work might become, I also resolved to keep in mind the alternative that the totem symbolized. If the situation became completely unbearable, however, I would attempt to contrive my dismissal on the grounds of "incompetence" or "laziness."

4

The Years of Apprenticeship

1

With identity and social security cards in my pocket, I set out to the main MfS headquarters on the designated day of my medical examination. The streetcar contained a large number of well-dressed persons, most of whom exited with me at the Magdalenenstrasse station.

I was struck by the sheer enormity of the MfS complex. It was also well guarded by high, electronically equipped walls and by uniformed NVA soldiers who checked the official identity cards of all MfS employees.

My destination was a low, two-story building bearing the name "GDR Workers' Political Clinic." After the guard had taken my identity card and checked it against a long printed list of names, I was given an itemized schedule and an extensive medical questionnaire to complete. For five long hours, I went from room to room to be poked, prodded, and listened to—all in a most serious and dispassionate manner. At the end of this ordeal, my identity card was returned, and I could leave.

Two weeks later, Werner told me that I had received a top fitness rating and that the only remaining hurdle was the "Authorization Commission." Although I had little clue as to its actual function, Christian notified me about a month later that my official appointment had been approved. He instructed me to tell Linke that I was joining the NVA as a civilian worker in order to earn more money. When I informed Linke, he responded with an unintelligible grumble and made certain that I had no spare time during my remaining weeks at the society.

On August 1, I boarded the streetcar again to report for my first day of work. Following Werner's advice, I was properly attired in coat and tie. My mood was a mixture of excitement and curiosity. How, I wondered, was such a gigantic apparatus organized? What would the working atmosphere be like, and what specific assignment would I receive? Had Küster's friend prophesied correctly regarding my promising career?

This time I took a different exit from the streetcar station and followed a route that brought me to a dirty gray, five-story building with the nameplate "Council of State of the German Democratic Republic—Ministry of State Security—Visitor's Entrance." All the windows were barred, and a television camera was positioned over the door to monitor the street outside. Taking a deep breath and blinking once more into the morning sun, I entered the building.

When the door closed behind me, I noticed that there was no inside knob. To my further astonishment, all I could see was my reflection in a full-length mirror on the left wall. Otherwise this cell-like room was completely empty. A grimace on my face provoked some muted laughter. Then the mirror moved to the side, revealing two grinning guards seated at a counter.

"What do you want?" one of them asked in an official tone of voice.

"I've come to start work," I replied.

After finding my name on a printed list and closely scrutinizing my identity card, he buzzed a door on the opposite wall. I was told to wait in the visitors' room until someone came to fetch me.

Nearly an hour passed as the ten persons ahead of me were called individually and escorted away by a guard. Finally Karl-Heinz from the personnel department appeared and, passing through another guarded door, took me to the inner part of the building.

It was a hive of activity. Karl-Heinz silently guided me through a confusing maze of stairs and corridors until we reached another guard, who again inspected all of our papers. We then crossed a courtyard full of parked cars and entered a six-story building. Another uniformed guard checked our papers.

As we proceeded to Karl-Heinz's office on the third floor, I noticed that all the office doors were designated solely by numbers. His own office contained only two desks, a wardrobe, and two steel cabinets with seals on the doors. In stark contrast to the Physics Society, these antiquated furnishings seemed more befitting a provincial postal official.

Karl-Heinz asked me to sit down and then removed several sheets of paper from one of the file cabinets. "Is everything all right?" he asked.

After I answered affirmatively, he continued, "Are you now prepared to become an MfS officer?"

Liking the sound of this new title, I again replied positively.

"Here is the text of your commitment. It's compulsory, so read it through and then we can clear up any questions you may have."

The contents of the six typewritten sheets differed from my earlier agent commitment only in the amount of detail. Three pages alone spelled out what was expected of me and what was forbidden. I was bound, for example, to register all friendships and acquaintanceships as well as any attempted contacts by an "imperialistic institution." I was to be reachable at all times. I was to educate my family in accordance with SED standards. At the same time, I could not divulge any of my activities, even to another state agency. Further, I could not visit a doctor outside the MfS or have any unofficial contact with the West.

One section made me feel particularly uneasy. I had to submit to the military jurisdiction of the GDR, recognizing that a broken commitment would bring the full severity of the law to bear on me. Nevertheless, after Karl-Heinz answered my questions, I copied and signed each page. He then checked the document very carefully and placed it in a thick file. Explaining that he was the personnel instructor responsible for my service unit, he advised me to refer any future questions to him.

This session lasted about an hour. At its conclusion, Werner returned and added his personal congratulations. As we left the building together, he informed me that, in spite of official regulations, fellow workers remained on a first-name basis; only higher ranks, such as the divisional head, required a formal "Sie." When I interrupted to ask about my own area of operations, he told me that that information had to be relayed by the departmental head, Christian Streubel.

After traversing several more courtyards, we came to what appeared to be a former apartment house. Indeed, on the fourth floor was a luxurious four-room unit, originally designed to house senior employees of the ministry. The growth of the MfS's specialized divisions, however, had forced the conversion of this structure into office space. Since it was noontime and the employees had gone to lunch, I could inspect the department's physical layout at my leisure. Werner explained that, while the bathroom and toilet remained unchanged, the kitchen had been made into an office for the departmental secretary. Werner shared a room with another comrade, but Christian, as departmental head, had an office for himself. I was allocated one of the three desks in what had previously been the living room. It all seemed very cozy and compact.

Upon their return, my new colleagues gave me a boisterous greeting. Surprisingly, three of them were already familiar figures. There was the fake intelligence dealer who had cleverly tricked me the previous fall during a practice exercise. Introduced as Second Lieutenant Peter Grosse, he had a wide grin on his face. Then came the less adroit "enemy agent" who had lost his umbrella during the Leipzig trade fair in 1971. In reality, he was First Lieutenant Horst Kiessig, a genuine Saxon, good-natured and instantly likeable. I further recognized the male half of the amorous couple from my table at the Leipzig nightclub, who turned out to be Lieutenant Werner Heintze.

The two remaining colleagues were Second Lieutenant Axel Huether and Lieutenant Olaf Junghanns. Although I had never seen them before, they had observed me during my embarrassing practice contact with Grosse and submitted a written report including suggestions for my improvement. This episode was now embarrassingly reviewed in fine detail. Afterward, Christian called me to his own office, where, after the standard but short political statement, I was presented with a great deal of new information to digest.

2

I was now a staff member of department one of division XIII of the Sector of Science and Technology of the Chief Intelligence Directorate (HVA) of the MfS. The HVA, charged with the task of obtaining intelligence from enemy and neutral countries, was organized according to various specialized areas. In this instance, the Sector of Science and Technology contained a division devoted to physics, chemistry, and biology. It in turn was divided into specific departments.

As Christian explained, "Our physics department is attempting to gather all available intelligence regarding our enemy's efforts in the field of atomic weaponry. The Federal Republic is our prime concern, even though some manpower must also be directed toward the United States. In addition, we are responsible for obtaining information about new and existing weapons systems based on advances in modern physics. While our Soviet comrades concentrate on the United States, we must be able to deal with West Germany by ourselves. Make no mistake, no one else in the GDR gets involved in this activity."

Although this sounded most impressive in theory, I later discovered that actual practice was more complicated. The department's overriding objective was to acquire any scientific or technical information that could aid the GDR's fundamentally flawed and ailing economic system. At the same time, the Soviets profited greatly, since they received copies of practically everything in our possession. Christian finally gave me some texts about the HVA to study, pointing out, however, that each comrade had to develop operating techniques based on his own particular skills and knowledge.

Hardly had I put these training books into my empty steel cabinet when Werner appeared with a list of official procedures to complete. First it was necessary to notify the HVA Party Office of my change of employment. To secure my steel cabinet, I next received a seal stamped with the number

6475. According to Werner, it was the only one in existence, although Christian also possessed a key and was authorized to open the cabinet. Presumably I would know if anyone else had been rifling my files.

The next stop was the photographer. Once the pictures had been developed, I received my official identity card, which was to be secured by its leather band inside my jacket. Losing this identity card, Werner warned, was nearly the worst transgression possible and would result in a stern punishment.

At the armory, I was given a regulation pistol and fourteen bullets. I also applied for a new apartment at the housing office. Although it would take approximately two years to acquire one, most GDR citizens had to wait a minimum of six years. Werner further noted the most important buildings in the complex: the counterintelligence headquarters; the main ministerial building in the center of the complex; the HVA headquarters; the staff officers' canteen, which the other workers referred to as the "Commanders' Hill"; and finally the MfS's own commissary, which was far better stocked than any normal store in East Berlin.

Just as I returned to my desk, Christian came over to take me upstairs to meet the divisional head. His secretary, Comrade Master Sergeant Iris Eschberger, had no compunctions about keeping us waiting. Despite a closed and leather-padded door, a penetrating voice could be heard. The man who emerged several minutes later bore the clear expression of having received a severe reprimand. As Christian and I entered his office, it was immediately apparent that Comrade Lieutenant-Colonel Horst Vogel, a tall, powerfully built man in his middle forties, was a commanding personality. Merely the way he looked at me produced a feeling of complete nakedness.

"Have you finished your monthly plan yet?" he asked Christian in a most disagreeable tone.

Christian, showing none of his normal self-confidence, meekly answered, "Not yet, Horst. I'll give it to you first thing tomorrow morning."

"If you can't stick to deadlines yourself, then I'll have to stop approving your requests." Vogel then turned to me and said, "So, you're Comrade Stiller. Welcome to my division. Tell me now, with what sort of expectations did you join the MfS?"

Having anticipated some further explanations about the division's work, I was startled by such a blunt question. "Comrade Lieutenant Colonel," I stammered, "right now everything is so new and strange for me . . . ."

"I'm not interested in your impressions," he interrupted. "I asked about your expectations!"

"Comrade Lieutenant Colonel, I know how much the GDR's security depends upon the MfS. Therefore I will attempt to fulfill all the demands made of me."

"I certainly hope so, both for your own sake and for that of your departmental head. You're a physicist, and as a part-time agent, you also showed an aptitude for intelligence work. We are expecting a lot from you, and if things work out, there are boundless possibilities for you. Let me take you to meet the head of the sector."

Comrade Colonel Heinrich Weiberg's office was located in the main HVA building. Vogel and I, however, had to wait for him to return from a meeting with Comrade Lieutenant-General Markus Wolf, the head of the HVA and a deputy minister of the MfS. Revealing a somewhat friendlier side, Vogel began to inquire about my background. Then, quite unexpectedly, he asked, "What do you think of Western television?"

In a bold-faced lie, I denied ever watching it. "I strongly recommend that you don't," he replied. "We're quite strict about matters of party discipline." Never wanting to have to confront Vogel because of some misdemeanor, I resolved for the moment to stop watching the two main West German channels.

A very impressive, elderly man with snow-white hair entered the room. Judging from the yellow stains on his teeth and fingers, he was doubtlessly a heavy smoker. In a thick Berlin dialect, and with a slight stammer, Weiberg said to his secretary, "Well, Jutta, Comrade Wolf must have gotten out of bed on the wrong side this morning. Try to find the statistics he wants and take them to his receptionist."

As Vogel rose to attention and started to introduce me, Weiberg beckoned us into his office. It was furnished much more modestly than I had imagined. Since Weiberg enjoyed recounting various stories from the sector's past history, the discussion that followed had a distinctly paternal tone. Even though he showed some signs of age by occasionally losing his train of thought, his irreverent Berlin humor was fully intact.

When we returned to our own building, Vogel remarked, "Comrade Weiberg is the person who founded the sector. Now that we count among the very best in the entire HVA, a large debt of gratitude is owed to him." According to my later calculations, the sector included roughly 200 officers and 2,000 agents at home and abroad.

As my first working day came to an end, I carefully sealed my file cabinet and got a ride home with Axel Huether, who lived nearby. After first serving in the Feliks-Dzerzhinskii Guard Regiment* and then in the Chief Section for Personal Security, he had joined the department in 1969. I appreciated his quiet, amusing manner. En route, Axel mentioned having witnessed some incredible things among the party hierarchy, but declined to elaborate.

That evening when I broke the news to my wife about my new

---

* Named after the founder of the Soviet Cheka, the Feliks-Dzerzhinskii Guard Regiment was an armed unit charged with protection of top party personnel, visiting dignitaries, and important government buildings. In this period it numbered about 4,000 men.

employment, a most unpleasant discussion ensued. Not only had her father served as a security official in a Hungarian munitions factory, but she had experienced the brutal suppression of the 1956 uprising, including the collaboration of some of her countrymen with the Soviet occupation forces. When I then stated that my duties would normally involve a seventy-hour week, we experienced our first marital crisis.

Fearful that her dislike of my occupation would intensify and create new problems, I decided to suppress my inner convictions and try to "reeducate" her politically. That proved to be a major mistake, for quite unexpectedly, she became a passionate advocate of the party line. When we later moved to an exclusively MfS apartment building, these beliefs were fortified by our neighbors, and our marriage never really recovered. Indeed, any discussion that deviated from official doctrine could not be tolerated.

Christian continued my departmental orientation the following morning. "Above all," he stressed, "we exercise the strictest secrecy among ourselves. Just as your work concerns only the two of us, the cases of your colleagues are strictly taboo. Everyone in the department controls a specific number of undercover agents in both East and West Germany. In time that will apply to you. For now, to help you better understand our work, you should carefully read these four dossiers."

I had hardly read one page before two of my colleagues appeared. One was Captain Günter Haering, the divisional party secretary, who proceeded to emphasize the extraordinary importance of political work within the MfS. In his opinion, this endeavor lay at the heart of the employees' continuing "education according to class doctrine."

By contrast, I took a liking to Captain Gerhard Jauck, the blond-haired, well built, and youthful-looking deputy divisional head. In a quite unconventional manner, he explained the functions of the other departments within our division. Whereas department one covered the fields of microbiology, bacteriology, and biological warfare, it was the task of department three to track down chemical weapons in the West. "Watch out for the members of department four," he cautioned. "Just because they are directly involved with the United States, they consider themselves superior to the rest of us. It's too bad their track record isn't any better."

Jauck further advised me to set realistic goals and to expect failure most of the time. "Despite all attempts to raise intelligence work to a science," he said, "it will always remain primarily a matter of experience, intuition, and luck. If one out of ten Westerners happens to respond to your overtures, you can consider yourself fortunate. But if everything goes wrong at first, don't feel discouraged. Some of our employees have yet to make one West recruitment after five years. An early success, on the other hand, would put you in the strongest position for the future."

Next came notification of an important meeting with the deputy head of the sector, Colonel Willi Neumann. Before leaving, I was warned by the departmental secretary, or "Sigi," as Master Sergeant Sigrid Brodehl was affectionately known, that a rapid promotion depended upon a favorable impression. When I entered Neumann's office in the main HVA building, his secretary, who turned out to be the other half of the Leipzig nightclub couple, gave me a beaming look of recognition.

A small, rotund man nearly sixty years old, Willi, as he was generally called, was known for his gluttonous appetite and never passing up an official meal. He also had a reputation for being exceedingly clumsy. In fact, our initial meeting was abruptly called to a halt after he managed not only to spill a fresh cup of coffee on his suit but also to upset the milk pitcher on his desk and then trip over his own overturned chair. Realizing that Willi was also the type of person to bear a grudge, I struggled to keep a straight face during this unforgettable performance.

3

Upon seeing the 1,500-page dossier marked "Gärtner" lying in front of me, Werner remarked, "So you've been given the big nuclear spy. You'll have fun with that one." Certainly the dramatic saga of Harald Gottfried, as he was known in reality, gave me some insights into the early operations of the HVA.

Born in 1935, Gottfried had been resettled with his family after the war in Thuringia. Unfortunately, his father, a provincial schoolteacher, happened to make a critical remark about the Soviet treatment of local women and girls. Although no Nazi, he received a ten-year prison sentence and, according to official reports, later died of pneumonia. As rumors began to circulate that the man had actually been tortured to death, the remaining members of the family, with the exception of Harald, decided to immigrate illegally to the FRG. More concerned about making a career than with his father's fate, Harald continued his studies in pedagogy in Dresden, and, to avert any suspicion of himself, became an active FDJ member.

The interest of the Dresden State Security branch was triggered when Harald applied for an exit permit to visit his mother and sisters. That he took such a formal step, when fleeing the GDR in those years involved nothing more than a streetcar ride from East to West Berlin, convinced these authorities that Harald would probably return. They could not, however, exclude the possibility of his employment by a Western intelligence agency. When confronted by MfS officers, the young man maintained that he felt burdened by his father's "guilt" and disapproved of his family's move to the West. In addition, he considered himself a loyal GDR citizen as well as a true Marxist-Leninist. At a second meeting, Harald even agreed to compile reports on those fellow students who displayed signs of ideological weakness.

His following assignment—to stop in West Berlin after a visit with his family and penetrate an organization of lawyers actively opposed to the GDR regime—was also carried out to his superiors' satisfaction. At this point, Willi Neumann, sensing an opportunity in Harald's admittedly thin file, summoned him to the MfS headquarters in East Berlin and obtained his commitment to work as an undercover agent. A month later, upon completion of the necessary administrative inquiries, Harald received the codename "Gärtner."

At that time, the West German government was finishing plans to construct a nuclear research center in Karlsruhe. Fearful that the FRG might violate its stated pledge not to build nuclear weapons, the Soviets and East Germans viewed this new facility with heightened concern. Yet it should also be noted that they possessed a keen curiosity about all scientific investigation, regardless of its application. They further knew that no field could be better guarded from outside observation than nuclear physics.

According to Neumann's plan, Gärtner was to obtain West German citizenship and enroll at the Technical University in Karlsruhe as a student of electrical engineering. The MfS would provide a monthly stipend of 150 West German marks. When Neumann alluded to his family history, maintaining that there was "a certain debt to society to repay," Gärtner unhesitatingly agreed. Nevertheless, one unforeseen obstacle remained, for in the meantime Gärtner had enrolled in the SED. That awkward fact ruled out using the organization of West Berlin lawyers to facilitate his naturalization. Instead he should appeal to the emergency reception office in West Berlin, declaring that he could no longer reside in a state that had murdered his father, and that his party membership was solely to protect his place at the university.

The ploy worked, and in the following years Gärtner proved to be a hard-working, inconspicuous student. On his occasional trips back to East Berlin, he received additional instruction in ciphers, radio transmissions, dead-letter drops, and secret photography. Still, despite his solid reports on fellow students and teachers, he began to show those familiar signs of ideological softness that come from living for extended periods in the West.

To combat this backsliding, MfS officials applied more psychological pressure, reminding Gärtner especially of his father's guilt and subsequent fate. At the same time, having just discovered the enormous potential offered by the many unmarried governmental secretaries in Bonn, they decided to use him for a somewhat different assignment. Gärtner was to seek out women who worked in important ministerial offices and establish a romantic liaison. Not unattractive in appearance, he quickly became absorbed in this activity, completely neglecting both his studies and his MfS obligations. Rethinking the situation, Neumann abruptly ordered him back to the university and also reduced his funds.

Upon Gärtner's graduation in 1961, the MfS was in a quandary as to how to proceed. To submit an employment application to the Nuclear Research Center in Karlsruhe raised the possibility of a thorough security check and the discovery of his former SED affiliation. On the other hand, the enormous Soviet interest in this new facility could not be ignored, and this finally persuaded Markus Wolf, the already experienced head of the HVA, to risk this important placement.

As it turned out, Gärtner received a position without difficulty and began relaying films of various unclassified documents. Soon enough, however, he fell into new personal difficulties. Despite all the warnings of the MfS, he decided to marry a divorcée with two children. Besides his new wife's pronounced dislike of the GDR, Gärtner's added family responsibilities caused the flow of information to decrease. To remedy the evident "lack of discipline" shown by their agent, the MfS transferred responsibility for Gärtner to the local resident codenamed Hartmann. In addition to reducing the number of Gärtner's trips to East Berlin, this arrangement kept him under tighter control and resulted in more and better information.

Several years later, however, Gärtner committed another major error by confiding his MfS work to his wife. While she emphatically disapproved of his "part-time job," he obtained her pledge never to betray him. As past experience had made the MfS highly skeptical of such promises, the tie to Hartmann was immediately severed to protect the rest of his residency. Gärtner was left to fend for himself, although once it seemed certain that his wife was keeping her word, a so-called "instructor" met him at regular intervals in the FRG. As a further precaution, Gärtner was ordered to bury his secret coding machine and other equipment somewhere outside his own property.

This new setup initially yielded impressive results. Hilde Klein, who had assumed the role of instructor "Gross," was a skilled undercover agent, and the exceptionally valuable information obtained soon resulted in large stipends and various awards for Gärtner. Naturally these documents contained no references to atomic weapons, but they still gave the Soviets substantial data regarding the development of nuclear power stations.

In October 1968, however, Gärtner was suddenly arrested in Karlsruhe by the provincial criminal police and charged as an enemy agent. En route to a meeting with him in Heidelberg, Hilde Klein happened to see the headline "GDR Atom Spy Arrested" with an accompanying picture of Gärtner, and beat a hasty retreat back to East Berlin. While her safe return was greeted with great relief, everyone seemed completely baffled as to how Gärtner's cover had been blown. Had his wife betrayed him? Or had he himself been careless when procuring and photographing the documents?

Clearly Gärtner had not followed the earlier order to dispose of his technical equipment. In fact, when the police later discovered it in a trailer outside his house, he again ignored the MfS rulebook and made a full confession. For the MfS, the pressing question was whether he had implicated Hartmann as well. The two men had met often enough, although Hartmann's real identity had never been disclosed to him.

In the suspenseful days that followed, the MfS undertook its own investigation to discover what had originally gone awry. At this point, several pages were missing from the file, and the narrative became somewhat hazy. Despite receiving an eighteen-month prison sentence, Gärtner was released after six weeks, allegedly because the period while awaiting trial had been taken into account, and returned to the GDR. What drew my particular attention was a sentence in the final summary: "In light of all known evidence, Gärtner's arrest had been caused by the betrayal of a double agent named 'Alois.' "

Having seen nothing previously in the file regarding a double agent, I asked Christian for an explanation. "That's a long story," he replied. "You should ask Werner to explain it to you. Though hardly a glorious chapter for us, it will help you understand why we can never be careful enough."

4

The following Saturday, over a pot of coffee at the office, Werner told me the complete story of Alois.

The decade of the 1950s was a golden age for HVA recruiters. By thoroughly combing the East German universities, students possessing a degree of sympathy for the regime were first identified and then given a perfunctory security check. They were to pursue those studies in the West that would later give them access to valuable intelligence material. Because the allure of life in the FRG far outweighed the risk of detection, it was possible to attract large numbers of so-called prospective agents. With the open border in Berlin, they were also easily placed.

The erection of the "Anti-Fascist Protective Wall" in 1961, however, created a number of problems for the HVA. Not the least was the maintenance of this large body of agents already in the West. At the time of their transfer, they had purposely received little technical training in espionage. To be sure, fearful that they might later reveal themselves to West German counterintelligence, the HVA had strictly followed the maxim that information regarding operational procedures should never reach the enemy. Then, too, the majority of these agents had yet to complete their studies and had nothing of interest to convey. Put simply, the amount of money and effort involved hardly seemed justified by the meager results.

To remedy this situation, various residencies, like the Hartmann one, were set up in the FRG. A number of agents would then be assigned to a resident, normally someone residing in the area as an "immigrant." The principal work could then be handled in situ, although maintaining contact with East Berlin through couriers and instructors continued to be a problem.

Also at this time, Linke was a full-time employee in our department. At the Leipzig trade fair, he encountered a West German full of praise for the GDR and quickly recruited him under the name "Alois." Even though his business offered nothing of interest to the HVA, Alois had to make frequent trips to West Berlin. Linke therefore assigned him to the Hartmann residence as a courier. In exchange for money, Alois was to bring the contents of a dead-letter drop in the Frankfurt area to East Berlin on a regular basis. Given the FRG's minimal security checks at the time, this arrangement worked smoothly for many years.

Meanwhile both Linke and his departmental head, Major Günther Heinrich, had developed a great fondness for alcohol and began to lose their "revolutionary vigilance." Specifically, they permitted Alois to function as an instructor without making any further inquiries. Besides contacting Hartmann at his own apartment, Alois came to know everything about the residency's operations, including individual names and addresses. Obviously this constituted a severe violation of existing rules, but no disciplinary action was taken.

The arrest of Gärtner, however, gave a sudden jolt to Linke and Heinrich. Once the HVA's internal investigation was under way and suspicion increasingly began to center on Alois, they had to face some highly embarrassing questions. That their days in the department were now numbered seemed a foregone conclusion.

While Alois knew nothing of the ongoing HVA investigation, the case against him was building from another direction. Anxious to send a report to his East German superiors, Gärtner had managed to enlist the help of a fellow prisoner named Wolfgang, who was soon to be released. Also in clear contravention of MfS procedures, Gärtner had even confided the secret telephone number of his case officer. Upon arrival in East Berlin, Wolfgang decided to circumvent the lengthy entry procedures by loudly proclaiming that he possessed vital information for state security. Eventually, after much hubbub, he delivered Gärtner's report and explained the circumstances surrounding it.

When the news of this incident reached his office, Willi Neumann, convinced that Wolfgang had to be an enemy agent, flew into an instant rage. Afterward, however, he took a closer look at Gärtner's report and noted one sentence in particular: "During an interrogation, the name 'Ulli' was mentioned, although it had never passed my lips before." Ulli, as it turned out, was Hartmann's real first name. As Gärtner's wife and lawyer also supported his contention of never having mentioned Hartmann's name, West German authorities must have learned it from another source. Since the headquarters staff remained above suspicion, only Alois was left.

After thoroughly reviewing the files of everyone involved and then interrogating Linke about what Alois might have known, Neumann contacted Weiberg. Reluctantly the two men appeared before Markus Wolf with the news. "You've got four weeks to deliver this double agent," Wolf replied. "Since the Hartmann residency is in great danger, all operational work must be halted immediately and any incriminating evidence destroyed."

"Comrade Lieutenant General," Weiberg responded feebly, "I'm afraid we weren't dealt a very lucky hand this time."

"Instead of a hand, you should have used your head," Wolf said in a retort that later became famous in the ministry.

Although further departmental investigation strengthened the case against Alois, it seemed puzzling why the West Germans had not yet made their move against the Hartmann residency. The most probable explanation was that Gärtner's long separation from the residency had made him vulnerable and that a "hands off" policy was being pursued for the moment. That meant proceeding as cautiously as possible, for a sudden or indiscreet move against Alois could result in the capture of everyone connected to Hartmann.

During his next visit to East Berlin, Alois cinched the case against himself by falling into every trap laid by the HVA. Besides writing down the automobile license plate number of his case officer, Manfred Terber, he used the man's short absence from the room to search his briefcase and photograph several interesting documents. Nevertheless, since the Hartmann residency had not been completely dismantled, no action was taken, and Alois returned safely to the FRG.

Once preparations for the retreat had been completed, the hard question was whether to summon the residency immediately back to the GDR—and thereby lose Alois—or to risk the residency by waiting for his next trip to East Berlin. Although the top HVA leadership, including Wolf, preferred the former alternative, none of them wanted to take responsibility for the final decision. The matter was ultimately resolved by the head of the MfS, Erich Mielke, who demanded Alois's capture at any cost.

After another anxious period of waiting, Alois finally returned to East Berlin, accompanied by his wife. Instantly the GDR border patrol sounded the alarm for Hartmann and his group to leave West Germany as quickly as possible. Meanwhile the abundant hospitality of the MfS guesthouse "Wald" was extended to the couple in the usual manner. In order for the two departmental employees stationed outside to monitor the listening devices and also prevent Alois's escape, Terber had locked the window shutters before leaving the couple that evening. That gave Alois his first uneasy feeling. After then discovering that both his passport and miniature camera were missing from his luggage, he sank into an armchair and told his wife to remain quiet. An attempted telephone call to Frankfurt was denied because of "temporary technical difficulties," and a long, sleepless night began.

In the calculation that the double agent might inadvertently reveal some additional information, the actual confrontation—to be played out in a quite perverse fashion—was delayed until the following day. While Terber took Alois's wife on a downtown shopping tour, Alois was invited by Neumann to a substantial noon meal at the guesthouse. As Alois was passing the vegetables, Neumann stated that the MfS knew his identity as a Western agent and that their talks would be continued at another location. Alois was given a faint glimmer of hope that some sort of bargain might be struck. Once Neumann had eaten his fill, however, Alois was placed under guard and driven to the MfS's interrogation prison. Yet, despite the insults, threats, and bribes that followed, he maintained utmost discipline, admitting nothing other than his rank as an American colonel and calmly accepting a sentence of life imprisonment.

Having developed a certain admiration for Alois, I felt troubled by this outcome. Certainly his life sentence seemed unfair compared to the mere eighteen months that Gärtner had received in the FRG. When I sought an explanation for this discrepancy, Werner replied, "They're just trying to maintain the pretense of having a democratic system."

There remained several other sequels to this story. Whereas all the members of Hartmann's residency arrived unscathed back in East Berlin, Linke and Heinrich, still subject to the internal investigation, began to take increasing solace in the bottle and were later transferred. The downfall of Manfred Terber was also not long in coming. In a moment of romantic indiscretion, he revealed some information to a woman who subsequently tried to enlist his cooperation with an American intelligence agency. Realizing that he had already gone too far, he made a complete confession to his superiors and, in return, received a six-year sentence in the high-security prison at Bautzen.

Gärtner's return to East Berlin in the fall of 1969 happened to coincide with the celebration of the GDR's twentieth anniversary. Not wanting to be left out of the massive propaganda display surrounding the event, the MfS decided to make a special television film devoted to the nuclear spy and his struggle for peace on the "invisible front." In fact, I had found in Gärtner's file not only a copy of the final broadcast but all the various drafts, beginning with the initial concept. Significantly, too, the scriptwriter and director turned out to be Christian, who had succeeded Heinrich as departmental head.

The film itself embodied a complete falsification of the case. Contrary to what had really transpired, Gärtner was depicted as having discovered the nefarious production of nuclear weapons in Karlsruhe and then been subjected to a brutal interrogation and confinement. Yet, as the MfS records themselves indicated, the West Germans had made no attempt either to manufacture nuclear weapons or to obtain a supply from abroad. Moreover, indicative of the almost cordial treatment by FRG authorities, Gärtner had left prison several pounds heavier and with a newly acquired knowledge of French.

But that was not all. To lend credence to this spurious documentary, three of the scientists belonging to the Hartmann residency—Herbert Patzelt, Ehrenfried Petras, and Heinz Wieczorek—began to give well-publicized press conferences to explain their "defection" to the "true German fatherland." Repeatedly they maintained that their consciences had forced them to leave an imperialistic state readying itself for nuclear war. As I also discovered in Gärtner's file, this final twist enabled the MfS to record the retreat of the Hartmann residency not as a preventive measure but as an "offensive" gain.

Such a brazen disregard for truth brought me to a new realization. The lie was not used just to cover up certain instances of mismanagement, but formed an intrinsic element of the Marxist-Leninist state. In the GDR, the determination of all matters from a so-called proletarian point of view, regardless of actual facts, had led to the SED's exercise of unbounded power.

Curious about the attitude of my MfS colleagues, I once very cautiously alluded to this shrewd arrangement. "You can only harm yourself with such questions," replied one of them. "Learn as fast as possible what can and cannot be said—and also learn to ignore many things or forget them completely afterward."

5

The next two files that I was to examine proved considerably less interesting. One concerned Heinz Felke, a physics professor at Dresden, whose recent recruitment had been effected by using the fact that certain members of his family were former Nazis. Assigned the codename "Erich," he never showed any signs of cooperation and completed his assignments only reluctantly. His file therefore was officially classified a dead one. Even though Erich remained subject to future reactivation, I was never to meet the man during my MfS tenure.

The other file, involving Rudi Rockstroh, a physicist at the East German Central Institute for Nuclear Research, fell into the same category. By stressing that all loyal SED members must make some contribution to the defense of the state, Linke had recruited him in the mid-1960s under the name "Falcon." In the meantime, however, the lack of a suitable placement meant that he had been left alone.

It was the fourth dossier, marked "Günther," that held much more promise. Already known to me under his real name, Alfred Büchner, he had headed the Physics Society just prior to Linke. His many years in that position had enabled him to know virtually every major physicist in the FRG. Yet in the early 1950s, Büchner had also offered his services to the MfS and had become a specialist in "skimming the cream," or the acquisition of semi-confidential information, from his West German colleagues. His technique was to pose as a "liberal" scientist, lamenting the poor connections between the physicists of a divided Germany and pointedly criticizing the GDR leadership. Because of their idealistic belief in the freedom of science, many West German colleagues responded by giving him some of their unpublished reports and other valuable tips. They remained, however, completely unaware of the important assistance they were extending to the GDR's own unproductive research program.

Although the quantity of documents acquired by Büchner had established him as a major departmental asset, he had unfortunately run afoul of the GDR's own laws because of his attraction to underage girls. For the powerful MfS, it was easy enough merely to file the state attorney's charges in the wastebasket, but Büchner nonetheless had been barred from further travels to the West.

Even though these detailed files had made for instructive reading, I felt puzzled and asked Christian how next to proceed. He first announced that I was about to attend an introductory course for all new MfS employees, to be followed by three months of theoretical instruction at a special HVA school. My other task was to become acquainted with Büchner and direct his activities at the Leipzig trade fair. To supplement my assignment, Christian gave me a series of pamphlets stamped "confidential," which explained the various stages in the development of potential agents.

The introductory course turned out to be a farce. For two long weeks, thirty of us were compelled to hear members of the main personnel and training division making their verbose condemnation of West German imperialism and extolling the MfS's supreme importance in the defense of the state. Besides being reminded of the need for secrecy and "revolutionary vigilance," we were shown training films designed to arouse our class hatred. So that even the new kitchen employees would understand what was expected of them, the entire presentation was pitched on a very elementary and boring level.

When I returned to MfS headquarters, preparations for the fall trade fair were in full swing. Since the HVA course was not to commence until later in the month, it would be possible for me to attend the fair as well. In fact, as Werner explained, this biannual event afforded so many opportunities for Western contacts that nearly the entire HVA had become regular visitors. Besides welcoming a return to the site of my university studies and the chance perhaps of seeing some former classmates, I also wondered whether someone from the "other side" might attempt to contact me. Yet in reality, I knew that the constant presence of numerous MfS colleagues would virtually eliminate any such possibility.

My companion on the trip to Leipzig was Peter Grosse, a former professional soccer player who had joined the department about a year before. A joint injury, he explained, had ended his undistinguished career in the GDR league and led to his decision to attend an engineering school. While a student, he had been recruited by the MfS and given a short training session. Because of the aptitude he had shown for intelligence work, Grosse was repeatedly sent to the FRG on different assignments. One of his main tasks involved shopping at specified stores for various items— mostly textiles and electronic products, but also some luxury goods—and returning with them to the GDR. No explanation was ever provided, but occasionally he received permission to keep something for himself.

As these shopping lists grew longer and came to include sex-shop items, the pretexts for his trips became flimsier. When one assignment merely consisted of writing down all the license-plate numbers in a Stuttgart parking lot, he began to question his case officer about the legitimacy of these trips. Despite assurances that all was proper, Grosse decided to terminate this activity after being told to readjust his traveling vouchers in a blatantly fraudulent manner.

Reassigned to new duties, he was to make regular trips to Bonn and, like Gärtner, attempt to ensnare some lonely governmental secretaries. That he already had a wife was merely brushed aside by his case officer, and soon Grosse's good looks and manners proved irresistible to many targeted women. Through some indiscreet remarks of his case officer, however, Grosse's wife learned of this activity and threatened to make an official complaint against the case officer, who responded by offering Grosse a well-paying headquarters appointment if the Bonn episode was completely forgotten.

Although the couple accepted the deal, the new position failed to materialize, and Grosse was placed in our department. Soon enough, however, Christian extracted the full story of his past assignments and proceeded to initiate disciplinary action against the former case officer. While the man was eventually dismissed and disappeared into the gray working masses, his crime turned out to be not the extensive shopping lists but rather the attempted manipulation of the travel account.

Since both matters plainly involved the embezzlement of state funds for private purposes, I expressed my confusion about the official verdict. Grosse explained that the case officer had tried to siphon the travel money into his own pocket, whereas the order to buy Western goods had originated with Vogel and other high-ranking officers. "It won't take long before you notice a most unequal application of socialist morality and legality," Grosse continued. "For a lowly MfS worker, the rules are strictly enforced without exception. The higher the rank, however, the larger the bounds of permissiveness."

Because of his evident candor, I decided to ask about the chances of a headquarters worker ever receiving a Western assignment. "None at all," he answered. "It is simply too dangerous for HVA officers possessing such valuable secret information."

His definitive reply made me think that I had perhaps miscalculated and was now more restricted than before. I decided to probe further. "But how can I properly dispatch my agents to the West without any first-hand experience myself?"

"The first commandment of the MfS is security, and the headquarters staff receives top priority." It was an answer that I wanted to resist believing. In fact, as I later discovered, there had been several well-justified instances when a case officer traveled to a Western country. Yet the complete trust of one's superiors, developed over a period of many years, was an absolute prerequisite.

When we arrived in Leipzig, we went directly to the student barracks that regularly served as the sector's headquarters during the fair. In the outside lot, I was astonished to see several luxurious Western automobiles with GDR license plates parked among the usual East bloc makes. Grosse explained that all the divisional heads had a strong craving for beautiful and expensive Western cars and attended the fair specifically to see the new models on display. Brigadier-General Fruck, the first deputy head of the HVA, had first choice and usually bought the entire collection, which he then distributed to the divisional heads according to their individual preference. Since Mielke disliked seeing these vehicles on the streets of East Berlin, their use was restricted to official trips such as this one.

Grosse anticipated my next question about the source of payment. "Just because the GDR lacks hard foreign currency doesn't mean that the HVA does. Each divisional head has a secret fund completely at his disposal. When I once indignantly asked Christian how such a situation could be reconciled with the socialistic ideals of thrift and simplicity, he shouted back, 'Prove that you have some ability yourself before asking any more questions like that.' Yes indeed, our state also holds to the principle of every person for himself. The sooner you realize this, the better your chances of enjoying the good life."

Following the assignment of our living quarters, Christian assembled the departmental staff to talk about the world political situation and the operational possibilities at the fair. Afterward, he met individually with each of us. In my case, as I had already instructed my agent "Günther" to come to Leipzig, there was relatively little for us to discuss. Still I was encouraged to observe the technique of my colleagues and look at several Western visitors.

To prepare our meals, an entire kitchen crew had been brought to the fair. That evening, dressed in more casual attire, we were able to enjoy a first-class steak dinner at the sensationally low price of 1.25 marks. This prompted Grosse to repeat his earlier advice. "Just remember, the bosses are at the top, and the ordinary citizens at the bottom. We're therefore in a position to enjoy certain 'middle-class' privileges. It actually takes a touch of corruption to understand how the whole system works."

As a further perk, there was genuine Pilsner beer from Czechoslovakia, a rarity in the GDR. Because I was the newest departmental employee, the first round belonged to me, although the money spent was soon gained back by my winnings in the all-night card game that followed.

The next day, still feeling ill at ease with such privileges, I decided to broach the subject with Werner Heintze, another colleague who seemed friendly as well as intelligent. Given his high position as second divisional party secretary, I expected his reaction to be totally different from that of Grosse. That proved to be another miscalculation.

"As a newcomer, I also believed that the MfS had a particular responsibility to uphold the ideals of socialism," he said. "But you'll be better off remembering that we're only human beings and keeping your ideological bellyaches to yourself."

6

Despite the meager representation of Western firms involved in nuclear technology, I was excited by the prospect of assuming the role of case officer for the first time. As soon as Günther arrived in Leipzig, Christian accompanied me to a morning meeting at the Café am Ring. A small, plump figure—his inferiority complex toward adult women seemed quite understandable—Günther immediately reciprocated Christian's warm greeting. But upon learning that I was now his new case officer, he kept a noticeable distance. I began to wonder whether my youth and inexperience would preclude a relationship with someone so worldly and knowledgeable.

Over Irish coffee to mark the occasion, the discussion came to focus on current scientific issues and remained generally free of Christian's normal political injections. Because of my recent studies, I succeeded in making a good impression, and Günther's expression brightened. Once the two of us were alone, Günther explained his initial mistrust. It turned out that my predecessor, Olaf Junghanns, possessed little understanding of physics and had subjected him to constant political sermonizing, despite Günther's own thirty years in the SED.

"At the last fair," he continued, "Olaf made me present myself to Western visitors as a member of the GDR Peace Council and practically beg them to contribute something to the socialist cause. I hope that you won't make me repeat that."

This quaint little man made me smile to myself. After assuring him of my very different approach, I pointed out a group of French exhibitors of nuclear power equipment. Because of their broken German and his excellent command of French, he should offer his assistance as a translator and try to break the ice with one of them.

"The only difficulty," he replied, "is that my superiors in the Ministry of Science and Technology must approve any Western contact."

"If they ever find out, it only means that you've done a poor job," I stated firmly. "Just tell the French representatives that you're acting in a private capacity and make some complaints about the GDR's restrictive policy regarding contact with Westerners. That should produce a more intimate atmosphere."

Noting that Olaf had always stuck to the rulebook, Günther eagerly accepted my unorthodox suggestion. "How far though am I allowed to take them?" he inquired.

At that point, I admitted my greenness in such matters and deferred to his long experience. This move seemed to cement our relationship. "At last someone honest has joined the outfit," he remarked with evident satisfaction.

Back at the barracks, I ran into Werner Hengst, who offered me a bottle of beer and started an informal conversation. When he inquired about my first impressions of the department, I responded favorably and pointed out the friendliness of even my superiors.

"That may well change," he warned. "Appearances notwithstanding, there is much ambition and in-fighting. Some positive results will certainly put you in good standing with the bosses, but your colleagues' envy will also be aroused. On the other hand, while the absence of results might elicit some personal expressions of sympathy, you'll be officially admonished for your poor showing. Try therefore to make a Western recruit as soon as possible, preferably within the next two years if you expect to be promoted rapidly. Can you imagine Vogel's reaction when someone requests a higher position after five years of no recruitments?"

Taking another swallow of beer, Werner continued, "Also remember to keep your big mouth shut about politics."

As I started to object, he interrupted, "Whom are you trying to fool? After all, I was the person who processed your MfS application, even if my final report omitted some things about you."

"If there had been any doubts, why then did you approve my candidacy?" I asked.

"In contrast to many other employees in the division, you seemed to have the makings of a good intelligence officer, including the capacity to adapt." To be sure, as I increasingly discovered myself, it was a certain calculated conformity that made for a successful MfS career and also gave stability to the entire system.

In the meantime, Günther had arranged to have dinner with one of the Frenchmen and asked me to join them. We agreed that I should be introduced as his assistant, using my old cover name, "Schilling." During the meal, I remained superfluously in the background, particularly since the conversation was mostly in French. After the rather enigmatic man left, I eagerly asked Günther for his assessment.

"I think we've made a good catch," he said. "He's a shady type and obviously short of money. When I made the half-joking suggestion that he privately sell me some of his firm's 'know-how,' his demeanor became very serious. He wants to talk more about my offer, but unfortunately his next visit to the GDR is a long time away. When I offered to meet him in France, he responded with an invitation. I hope that the trip will be possible."

My hesitant reaction—this initial meeting had perhaps gone too far— quickly dampened Günther's feeling of accomplishment. "Not only did you give me a free hand, but opportunities must be seized when they appear," he stated, obviously offended. To be on the safe side, however, I decided to seek Christian's advice before proceeding any further.

Not surprisingly, my story aroused Christian's extreme indignation. "Did you take leave of your senses? Hardly three days in the department and you permit your agent to attempt a recruitment without making a prior investigation of the man or applying for official approval. It will certainly be lively with you around here!"

Christian's anger had obviously been feigned, for immediately afterward I received instructions to run a check on the Frenchman. The next day I obtained a report from Division "R" (records). As no previous entries had been found, the man was now considered mine and could not be claimed by any other MfS officer. In addition, all new information about him, regardless of its source, would automatically come to me.

Soon after the fair ended, Günther received a written invitation from the man to continue their "interesting" conversation in France. Christian seemed greatly pleased and approved the trip. "Still it could be a trap," he cautioned, "and no agreement should be concluded there. Instead, the contact should be strengthened and then the man invited to East Berlin for more serious talks."

Because my HVA training course was about to begin, the necessary arrangements were left in Christian's hands. Yet before the trip could materialize, Günther was hospitalized, and died three months later from a heart attack. A letter was subsequently sent to the Frenchman, purportedly from Günther, but it went unanswered.

7

On the eve of my departure for the HVA school, I returned to the office to bid my colleagues farewell and to collect my service pistol, gas mask, and submachine gun. I then notified Vogel of my impending three-month absence. Although I purposely stressed to him my strong sense of purpose regarding this training, the mere prospect was repellent to me. Indeed, as a number of former participants had testified, the actual instruction had little practical content and was comprised mostly of ideological indoctrination. My only curiosity was to discover the precise location of the school, which no one had seemed willing to reveal. The instruction sheet merely indicated that it was approximately sixty miles from East Berlin.

The only other trainee from my division was Peter Bertag, who had already become known as Vogel's protégé. Thirty years old, he had earned his doctorate in chemistry from the technical university in Merseburg and had also served as the full-time FDJ secretary during his final years. Besides working with the arrogant United States specialists of department four, he seemed excessively bound to the party line and prone to political bombast. My first impression was hardly a favorable one.

Although the HVA's actual size remained a closely guarded secret, the fact that there were forty participants in our group allowed me to make a rough estimate. On the basis of two such mandatory training courses every year and twenty-five years as the average length of service, I arrived at the figure of approximately 2,000 officers, which later experience also confirmed. There were, of course, many other people involved in espionage work, including the various branches of the MfS counterintelligence section. The NVA also contained a surveillance unit, but no one took it very seriously.

It was a beautiful fall morning as we headed south on the autobahn toward Leipzig. To make certain that no unauthorized person had boarded the bus, our official identity cards were checked a second time against a printed list. To pass the time we played cards.

After leaving the autobahn, the bus continued through the old but shabby town of Belzig and stopped at a barrier about a mile and a half down the road. A sign read "Central School of the Society for Sport and Technology, Edgar André." A uniformed guard lifted the barrier, and we drove on to the main complex.

Almost immediately, we found ourselves sitting in a lecture room waiting for our first session to begin. At the abrupt command—"Comrades, officers, attention!"—all of us rose in military fashion, despite our civilian clothes, and a flock of teachers entered the room. Their elderly leader, Colonel Otto Wendel, greeted us with a short, friendly address before handing over the meeting to his less agreeable assistant. For the next two hours, one political cliché followed another.

Based on the reactions of my fellow classmates, I discerned two distinct groups. One was a small number of fanatics, who gave the impression of complete absorption. The other, far larger group was made up of mode-rates, who could barely hold back the boredom from their faces.

To obtain our room assignments, we then proceeded to the barracks, located next to a soccer field. From the quartermaster, each of us received a GST uniform to help give a measure of plausibility to the school's official cover. Finally, our official identity cards were exchanged for small gray cards stamped with an "S," which would allow us to enter and leave the various school buildings.

After a hearty lunch—the food proved to be excellent—we were told to maintain absolute secrecy regarding the real purpose of the school. Trips to Belzig could be made only to purchase the most essential items, and all contact with the local populace was expressly forbidden. Even our regular HVA work should not be discussed with members of other units. As a further precaution, our instruction material was locked away in a safe every evening. In fact, when one member of our group happened to walk across the courtyard with an uncovered training manual, he received a sharp reprimand.

One of my roommates was Second Lieutenant Klaus Bellmann from the Border Work Patrol. Having never heard of this unit before, I pressed him that evening for an explanation, but he refused, referring to his strict orders not to divulge any information. Over the next weeks, however, his resist-ance weakened, and some details began to emerge. This patrol had the responsibility of clandestinely guiding MfS agents through the minefields in both directions over the border with West Germany. I also learned the reason for such extreme confidentiality. At a training session the previous year, one participant, after ascertaining the exact location of these un-guarded border paths from his roommate, had used that knowledge to escape to the FRG. Later I discovered that a number of MfS officers had made similar attempts, although only a few had been successful.

My other roommate was Lieutenant Klaus Gey from division one. When he related the details of his posting to Munich as an East German tourist during the 1972 Olympic Games, I listened with great envy. Yet to prevent his description of the Bavarian capital from sounding overly enthusiastic, he carefully added, with a touch of class consciousness, "Naturally it was all stage-managed to make West Germany look good during the games."

When our classes began the following morning, the first area to be explored was Marxism-Leninism. Despite the attempt at a more theoretical treatment, the message seemed so familiar that general boredom prevailed. The only real debate in this session concerned the possible effects on the MfS of a new treaty about to be ratified with the FRG. While some believed that relaxed relations would offer more potential contacts in the West, others feared an ideological softening in the GDR and greater complica-tions for the MfS. The issue was finally resolved when our teachers presented the "correct" point of view. Whereas some aspects of our work would certainly become easier, we were also warned not to misinterpret the advent of a friendlier relationship. In Marxist terms, it signified merely a change in the external conditions of the "struggle against the class enemy." If Western imperialism was to be defeated, an even harder fight must be waged on all fronts.

There was the further question of whether the enemy would acquire increased potential for the "subversive penetration" of the GDR. We, however, received the firm reassurance that the MfS possessed the where-withal to deal with any new activity. Moreover, the political process involved in these negotiations would result in an objective weakening of the imperialist West. As one of our teachers noted, "This agreement will naturally contain minimal compromises on our part and maximum conces-sions from the FRG."

The next area of instruction—"operational regime conditions"—was an MfS term indicating everything currently known about the FRG. That involved not just the police, military, and intelligence forces, but all other facets of life, including their regional variations. As in the sessions on Marxism-Leninism, the general presentation had a highly tendentious tone. Nevertheless, this exposure to life on the other side of the border contained some intriguing information, and I began to draw my own conclusions. To be sure, despite all the efforts to frame the "central questions" around such issues as strikes, unemployment, and general repression, it seemed clear that the FRG not only had a higher standard of living but also tried to deal with problems in an open and democratic manner.

Our discussion of how to put this knowledge of the enemy to practical use was drawn from one hypothetical case. It assumed that an already married GDR "immigrant" had succeeded in enticing an unattached middle-aged secretary to work for the MfS. Because this woman also became increasingly insistent on marriage, the question therefore arose as to the proper response of the case officer in charge. While I was immediately struck by the similarity of this example with the actual stories of Gärtner and Grosse, the coincidence did not stop there. Indeed, many "lonely hearts" cases were subsequently uncovered in the FRG, only underscoring the importance of this technique for the HVA.

By mid-December the training courses had been concluded, and we had a week to prepare for the final examinations. Anxious to leave the school with good marks, I studied especially hard. My first question—how could a case officer spot a potential double agent placed by the enemy—took the form of a one-hour oral presentation. Fortunately, I was well prepared and able to draw on the dossier of "Alois." My teachers seemed most attentive, for although they had heard about the case, they knew none of the details. The next two questions concerned the functions of the FRG Border Police and were much less difficult. In the final section on Marxism-Leninism, I launched into an intense monologue and hardly gave the examiner a chance to speak.

The following day we assembled to receive the examination results. Emphasizing the significance of the occasion was Brigadier-General Horst Jaenicke, the second deputy head of the HVA, who had made a special trip from East Berlin. As he handed out the final marks himself, each of us was required to come forward and shake his hand in a stiff military fashion. I had earned the best grade possible, placing me among the top four students in our class. Of the other three, two held degrees from the Moscow diplomatic school and one was a former journalist.

8

However satisfactory my performance at the HVA school, the task now, as Christian stated, was to achieve a similar degree of operational success. Yet before starting to deploy agents to the West, I needed to establish a solid "rear" base in the GDR. That meant building my own network of recruiters, instructors, safe houses, and cover addresses. In addition, since immigration remained one the most prized techniques of placing agents in the FRG— even more than a Western recruitment—I was to be on the lookout for possible candidates, preferably married couples.

When the Berlin Wall was built in 1961, it eliminated not only the simplest escape route to the West for ordinary citizens but also the main point of entry for HVA agents. To reach the FRG now, they had to resort to the same arduous techniques as real refugees. Frequently these agents posed as tourists at the Black Sea and then "took flight" through Bulgaria into Turkey and Greece. Also on HVA orders, they might attempt to swim across the Elbe River or scale the Wall itself. Yet due to a lack of coordination, the results were far from satisfactory. More than once an HVA agent was arrested at the Bulgarian-Turkish border or even shot to death by vigilant GDR border troops.

Quickly enough, however, the HVA devised a new scheme to place their agents. By assuming the identity of Germans who had earlier immigrated to countries like Canada, Australia, and New Zealand, they gained admittance to the FRG as "repatriates." Then, after making a series of zig-zag moves, they applied for a new passport and found employment in a position "interesting" to the HVA. I now learned that my own name had been on a list of potential repatriates just prior to my marriage.

Although this method was discontinued several years later—in 1976 West German counterintelligence caught on and made a spectacular arrest of more than thirty agents, while another 120 fled back to the GDR—the HVA continued to value its effectiveness at the time. According to Christian, this type of agent should meet the highest criteria, including reliability and ruthlessness. To reinforce this point by a negative example, he described how a new agent, after a long and expensive training period, became so unnerved at the sight of two patrolling policemen upon his arrival at the Frankfurt train station that he immediately returned to the GDR via Prague.

I had to begin practically from scratch. Despite occasional tips from certain students and young scientists, I lacked my own regular group of agents. Since Günther's death, there was only Gärtner, who was now completing his doctorate in electronics at Humboldt University. Still the fear lurked that the West Germans might have recruited him while in prison. Particularly because his file contained an explicit note of warning signed by Neumann, I refrained from approaching any of the numerous persons Gärtner had suggested.

My first decision was where to concentrate my efforts. East Berlin, according to all my colleagues, was so saturated by both the MfS and the KGB that few opportunities existed. In addition, one had to work with the East Berlin counterintelligence division, which had notoriously poor relations with the HVA. The northern university towns of Rostock and Greifswald similarly held little promise, for even if I had had a driver's license, they lacked good connecting highways. Since Jena and Magdeburg had been the site of so many bad experiences for the MfS, the departmental heads rejected in principle all candidates from these universities. Finally, Leipzig had to be eliminated because I was still too well known in student circles.

There remained only three universities that had graduate faculties in physics: Dresden, Karl-Marx-Stadt, and Halle. That they were all located in Saxony turned out to be quite advantageous. In contrast to the East Berliners, whom the MfS regarded as "ideologically embittered," the Saxons seemed unusually open to our advances. Their poor reception of West German television and nearly total dependence on GDR news broadcasts may well have accounted for the difference.

In any event, by approaching them in a very collegial manner, I gained the assistance of the personnel in the three local MfS offices. Besides giving me some helpful leads, they allowed me to peruse their collections of individual questionnaires and résumés. After several trips to each city, I had compiled a long and detailed list of potential candidates. In making my final selections, however, I knew that my own credibility would be lost if personal feelings played a role. Loyalty to the regime stood as the main criterion, and my choices had to be made on that basis. However imperfect an indicator, any person not belonging the SED was automatically excluded from a Western assignment.

Having made my selections, I submitted their names to the administrative registration office, or division XII, of the MfS. Utilizing advanced data processing, it maintained records on a wide range of persons, including informers, agents, political dissidents, and suspected Western spies. Also included in these files were the names of those persons possessing incriminating evidence, as well as a list of everyone who had ever worked on these cases or submitted a request for information. There was even an archive that housed all the processed material, either in its original form or on microfilm. According to my estimates, section XII maintained files on approximately two million GDR citizens and on many important West Germans and other foreigners as well.

A negative response from division XII—indicating no file on the person—was a green light to proceed further, whereas a positive response meant that the person was already "taken." In that event, one received the name of the MfS unit that had made the initial registration. Its permission was necessary before making any advances to the person in question.

When many of the names I had submitted turned out to be taken, I started to compile a list. Christian, however, caught me in the act and noted that MfS regulations strictly forbade keeping such records, for they could provide the enemy with the names of persons having some connection to security operations. Yet precisely because these lists would later be of great value to the BND, I ignored Christian's threat of severe punishment and continued my compilation. As it took only a telephone call to a colleague to ascertain the reason for a person's file, I included that information as well.

Those persons whom division XII indicated as "not taken" now belonged to me, and I could begin building my own dossiers on them. The first step was to contact the local MfS counterintelligence section, where I had made my initial inquiries, and obtain a copy of everything on record. I next sent an investigative order to division VIII of the appropriate MfS regional office. As a result, full-time field workers descended on the area where my "agent-candidate" lived and worked. By questioning everyone who had had any dealings with the person—from his employer and coworkers to the local party secretary and the postman—they attempted to collect as much information as possible about his habits and opinions. Because the MfS had cultivated a reliable group of informers in practically every corner of the GDR, the sheer scale and density of this investigative network can hardly be conceived.

Hoping that several true and unblemished "sons of the party" would emerge in the end, I had purposely submitted a long list to be investigated. Yet as this process continued to eliminate more and more names, I began to think about my own processing four years ago. Had Leo and Werner probed me then with the scrupulous methods of my current investigation, I would never have gained entry into the MfS. Having now seen the number of possibilities at its disposal and knowing that internal security checks were an ongoing, undisclosed operation, I resolved to be far more discreet with my own comments.

In any event, Christian seemed quite pleased with the bulging files I had amassed. After he had approved my proposed agent-candidates, I narrowed the list to five persons, three in Karl-Marx-Stadt and two in Halle. I visited each of them at work, quietly introducing myself as Werner Schilling, a member of the MfS, and stated my desire "to clarify several important questions." I carefully noted their reactions.

Since an overt approach had been made, they were now classified as "contact persons." After setting a time for the first real meeting and emphasizing the importance of utter secrecy, I then went to the local MfS office to obtain the names of several ideologically suspect scientists in the area. When I next saw my contact person, these names would be presented to him and a written assessment requested for the following meeting. Besides stressing the need to support the MfS's struggle against enemy subversion, I used the standard method of opening the political discussion with a topic of current interest.

On balance, the results seemed quite satisfactory. Although the three weaker candidates had to be eliminated after several meetings—one frightened man behaved as if he were in an interrogation cell and refused to write reports on the grounds of conscience—there remained two with considerable promise. One was Holm Arndt, a physics instructor in Halle; the other was Peter Noetzoldt, a graduate student in physics in Karl-Marx-Stadt. Both appeared relaxed and confident, actively participating in the political discussions and showing no reservations about assisting the MfS. Descended from two generations of communists—including a father who had been placed in Buchenwald by the Nazis—Arndt not only possessed a favorable background but had also revealed a distinct lust for adventure. Noetzoldt had displayed a similar excitement about undercover work, but his living circumstances were far more modest. When I asked why his marriage had produced no children, he pointed to the lack of necessary material support. Knowing that a resettlement couple was required to be childless, I began to consider him and his wife as prime candidates.

Precisely because the reports submitted by Arndt and Noetzoldt were so excellent, I was placed in a difficult situation. Their political assessment of various colleagues had to be passed on to Christian, who always wanted action taken against anyone showing signs of skepticism or hostility toward the regime. Yet whenever Christian wrote the comment "forward to counterintelligence without fail," that document was placed in my drawer and later destroyed. Although his excellent memory increased the risk involved, he only once questioned whether a report had been sent along. On that occasion I lied. When he checked with counterintelligence officials several days later and found the report missing, I responded by blaming the divisional secretary, who was notorious for her negligence.

As I had discovered, the scope of the HVA was not limited to foreign intelligence activity. To be sure, we had the obligation to inform the appropriate counterintelligence authorities of any evidence of domestic dissidence encountered in our investigations. Besides contributing to the overall mission of the MfS, this order played an important corrective role within the HVA. Simply because of our constant preoccupation with the West, we could easily develop a weakened "class consciousness" and a faded "picture of the enemy." Mielke himself took a dim view of the arrogance shown by certain high-ranking, well-salaried HVA officers toward the members of counterintelligence. Within the MfS, it was also no secret that even Wolf, despite his many successes, had a troubled relationship with the chief minister. Thus, to eradicate any elitist attitudes and keep the realities of the GDR in focus, all HVA officers were required to make a domestic contribution.

It was not long before my two exemplary candidates were ready to enter a more formal relationship with the MfS. Just as I had done several years previously, they unhesitatingly signed a written agreement to work as agents. Since Noetzoldt served as the head of his university's FDJ unit, I gave him the codename "Secretary." Arndt, who taught at Martin-Luther University, was now to be called "Martin."

9

After one year of service, I had gained a good overall view of HVA operations, including the role of our department within the Sector of Science and Technology. That we clearly held the preeminent position was officially confirmed during the 1973 MfS anniversary ceremony. On that day, three members of the department—Christian, Werner, and an agent unknown to me at the time—received the Friedrich-Engels Prize First Class, the GDR's highest award in military science. It marked the first time that the honor had ever been bestowed on any HVA member.

The reason lay in the information gathered by the department, which was later utilized to equip the HVA with a electronic data processing system of the most recent vintage. Despite the barrier of internal secrecy, I also learned that the department's relatively large number of West agents* helped account for this success. One colleague, for example, maintained at least five agents, including several who delivered consistent, top-quality information. Having yet to place an agent in the West myself, I listened very

---

* The term "West agent" (*Westagent*) is used to designate an HVA agent stationed in the West; a Western agent, by contrast, is someone engaged by a Western intelligence organization.

carefully whenever recommendations were made at departmental conferences concerning methods of travel, proper behavior at border checkpoints,
and emergency measures in the event of an arrest.

Not surprisingly, party work proved unavoidable, but it seemed no
greater a burden than at the university or the Physics Society. At the
departmental level, all personnel attended the meetings—the divisional
head also made an occasional appearance—and we discussed current
intelligence and security problems. By contrast, the divisional party
meetings were stiff, formalistic rituals. One person gave a presentation on a
previously assigned topic, which was then debated by four members chosen
from each of the departments. To avoid any incorrect turn of political
phrase, however, the proceedings were always carefully planned in advance. Not even disciplinary actions, the normal spice of party life, found a
place on the agenda. Vogel had the division firmly under his control, and
infractions rarely occurred.

This situation, however, was far more the exception than the rule. A
secretary in the sector's electronics division, for example, had taken
advantage of the lack of proper financial controls and embezzled 45,000
marks over a period of time. When confronted with the evidence, the
woman threatened to reveal the sexual affairs rampant in the division,
including the names of high-ranking officers with whom she had slept
herself. In the end, she was dismissed, but fearful of a major scandal, the
MfS permitted her to keep the funds as "hush money."

As I began my second year, there arose a new possibility for gaining a
Western assignment. With the signing of the 1972 Basic Treaty between the
two Germanys came the worldwide diplomatic recognition of the GDR.
That meant the opportunity to follow the example of the Soviet Union and
other East bloc states and establish permanent intelligence residencies
protected by diplomatic status. Because the HVA was officially charged
with foreign espionage, the personnel for these missions would be drawn
from our ranks. A new division within the Sector of Science and Technology
was soon established to determine which persons would be sent abroad as
"scientific attachés." Despite Vogel's assurance that all of us could reckon
with a lengthy posting sooner or later, it was clear that only the most
reliable persons would be selected. I therefore began to work even harder.

As more individual reports landed on my desk to process, I began to grasp
the totality of the MfS registration system. At that time, hundreds of
thousands of West Germans along with many other West Europeans and
Americans visited the GDR each year. Beforehand, however, every person
had to have a designated "receiver" in the form of a relative, a company, a
university, a research institute, or a travel agency. Moreover, a detailed
entry application for the visitor had to be submitted by each receiver in
advance. These forms were then forwarded to Main Division VI of the MfS,

which carefully evaluated them in terms of intelligence potential. Persons of particular interest ranged from government and party officials to journalists, lawyers, and scientists.

In order for special HVA work groups to process this information, a sophisticated computerized grid system had been established. In the case of a visiting physicist, a comprehensive summary of personal data would be sent to our departmental head. On the basis of that material, he would decide whether to assign a case officer in advance of the person's arrival or to simply leave him alone.

The border checkpoints were also well equipped to spot persons with intelligence potential. Everyone entering the GDR was checked against an extensive computerized catalogue of professions and geographic regions deemed important by the MfS. If a person fell into one of those categories, the border official would begin a seemingly friendly, noncommittal conversation in order to ascertain more personal details. Should the person prove unresponsive, his baggage could be thoroughly searched by a well-trained customs agent. The results of this inspection would be included in a report sent by the border official to the relevant HVA unit as well as to Main Division VI. A lay person normally remained unaware of how much could be gleaned in this manner.

The HVA officer assigned to a case had a variety of possibilities at his disposal. Naturally the receiver in the GDR was automatically investigated. If the officer thought that the contents of his mail would yield some information, he simply filled out three small gray cards and obtained the routine signature of his divisional head. These cards then went to division "M," as it was called in the MfS. Possessing a large staff to handle the volume of such requests, this division had developed expert techniques of opening letters, copying the contents, and resealing the envelopes for normal delivery. After also hearing that numerous employees of "M" also opened mail solely out of curiosity, I asked how such practices could be reconciled with the privacy of the post, but my colleagues merely roared with laughter.

In fact, the more I learned about the tools of the trade, the harder it was to repress my distaste of serving a regime so totally at odds with the fundamental rights of its citizens. Admittedly, I found the departmental atmosphere pleasant, certain colleagues very appealing, and the work quite engrossing, but these compensations were becoming increasingly insufficient. To appease my conscience, I began to ponder how an escape to the West might be combined with striking a blow to the regime. Although nothing definite came to mind, it was apparent that any venture would entail great risk.

Returning to work, I soon realized that the efforts involved in pursing these so-called "entry leads" were hardly rewarded by the results. However sophisticated the means of detection, the case officer not only had to wait until the person's second visit before making a direct approach, but could never anticipate his reaction. It thus seemed better to concentrate again on building up my domestic network of agents.

My next potential candidate was Gertraude Sumpf, an assistant professor of art history at Humboldt University. As her impressive file revealed, Sumpf had worked for the KGB when she was a student in Moscow. Despite the absence of details, she had been given high marks for her recruitment of a Japanese classmate. Upon the completion of her studies and her return to the GDR, the Soviets transferred her file to the MfS. Christian, who had also been studying with her at the time, vouched for her absolute political reliability.

I further learned from the file that her parents had been longtime agents of another MfS unit. Interestingly, they had been so gratified by the reward of a handsome new apartment in downtown East Berlin that they permitted the MfS to use one of the rooms as a safe house. Equipped with this helpful background information, I set out for what was to be the easiest recruitment of my career.

When we met at her office, I showed her my official identity card and made the standard introduction. "Are you asking me to work for you?" she said, with absolute composure. "If you want a quick answer, it's yes. There's no reason to beat around the bush." Training her was also a simple task, for the KGB had done its job very well.

A major event planned for the summer—the World Youth and Student Festival—had already begun to preoccupy the MfS. Since the festival was to be held in East Berlin, the GDR leaders wanted no effort or expense spared in creating the most favorable impression of the "new Germany" for the foreign visitors. That meant conducting a vast number of security checks on all prospective members of the GDR youth delegation. At the same time, East Berlin was to become off-limits to any young person with a record of political dissent. While the most dangerous suspects were placed in provisional protective custody, all undesirable young persons from East Berlin were assigned to special summer camps and agricultural work units. Even the numerous prostitutes were temporarily barred from the city.

At the event itself, members of the Feliks-Dzerzhinskii Guard Regiment, wearing FDJ gear instead of their customary uniforms, were positioned among the delegates in order to take immediate action should a hostile demonstration erupt. Likewise, the HVA's overriding concern was internal security. All vacations had been suspended, and we had to sleep in the office every other night.

By no means, however, were the many opportunities for new recruitments ignored. Indeed, by utilizing the festive atmosphere of the attractively decorated city, our younger East Berlin agents succeeded in making a large number of Western contacts. As the HVA's annual report later confirmed, operation "Banner," as it was officially known, had resulted in a dramatic increase of new student agents.

I had been assigned to a special support group for the Main Division for Personal Protection, or simply "PS." It had the important function of protecting both the GDR leadership and dignitaries from abroad. Because every state visit required some additional security personnel, we were routinely dispatched in these special units. Prepared to take any necessary action with our concealed pistols, we stood in groups of two for hours in advance along the designated route. Most passersby, however, easily recognized our MfS affiliation by our conspicuously inconspicuous behavior.

On this occasion, my PS unit was responsible for the protection of Yasir Arafat. Before his arrival, we had received a lengthy lecture stressing the importance of good relations between the socialist camp and the Arab world. In fact, his visit to the festival had been purposely arranged to coincide with the SED's official recognition of the PLO.

Given such a controversial and potentially targeted figure, a total of fifty men had been assigned to this PS unit. Ten of us had the specific task of securing in advance any route that Arafat might take either on foot or in an automobile. That meant searching garbage containers, inspecting parked cars, and apprehending all suspicious strangers. Yet to our great frustration, a route was hardly declared safe when Arafat suddenly changed his plans, and we had to begin anew. Nevertheless, all these efforts found a certain compensation at the conclusion of his visit. At that time, the regular PS personnel told us various off-color stories about his personal habits, including how the MfS had generously satisfied his strong desire for female company.

During this period, however, there was also a much less amusing case. Shortly before the festival began, I received a call from a local MfS official in Halle regarding one of my "claimed" candidates, a physics student named Hans-Ullrich Doerge. Having yet to make an approach myself, I agreed to my colleague's request that he be "loaned out" to help with the security arrangements of the Halle student delegation. It quickly became apparent that Doerge was an extraordinary source of information, providing exhaustive lists of everyone overheard making disparaging remarks about the GDR.

At the end of the festival, my colleague from Halle offered to exchange two of his "good" people for Doerge. Although some hard bargaining on my part managed to secure an even higher "price," I felt reluctant to lose such a natural-born informer and thus declined the exchange. Our first meeting occurred shortly afterward, and within a matter of months, he counted as one of my official recruits. Coming from a humble background,

Doerge was intelligent and industrious as well as a party fanatic to the core. Not only did he consider Honecker's latest speech to have the binding force of law, but he even found ideological fault with many loyal, long-standing SED members. In the end, he created enormous difficulties for me. His fanaticism turned into a persecution complex, and I had no choice but to have him placed under psychiatric care.

5

The Daily Grind

Shortly after the World Youth and Student Festival, one of my departmental colleagues, Axel Huether, was reassigned to pursue advanced studies at the MfS institute in Potsdam-Eiche. Although I regretted his departure for personal reasons, it marked the beginning of a new and important phase of my career. Laying a stack of files before me, Christian stated that I was to be one of the principal recipients of Axel's agents. Such a display of trust was a clear and welcome reassurance.

Among the files was my first active West agent. Since a meeting with "Sperber" was imminent, I quickly began to study his background. Born in 1935, Rolf Dobbertin, as he was actually named, had shown a scientific bent in his high school studies and later obtained a degree in physics from the University of Rostock. As the son of a communist, he had also displayed the "correct" political attitude. In 1954, when a group of militant FDJ members including Dobbertin deliberately clashed with West Berlin police during a so-called "peace march" and was forced back to the Soviet sector, his name came to the attention of the MfS.

Soon thereafter, Dobbertin was handily enrolled as a contact person. Nevertheless, the information he delivered was not especially valuable, and his sharp intellect began to question the discrepancy between Marx's teachings and certain SED resolutions. His case officer, feeling increasingly exasperated, finally sought to have him transferred elsewhere, a not uncommon procedure in the MfS. Because the HVA was eagerly seeking candidates for resettlement in the West, it was decided to forget about his political shortcomings and prepare him for a new assignment.

The transfer to foreign intelligence had a salutary effect on Sperber, as he was now called. Perhaps owing to the prospect of adventure abroad, he suppressed all his ideological doubts and showed no signs of wavering from the party line. In 1956, after a short training period and a perfunctory security check, he was declared ready for deployment.

Utilizing an ingenious variation of the standard resettlement procedure, the HVA instructed Sperber to proceed via West Berlin to Paris. Thanks to the earlier efforts of Rompe, a French physics professor known by the codename "Ludwig" had agreed to an arrangement whereby HVA agents could enroll in his institute disguised as East German refugees. Everything went as planned, as Sperber obtained the proper naturalization papers and continued with his studies at Ludwig's institute. To provide him with funds for his living expenses, the HVA turned to another agent, the co-owner of an import-export firm in Switzerland. According to the terms of a fictitious "study grant," he was to send Sperber a specified amount every month. Naturally the HVA provided both reimbursement and a commission.

At the completion of his scientific studies, Sperber was well equipped to function as an agent. Besides having received exhaustive training during his periodic trips to East Berlin, his own aptitude for foreign languages had resulted in a firm command of English and French. The question now was where to place him for maximum results.

Two possibilities appeared. One was the United States, an object of mounting interest for the HVA. Although Sperber had consented to go, the detailed information form required of all immigrants posed a major hurdle. Whereas the fact of his former SED membership had simply been omitted from his earlier FRG application, too many persons from the Rostock physics department had now fled to the West and could testify to Sperber's party affiliation. For the HVA, the danger of exposure was too great.

The other possibility was the FRG, specifically the nuclear research station in Jülich. In this instance, however, Sperber's own personal life turned out to be the complicating factor. He had become romantically involved with a young West German girl, and she firmly refused to leave Paris. When Sperber and the girl decided to marry, the HVA had no alternative other than to accept the situation. Even so, he proved quite valuable, cultivating a wide circle of French physicists and sending a steady stream of research data back to East Berlin.

The next set of complications arose during his vacation on the North Sea island of Sylt. In his wife's absence, Sperber proceeded to have an intense, brief affair with a young unmarried student from Dresden, who was visiting relatives in the FRG. Ignoring all his previous training, he divulged to her his Western assignment on behalf of the HVA. As it happened, she too worked for the MfS, and later reported the tryst to her Dresden case officer. Hardly had Sperber been officially reprimanded than he received a blackmail threat from the girl. She had become pregnant, and unless financial support was forthcoming, the father's identity would be revealed. Knowing that his wife was in no position to take offense because of her own extramarital affairs, Sperber simply made an open confession.

He next pondered how best to inform HVA headquarters of what had transpired. Rather than arranging a meeting, he sent a letter, carefully written in special ink, that described the attempted blackmail. Immediately the girl was taken to task and swore never to resort to such tactics again. Sperber, however, sensed that trouble was afoot and ignored his instructions to come to East Berlin for an emergency meeting.

At this point, with no better option available, the HVA decided to pay the child support and take a more conciliatory approach toward Sperber. Certainly the department was loath to lose one of its top producers. Besides conveying nearly one hundred documents each year, he had established contact with some American physicists and was beginning to receive direct information from Princeton, Berkeley, and Lawrence Livermore. It was not long before Sperber received his first medal for outstanding service.

Lacking any firm political guidance, however, he had fallen under the influence of French intellectuals and took the Chinese side regarding the Sino-Soviet split. To rectify this situation, the HVA turned to "Armin," a new agent who had recently been resettled with his wife in the FRG. Not only was he especially intelligent and capable, as was true of most new HVA personnel since the building of the Wall, but he had yet to receive a specific assignment. Armin thus became Sperber's resident and soon managed to bring him back into political line.

Although the file ended on a positive note—the information flow continued to be plentiful, and no ideological doubts had reappeared—I had an unsettling conversation with Axel prior to his departure.

"You must be awfully careful," he said. "Sperber's position is very shaky. The top HVA people are worried about the high risks in France and would prefer that he return immediately. You should therefore take great pains with the phrasing of your reports. Also, don't think he's stopped his crazy political thinking. The Soviet Union is still a particular bone of contention. Since a counter-revolution presumably took place under Stalin, he feels that the communists can make no moral claims to the leadership of the Soviet Union. When you hear such wild theories, it's better just to let him talk and not get involved in a serious conversation."

Axel also told me the cover address in East Berlin where Sperber sent his letters. In this instance, a schoolteacher and local party secretary codenamed "Wild" had put his mailbox at our disposal for clandestine correspondence. The first letter that arrived from Sperber appeared to be an innocuous vacation greeting signed by "Uncle Manfred." After noting its postmark and date of delivery, I gave it to the HVA's department C, which had the task of coding and decoding secret messages. The following day the key words had been broken down: "father" signified a meeting with Sperber in East Berlin, and "July 30" really meant three days earlier. Such double-coding was a standard precaution in case enemy counterintelligence should intercept the message.

There were other safeguards as well. Besides using special ink, the agents had to print their messages to avoid the possibility of handwriting comparisons. There were not only special codewords for meeting places like Amsterdam or Düsseldorf, but also various passwords that an unknown contact person would have to use. In Sperber's case, a specific type of Parisian subway ticket would also be needed as sign of recognition. To relay a message to him in Paris, there existed a designated public mailbox and a set of simple signals.

I next applied to the divisional secretary for the exceptionally large sum of 4,350 West German marks, all earmarked for Sperber. The first 1,350 marks was a standard supplement to his salary, 1,000 marks was to reimburse his travel expenses, and 2,000 marks was to cover so-called operational costs. This last amount was unusual, for resettled agents did not normally receive additional money for the delivery of material. Sperber, however, seemed to be in constant financial straits, due primarily to his wife's extravagance, and demanded this extra sum. Incidentally, a substantial monthly payment went regularly to each agent's special account in the GDR. Besides covering the required party dues, this money was held in reserve in case of an emergency retreat.

Just prior to my first meeting with Sperber, Christian gave me some words of warning. "Most agents seem to feel uneasy at the change of case officers." He further cautioned me that Sperber was a "nervous type" and that certain "idiosyncrasies" should be expected.

After picking up Sperber outside the state travel bureau, Christian introduced me as "Werner" and announced my new role as case officer. As Sperber silently scrutinized me, I returned a similar look, albeit with a more friendly mien. Dressed in a dirty corduroy suit, he gave the initial impression of someone much younger than his forty years. Then I noticed the premature wrinkles around his eyes and the unhealthy gray tone of his complexion. In addition, he made a peculiar rasping sound approximately once every minute.

We then drove to Christian's safe house, where a delicious noon meal had been prepared by the housekeeper. Over the years she had grown fond of Sperber, and he regularly brought her bottles of cologne from the West. When Sperber announced that his wife was planning a trip to Lebanon and expected him to pay the expenses, Christian frowned, knowing that the department would eventually have to provide the funds.

The discussion, however, turned to more pressing matters. Presenting a key to a luggage locker in the Friedrichstrasse station*, Sperber explained that his American sources had sent him some new information. Moreover, he wanted to go to the United States himself to pursue several promising leads. As work was only beginning regarding the use of heavy ions in nuclear weaponry, the Pentagon had yet to declare a secrecy ban, and access through his contacts was relatively easy. In addition, Sperber planned to consult with another physicist acquaintance working in the field of radiation weaponry. Apart from his specialization in an obscure field that combined mathematics and physics, his scientific knowledge exceeded what my university training had provided. Nevertheless, I could follow his explanations reasonably well, while Christian remained noticeably silent in the background.

When this five-hour session had ended, I was given the luggage locker key by Christian and told how to proceed. My first stop was the divisional secretary, who filled out a so-called "special duty order." Once her chief had received the approval of my departmental head, I received a GDR passport and a special permit to enter the border zone. The identifying signature on the passport read "Brückner," and all the inside pages had been glued together. I was then driven to the Friedrichstrasse station.

After finding the entrance designated for border officials and employees of the "Reichsbahn," as the GDR railroad was still called, I pressed the buzzer next to a locked door. Through a small window appeared a person wearing the Border Guards uniform. In reality, like all officials at the Western border checkpoints and the East German airports, he belonged to Main Division VI of the MfS. Handling entry and exit formalities was considered too sensitive and difficult to be left to the regular Border Guards of the NVA.

When I showed my special permit, the door opened. The man then inspected my duty order, which contained the phrase "personal operational business." As I explained that some left luggage had to be collected, he nodded and stamped my permit. Another door opened, leading to the other side of the border checkpoint. The MfS referred to this part of the station as the "Western section," even though it was on GDR soil and controlled by our own security forces.

I then went downstairs to await the arrival of the next subway train. I joined the exiting passengers and returned to the main floor where the luggage lockers were located. I removed the old, tattered document case that Sperber had left and then went upstairs to wait for the next train from West Berlin. Once again joining with the exiting passengers, I proceeded to

---

* Dating from the Wilhelmenian period, this labyrinthine structure is located in the center of historic Berlin. At the time, it served as a major hub for trains from the FRG and other East bloc countries as well as for East Berlin commuter trains.

the passport control counter on the main floor. After briefly examining my papers, the official on duty gave me a discreet wink, for he knew that we were both MfS colleagues. A further signal to the customs officer allowed me to pass through without any luggage inspection. I was now back in the GDR without having ever really left it.

There was a simple explanation for this complicated procedure. For reasons of security, the MfS preferred that the identity of its agents not be known to the border officials. Since the espionage material had been deposited beforehand in one of these luggage lockers, no awkward questions would be asked, and the agent could proceed undetected. Incidentally, the same process also worked in reverse. Before an agent returned to the West, the case officer placed a needed object such as a special radio in one of these lockers. After clearing the GDR border control, the agent removed the object from the locker in the "Western section" and continued his trip.

Sperber had obviously been very active, for his case was completely filled with scientific documents. Although not classified as confidential, they had yet to appear in published form and covered more than thirty topics, including nuclear fission and laser technology. I compiled a complete list and forwarded the documents to division V for scientific-technological assessment. After "neutralizing" the material by removing all indications of its source, the division would place these documents at the disposal of various research and industrial teams within the GDR. Before the material was distributed, however, the KGB liaison officer had made copies of nearly everything to be sent to Moscow.

The next day, I visited Sperber at the safe house to discuss his planned trip to the United States. Besides warning him not to reveal his espionage activities to his wife, I stated that my superiors no longer wanted information from France because of the high risks entailed. I also gave him his money and set our next meeting date for September in East Berlin.

2

From Axel I also inherited my first safe house, a studio apartment with a kitchen, codenamed "fortress." The necessity of meeting agents in restaurants or requesting the loan of a colleague's safe house had now been eliminated. With Sperber dispatched for the time being, I next turned to four other files left by Axel.

The first concerned Herbert Patzelt, one of the scientists belonging to the Hartmann residency who had fled to the GDR. My dealings with Patzelt, however, were to be limited to a single incident. Unable to readjust his life-style after his exposure to the FRG, he had become severely depressed and turned to alcohol. One day I learned that he had killed a person while driving drunk. Even for the MfS, it was difficult to have a charge of this severity dismissed. Nevertheless, I was eventually able to place him in a rehabilitation center, and he began to receive monthly payments for the difference in salary that his move to the GDR had brought.

The second file, involving a Greek couple, Alexander and Marie Kontos, was more unusual. Two years earlier, they had presented themselves to the border control at the Friedrichstrasse station. According to their account, following the colonels' coup in 1967, they had been forced to flee Greece because of their membership in the Greek Communist Party. The couple then managed to find employment in a French nuclear research center and started to collect documents that would be of interest to their socialist comrades in the East bloc. Despite the quite valuable material they had brought with them, the MfS, like any other security organization, subjected such a "walk-in" case to utmost scrutiny.

All the details of their story checked out, and the case was assigned to Axel. Securing their recruitment as agents was easily accomplished and gave a big boost to his career. In this regard, the MfS considered only the fact of a recruitment, not the circumstances surrounding it. Unfortunately, however, Axel then made a completely uncharacteristic error. In assigning them a cover address in the GDR, he happened to confuse the name "Gerber" with "Berger." Only after a long period of silence and many inquiries did he discover that all the mail sent by the Greek couple had been returned by the post office as undeliverable.

In the meantime, when the Kontos couple arrived in East Berlin with a suitcase full of documents, not only was no one there to meet them, but the border official acted in a brusque and condescending manner. They returned to Paris in keen disappointment. A letter from Axel, who felt utterly despondent at this turn of events, produced only a frosty reply. Even though they later informed him of their resettlement in the Algerian town of Oran, the relationship was never revived. My efforts similarly produced no results, and nothing more was ever heard from them.

According to Christian, the next file contained "material with considerable potential." In early 1971, the GDR Ministry of the Interior had received a letter from Richard Teichner, a young physicist of German background currently living in Rome as an Italian citizen. Unable to find a position commensurate with his training, he inquired whether something appropriate might be available in the GDR. The ministry official quickly sensed that this was a matter for the MfS to handle, and Teichner's letter landed on Axel's desk.

Exercising considerable caution, Axel first confirmed the name Richard Teichner and his stated address in the Rome telephone directory. He then wrote a reply using the name "Seifert," one of his standard aliases. In a completely fabricated story, Axel maintained that Teichner's letter had been forwarded to him from the Dresden Technical University. As the director of the so-called East Berlin branch, he wanted to extend an invitation to a nonbinding discussion. Hardly had Axel received word of

Teichner's willingness to come than a second letter arrived asking for a postponement. Teichner's explanation—a sudden call to military service —struck Axel as highly improbable. In all likelihood Teichner had simply changed his mind, but despite his desire to shred the whole correspondence, Axel placed the file in his cabinet.

Two years later, an unexpected letter arrived from Teichner. Now that his military service was over, he wondered whether the proposed meeting was still possible. Axel had replied affirmatively. That meeting, however, had yet to take place when I took over the file. As the agreed-upon date was rapidly approaching, I asked Axel why he had contrived something as complex as the East Berlin branch of the Dresden Technical University. With a sly smile, he handed me the remaining fourth file, a very bulky set of papers bearing the codename "Singer." Lacking the time for a thorough examination, I gave it a quick reading.

"Singer" was Gerd Stiller, a Dresden physics professor and specialist in computer programming. Interestingly, his famous brother Heinz Stiller not only presided over the GDR space program but was an agent of department one of our division. From 1956 to 1963 Singer had been an active MfS agent in various West German universities. When his position had become severely endangered, he was recalled to the GDR and awarded a professorship in appreciation of his undercover work. This move proved to be quite justified, for he developed into an important authority in his field.

According to Axel's plan, Singer's presence would give the meeting academic credibility and allay any suspicion that Teichner might have regarding its true nature. After Christian had generously put his safe house at our disposal, Axel prepared a special sign for the door: "Branch Office of the Dresden Technical University." Upon Singer's arrival, the three of us reviewed the details of the plan. We also decided that Singer should use another alias—Professor "Sänger"—and not reveal his actual identity. Although the possibility existed that Teichner might check the name against the faculty register or some readily obtainable material, we still felt too uncertain about our relationship to him.

I was already favorably impressed by Singer. A slim, black-haired man of average height, he had a full and sophisticated sense of humor. Later I noticed how he used that trait to mask his disappointment in the GDR, particularly its sterile and restrictive policy toward scientific research. By contrast, Singer felt a clear loyalty and gratitude toward the HVA. In part, this attitude had been skillfully cultivated by relatively open-minded and realistic case officers. Moreover, by also serving as one of the scientific-technological evaluators in division V, he could advance his professional reputation and stay abreast of developments from abroad. Nevertheless, during our frequent meetings he showed increasing signs of resignation and would have obviously preferred to return to the FRG.

The apartment bell rang punctually. Opening the door, I was surprised to see someone Middle Eastern in appearance and without a trace of a

Germanic background. Teichner had black curly hair and a thick beard as well as a soft, well-proportioned, intelligent face. Playing his role with real academic aplomb, Singer introduced Axel and me as his scientific assistants. When asked to talk about his own career, Teichner replied in broken German that it was first necessary to explain his decision to turn to the GDR.

3

Teichner's father had been a German-Jewish businessman in Breslau. With the advent of the Third Reich, he attempted unsuccessfully to immigrate to Palestine and resettled instead in Italy. Shortly after the war, he married an Egyptian Jewess, and Richard and his sister were born. The family circumstances were quite modest, and only a West German pension paid to his father as a victim of the Nazi period allowed the young Teichner to pursue his studies.

At Rome University, Teichner moved in communist circles and soon became a convert to Marxism-Leninism. Despite a strong showing on his doctorate examination, the best position he could find was teaching in an elementary school. Because his father could no longer work and the West German pension was inadequate to support the whole family, he reluctantly accepted the job.

Out of increasing frustration, Teichner first attempted to find a more suitable post in the FRG, but his applications yielded no positive results. He next considered Israel, where some distant family members had already settled. His communist friends in Rome, however, dissuaded him from such a move, pointing to the difficulties that his Egyptian mother and his leftist politics would bring. Instead, Teichner acted on their advice to investigate possibilities in the GDR, a state they considered as having already realized true socialism. As Italy had no diplomatic relations with East Germany at the time, Teichner made his initial inquiry at the Czechoslovakian embassy in Rome, and was advised to write directly to the GDR Ministry of the Interior.

Teichner then began to tell us about his scientific background, and produced several academic certificates. After carefully examining them, Singer posed a few questions to discover his level of knowledge. Teichner's answers made it clear that he was a physicist of considerable ability. I was curious about how he had gained entry to the GDR. His first stop, he explained, had been the newly opened East German embassy in Rome, where he presented his correspondence with us. He was then told to go the Friedrichstrasse station checkpoint. There the official, bewildered as to why the sponsoring institution had not supplied any advance authorization, gave him a day permit instead of a full visa. Axel and I exchanged glances. Wanting as few people involved as possible, we were not pleased that Teichner had gone to the embassy.

As our talks entered a more delicate phase, Singer acted quite cleverly. Confessing his surprise that a Westerner would want to work in the GDR, he presumed that Teichner was not applying for citizenship as well. Upon hearing that that was the case, Singer nodded understandingly and replied, "Naturally I will have to talk with the university administration before any decision can be made. You'll hear from me tomorrow." He then left the room.

After a short conversation, I asked Axel to take our guest to lunch and excused myself on the grounds of another appointment. Singer was waiting for me in his car at the next corner. We agreed that Teichner was authentic, and Singer could now return to Dresden. Back at headquarters, Christian seemed pleased by my report, and we began to plan the next stages of recruitment. As a precaution, however, Christian had the HVA directorate contact the MfS resident in the Rome embassy. All documentation pertaining to Teichner's visit should be sent to us, lest a non-MfS diplomat become involved and start writing troublesome reports to the Ministry of Foreign Affairs.

In the afternoon, I rejoined Axel and Teichner. Over coffee, we began to discuss politics in order to determine the specific nature of Teichner's ideological commitment. Whereas his theoretical grasp of Marxism was most impressive, he veered more toward pacifism than to armed revolutionary struggle and dictatorship of the proletariat, doubtlessly an influence of the "deviant" Italian Eurocommunists. So as not to weaken his chances of finding a good job, Teichner had also refrained from joining the party. From our perspective, that was actually preferable, since registered communists generally had fewer opportunities to be effective foreign agents. To prevent him from thinking that he was being courted in any way, Axel and I ended the meeting rather abruptly.

The following day, Teichner reapplied for a day permit and arrived at the safe house at the prearranged time. Immediately he asked whether any decision had been reached. Our reply was that matters did not normally move that fast, whereas in fact we wanted more time for a closer examination of his personality. To provide a note of encouragement, however, Axel informed him that the university administration had granted permission for him to be our guest for three days. We also took care that his accommodations would appear appropriately modest and not luxurious.

On the pretext of needing to arrange a visa at police headquarters, I left with Teichner's passport and visitor's permit. My real destination was division VI/K of the HVA. With the approval of one's departmental head, this unit could quickly prepare any type of required travel document, whether of presumed Western or GDR origin. In this instance, to prevent any subsequent reconstruction from the Western side, we preferred a so-called "paper insert" to a stamped visa. Two hours later, this permit bearing Teichner's name had been completed.

It was not until the last day of his visit that our carefully designed plan found its culmination. After apologizing for the absence of Professor "Sänger," who had allegedly been delayed on official business, I gave an elaborate explanation of the university's decision. To a socialist state like East Germany, the FRG's "guest worker" policy represented another example of exploiting the working classes from other nations. When I concluded that the GDR could hardly engage in such a policy and issue him a permit, Teichner sank back in his chair, deeply disappointed.

There was, however, another possibility. Because of the West's deeply antagonistic attitude, socialism had been denied access to many important scientific publications. Our proposal was that Teichner obtain Western material in the field of computer programming for us. Besides receiving a stipend, he could expand his own knowledge and thus improve his chances of employment. Teichner responded with boundless joy, maintaining that this offer was more than he had dared hope for. Not only was it possible to remain in Italy with his family and have a source of financial support, but a service could be rendered to a state for which he felt so much esteem.

To prove our sincerity, I told him that the university knew about his lack of funds and wanted to reimburse his travel costs in hard currency. Axel took 1,200 West German marks from his pocket and asked Teichner to sign a receipt. In his excited state, Teichner failed to notice that the document was blank and gave no indication of the issuing institution. Should any difficulties later arise, we could always enter the words "Ministry of State Security" and use the receipt as a so-called "compromisor" or means of blackmail. I also gave Teichner a list of topics that Singer had recommended and asked him to return in eight weeks' time to show us his first results. Our last advice was that he not mention the Dresden Technical University when back in Rome.

Just as we were about to part company, Teichner drew back and rather shamefacedly admitted to having another request. "Two evenings ago I went out dancing and fell in love with a girl, a pedagogic student. Since I want to see her again, would it be possible to stay for several days on my next trip to the GDR?"

Because his movements at night had not been monitored, Axel and I were completely taken aback by the disclosure of this rapid romance. Without revealing our deep distress, we simply stated our willingness to look into his request. Then, showing his skill in handling unexpected situations, Axel suggested that I take Teichner to a farewell dinner in a "quite decent" nearby restaurant. Because there were presumably matters that needed his immediate attention, Axel could not join us, but he would collect Teichner's luggage and meet us afterward. In our absence, Axel naturally hoped to find the girl's address among Teichner's belongings.

Two hours later, Axel arrived at the restaurant to take Teichner and his luggage to the Friedrichstrasse station, and I returned to the safe house.

Our final instruction to Teichner regarding his next visit was to apply for another one-day permit, and we would try to secure an extension. In the meantime, we had to discover the girl's identity and determine what her future role, if any, should be.

As it turned out, Axel had found no address, not even a name. Looking at my disappointed colleague with a somewhat patronizing smile, I proudly announced that the address was in my possession. Axel's first reaction was that I might have asked Teichner directly for the information. Assuring my colleague that I was not that foolish, I explained that Teichner had hung his jacket over his chair and a brief trip to the men's room had given me enough time to search his wallet.

Soon thereafter, Axel left for his new assignment, and I had sole responsibility for "Ernesto," as Teichner was now called. Investigating his new girlfriend was my next priority. By dialing a special number, it was possible to bypass the main telephone office and establish direct contact with the People's Police. To verify that the caller was from the MfS, a special tone also sounded on the line.

A woman's voice answered "oh-four," indicating the central registration center for East Berlin. It was also a voice that I had come to know quite well.

"Dear Comrade," I said, "this is the dear MfS." She laughed. "Please look up the card for Elke Ehrhardt, living in the Fredersdorfer Strasse."

A short while later my friend called back with all the personal data on record. Born in Königswusterhausen in 1953, the girl had been divorced once and was currently enrolled as a student. I also inquired whether she had ever received any registered Western guests, or if the card was marked with the red "K" designating an encounter with the criminal police. The answer to both questions was negative.

A similar police registration center existed in each district of the GDR. Obligated to give us any information we requested, these units were equipped with a number of different filing indexes. A request for a person's passport photograph, for example, came under the heading of "identity card application file." There was also a motor vehicle registration file, a foreigners' list, and a so-called "escapees from the republic catalogue" containing the names of all citizens who had fled the GDR.

I next filled out an MfS inquiry form and stamped it "urgent." The following day, I received confirmation that Elke had had no prior dealings with the MfS and was now registered under my name. We had to assume that Ernesto would have explained to her his reasons for being in the GDR. Before he made his next trip to the GDR, it was therefore necessary to know as much about her as possible.

Since he would probably start writing her letters, a postal control was placed on her mail. At the same time, I contacted division XX of the East Berlin district office, which had jurisdiction over Humboldt University, and requested her personal file. Incidentally, none of this snooping about caused me any pangs of conscience. Above all, I wanted to make my first Western recruit and thus improve my chances for an embassy posting abroad.

Fortunately, my investigation of Elke Ehrhardt revealed no complicating factors, and I could start preparing for the next meeting with Ernesto. Since Christian wanted to overhear the conversations between the two lovers, I was directed to division 26 of the MfS. The only requirement for having a listening device installed was the signature of Markus Wolf. Few scruples ever existed in this regard, and the approval of the HVA chief was practically automatic. As Christian once told me, Wolf had a preference for "liberal working methods" and felt that the available technology was not being utilized nearly enough.

After completing my application for a listening device, one of the officials of division 26 gave me a more detailed explanation. All the GDR's hard-currency "Interhotels" contained certain rooms permanently reserved for us and equipped with such devices. It was also possible to install a recording apparatus that switched on only upon the sound of a human voice in the room. The division merely needed to know the specific hours involved. I could later receive a transcript of the recording. In case of "Stadt Berlin," where Ernesto was scheduled to stay, there was so much background noise because of the elevators and the reinforced concrete beams that all the monitored rooms were on the upper floors.

Punctually as ever, Ernesto arrived at the next meeting with an extensive amount of material. After excusing the absence of Axel and Singer, I gave him his paper insert visa and the hotel room key. His gratitude was immense. In order to be certain that the lovers would make use of the monitored hotel room, I reminded Ernesto that his visa registration did not include his girlfriend's apartment. At the end of this very satisfactory meeting, Ernesto left with a new list of topics, a sum of money in his pocket, and some free time to spend with Elke. Confirming our assumptions, the transcript that I later received indicated a completely "correct" attitude in their intense political discussions and no suspicion about the presumed branch of the Dresden Technical University.

In consultation with Christian, I now began to devise a plan to make Ernesto an official West agent. That the relationship between him and Elke would soon lead to marriage seemed quite clear from the recorded conversations. In that event, Ernesto would probably want to live in East Berlin—a move that obviously had to be prevented. If we were eventually to place the couple in the West, Elke had to be won over to our side. As Christian bluntly stated, "We can let them come together, but we also have the means to keep them separated."

The fact that Elke was not a party member would make resettlement in the West all the easier. On the other hand, the lack of affiliation might signify weak political convictions on her part. Admittedly, the transcript of her conversations with Ernesto showed her in a very positive light, but then she might have been tailoring those remarks with another objective in mind. To know for certain, we asked Peter Grosse to put her to the ideological test. He, of course, was not made privy to the larger context of our request.

Peter had devised a clever scheme. First, he summoned Elke to a local police precinct and asked her about a fellow student who had recently escaped to the West. Her answers were open and sincere. Then, a month later, a second approach was made. After noting her earlier helpfulness, Peter asked whether she would assist in another very important matter involving the defense of the GDR. Although we anticipated some initial hesitation, she accepted without any further questions.

According to his concocted story, Peter worked as a specialist in the fight against those groups "subversively smuggling human beings"—the GDR's expression to describe any organization, whether humanitarian or commercial, that assisted people in fleeing to the West. Recently, he had arrested a young girl who served as an important liaison of such a group. Under interrogation, she had revealed that a courier was about to contact her with information about locating new "candidates" for their smuggling operation. It was Peter's intention to have this courier apprehended.

He needed, however, the corroborating evidence that Elke could supply by playing the role of the liaison. Since the courier and the real liaison had allegedly never met, there was no risk for Elke, and she agreed. As it turned out, Hilde Klein, the former instructor of Gärtner, was assigned the role of the courier. The actual meeting between the two women unfolded in true undercover fashion, replete with passwords, coded messages, and sealed instructions. To make certain that the incident appeared completely authentic to Elke, the courier was "arrested" upon leaving the tavern where they had met. For her valuable assistance, Elke was later given a special certificate and a substantial monetary bonus.

Our reward came in another form, for just as we had suspected, she had clearly enjoyed her supposed espionage assignment. Moreover, after receiving the money, Elke confessed to Peter that she had suppressed something that now ought to be revealed. To his complete puzzlement, she proceeded to give an account of her relationship to Ernesto. Nonetheless, Peter obtained a detailed written report from her, which was then sent to Christian and me. Not only was this document accurate in all respects, but she even stated her willingness to help the MfS verify Ernesto's political commitment to the GDR.

Needless to say, we felt quite satisfied. Apart from her talent for undercover work, there was now a definite event on record that could be used to secure her further cooperation. As for Ernesto, the deliveries and payments continued in the same manner. To lend some additional credence to our cover, I once took him to Dresden to see Professor "Sänger" again. It was also arranged that Singer would praise him for the amount and quality of his work and indicate the possibility of a permanent schedule of fees. This trip, however, purposely took place over a weekend. However naïve Teichner seemed to be, we did not want him wondering why the meeting was held in a restaurant and not in a university office.

4

As the time now seemed opportune to bring about the actual recruitment of Ernesto and Elke, I prepared the required draft report and received Neumann's approval. Certainly if Ernesto did not want to lose Elke, he would have to cooperate with us. Otherwise he would never set foot in the GDR again. Before making my approach to Ernesto, however, I needed to secure the recruitment of Elke.

To provide an introduction for me, Peter informed her that another MfS worker, who was especially interested in Ernesto, would soon pay a visit. When I went to her apartment, my resolve was to come straight to the point.

Hearing that I was Schilling from the MfS made her eyes open wide. "Schilling?" she replied. "Are you by chance the same university assistant in contact with Richard?"

When I confirmed her suspicion, she looked at me with astonishment. Yet soon enough she began to piece some things together.

"Was that smuggling business a set-up?"

"No," I lied. "It was real. That my colleague happened to choose you was pure coincidence. Actually my department was not involved, and I knew nothing about it."

The rest of our conversation continued without difficulty. Elke gave me her assurance that my double role would not be revealed to Ernesto, at least for the time being. Should he have any doubts after my recruitment offer and seek her advice, she would use all her influence in our favor.

Viewing her situation with absolute clarity, she asked, "If Richard were to work for you in the West, would I still be able to see him? We'd like to get married, and he wants to resettle here in the GDR."

Having received no authorization to answer that question, I attempted to stall. "Let's first see how Richard reacts and go from there."

Elke seemed to understand and remained silent. As a further precaution, however, I warned her not to disclose our conversation to anyone. Besides never seeing Ernesto again in the GDR, she would get into "trouble" for having betrayed state secrets.

After silently escorting me to the door, she made a most unexpected remark. "Even if it's imperative that Richard remain in the West and I must stay here, you'll still have my support." To my surprise, I had seemingly gained a very valuable ally.

Ernesto arrived from Rome three days later. When we met at the safe house, he appeared glad to see me again but also very anxious to rejoin Elke as soon as possible. After a short conversation, I made my bold announcement. "Richard, I am an officer of the Ministry of State Security, the intelligence service of the GDR. Having come to know you so well during the past months, we now want you to join us in advancing the cause of socialism together." Then, pointing to various examples of imperialist aggression as well as to his own bleak situation in Italy, I stated every supporting argument that could be mustered.

Completely stunned by this revelation, Ernesto had difficulty regaining his composure. He finally asked if Elke was also in league with us.

From his initial reaction, I realized that a lie was the only possible answer. If he were to learn about Elke's actual role, then we could be certain of never seeing him again. I mentioned that she should remain uninformed for the time being.

For a person with such a mild temperament, Ernesto proved to be remarkably stubborn. Any consideration of the offer, he stated, was dependent upon consultation with Elke. I hesitated awhile but then gave my consent. After all, she was my trump card in this situation.

At our meeting the following morning, Ernesto appeared more distant than usual. "What is it that you want me to do?" he asked.

"Actually, we haven't given that much thought yet. We mostly want to know how you feel about it."

"If I want to remain with Elke, there isn't much of a choice for me. Besides, in her opinion, it's an excellent opportunity to put my political beliefs into practice."

I had received permission in advance to go one step further. "If the two of you want to remain together, we've been considering the possibility of letting her go to the West. Of course, she must know nothing about this for the moment."

His face brightened, but there was one proviso. He wanted to acquire East German citizenship before signing any agreement. Should anything later go awry in the West, he wanted to be able to return with Elke to the GDR.

"That shouldn't pose any problem," I replied. Although such a request had not occurred to me beforehand, I did not want his recruitment to founder at this critical juncture. After two more hours of discussion, his optimism regarding the future had been restored.

Rather than ask him to sign a formal commitment now, I presented Ernesto with a receipt reading "Received from the MfS the sum of 1,500 West German marks for travel costs and delivery of information." His signature on this document thus allowed me to claim my first West agent. For the present, however, he was to continue gathering information in Italy and make no mention of his ties to the GDR.

It was clear that without Elke's assistance the recruitment of Ernesto would never have occurred. Moreover, lacking the requisite drive, agility, and willingness to take risks, he was not a natural-born spy. Precisely because Elke possessed those essential traits, I spent the next months concentrating on her development. As I had hoped, her response to this training was satisfactory in every respect.

Returning once a month to East Berlin, Ernesto also received some instruction in the basics of undercover work. When I asked about his request to become an East German citizen, there seemed to be no official obstacles. In fact, Christian merely laughed, remarking that he would then be more compromised than ever. Within a week, division VI/K had prepared a blue GDR identity card in the name of Richard Teichner. For the address we chose a so-called "restricted object"—a house that was registered under the MfS and not the police.

At our next meeting, I formally handed Ernesto this document. He was immediately overcome with emotion, not realizing, of course, that it did not entitle him to establish a residence in the GDR.

By sending him and Elke on a paid pleasure trip to the Egerland in Bohemia, we hoped that their future assignments would be carried out with greater motivation. In the meantime, I discovered that the paperwork involved in resettling an agent in the West was much greater than anticipated. After two intensive months, I had completed my part of the preparatory work for Elke's transfer and was ready to relay the file to the specialists in division VI. Besides enjoying the fact that other people were now beginning to work for me, I would not see this odd couple until they were resettled in the FRG.

My strong sense of accomplishment, however, was rudely shattered by a telephone call from Elke requesting a meeting. From the strange sound of her voice, I knew that something was amiss. When she then told me that a doctor had found her to be pregnant, I felt an almost uncontrollable anger.

Christian reacted to the news by making some off-color remarks about the couple. He then became more serious and advised me to salvage whatever I could. "Elke must have an abortion," he said, "but make sure that she thinks that it was her idea, for otherwise we'll be blamed if anything goes wrong."

At our next meeting, Elke appeared more relaxed and came up with the suggestion herself. Abortions were now easily obtainable due to a recent change in the GDR's birth control laws. I feigned some hesitation but then agreed that her pregnancy should be terminated.

Unfortunately, there was a further complication. Pending their transfer to the FRG, we had decided to reduce the frequency of Ernesto's trips to East Berlin. To provide some compensation to the couple, however, periodic telephone calls were allowed. Elke now confessed that in her state of shock, she had informed Ernesto about the pregnancy. While she felt convinced that he would have no objections to an abortion, I was decidedly more skeptical.

When Ernesto arrived several days later, my worst fears were confirmed. For him, an abortion was completely out of the question and would mean the end of their relationship. His position was also strongly supported by Elke's mother, a devout Baptist. As pressure mounted from both sides, Elke reconsidered the situation and decided that she wanted to have the child after all.

My superiors were naturally infuriated at this turn of events. Yet despite all our attempts to persuade her otherwise, Elke held firmly to her decision. Finally, Christian instructed me to make a new proposal to Ernesto: If he were to function successfully as an agent in the West for five years, then he could move to the GDR and become the child's legal father. However keen my own personal disappointment, I had come to feel a measure of compassion for the couple, and refused the assignment. A heated discussion with Christian ensued, but I continued to insist that he make the proposal himself.

Quite predictably, the meeting proved to be most unpleasant. Showing a side of his personality normally concealed from agents when all was going well, Christian resorted to the most brutal threats to secure Ernesto's cooperation. Ernesto in turn called us "blackmailers," but to no avail. I told him to apply to various institutions in the FRG and return for another meeting after receiving their replies.

When Ernesto arrived at the safe house several months later, his utter despair was written clearly on his face. Not only had every application been rejected but, more important, he had lost all faith in us. Christian advised me to keep tightening the screws and threaten to stop his trips to the GDR if his efforts slackened. Ernesto, however, reacted apathetically. I then tried to encourage him in a more positive manner, but even my most sincere appeals failed to reawaken any trust on his part.

Back at headquarters, I attempted to convince Christian of the futility of his methods. "What kind of intelligence officer are you?" he said scornfully. "It's our duty to get information, not to play marriage counselors. If Ernesto were 'one of ours,' it would be different. But he's not, and I'm not going to lift a finger for him. On the other hand, if you want to be taken in by his drivel, then that's your business. As far as I'm concerned, you can tell him that he can stop working for us whenever he wants. To get back into the GDR, however, he'll need the naturalization office's permission, and I'll make certain that doesn't happen. Anyway, how can I be sure that he isn't being positioned by the enemy as a mole?"

Having only recently vouched for his authenticity in writing, Christian knew very well that there were no grounds for this suspicion. The moment now seemed right to broach a plan that I had been considering over the past weeks. Convinced that Ernesto in his present state was completely useless to us, I suggested to Christian that we allow him to move to the GDR and erase all traces of his whereabouts in the West. Then, after a certain interval, a new "Dr. Teichner," a person thoroughly trained by us and possessing first-class identity papers, could reappear. Such an agent, I stressed, would be capable of accomplishing far more in the West than our Ernesto.

Despite having been subjected to all my powers of persuasion, Christian simply stared at me, mumbled something about "crazy ideas," and then threw me out of his office. I noticed, however, that afterward he headed straight to Vogel's office.

Within half an hour, I was sitting before Vogel myself. Although his greeting had been friendly enough, a frown now came over his face as if to underscore the seriousness of his words.

"How quickly will you be able to find someone in the GDR who matches Ernesto's papers?" he asked.

"It should be possible within a year," I answered.

"Good. Then I will approve Ernesto's move to the GDR. But if you don't find a replacement within a year, you'll be in deep trouble. In any event, check with 'six' to see what they can do with the existing documents and what papers will be needed for your plan."

After this session, Christian, who had also been present, appeared much calmer and clarified some details for me. I next went to division VI and explained my plan to Comrade Major Becker.

"It sounds good," he said. "Still, any trace of Ernesto's existence in Italy must be eliminated. That means acquiring all his papers, especially his West German naturalization certificate. In addition, I think that the resettlement of the new Teichner should be delayed several years—at least until the present passport has expired and the replacement person can submit a new application." All of this made sense to me.

The next morning I met with Ernesto, who appeared the very embodiment of misfortune and hardly capable of speech.

"Richard, we've won," I exclaimed.

He asked me indifferently what that meant.

"In six weeks you can move to the GDR, and I will help you with the resettlement."

"I don't believe you," he said, totally disillusioned. "I don't believe anything that any of you say anymore."

I then tried to convince him of our sincerity, but he remained suspicious. "Why is it that you've suddenly changed your minds?"

Forced now to gloss over Christian's brutal methods, I replied, "My superiors have realized that personal problems must take precedence." Ernesto, of course, received no hint of what our real intentions were.

After reinstilling a degree of optimism in his attitude, I had to make certain that he left no tracks leading to the GDR. "Richard," I began, "aren't you afraid that your father could lose his pension if your trips here ever became known?"

"No, I don't see any danger of that," he answered.

"Oh yes, that might easily happen. It would be better if nobody knows where you are. Tell your friends that you're going to West Germany and insist that your parents say the same thing."

By now Ernesto seemed much more amenable, and agreed. After I had given him some further instructions, he returned to Rome.

In order to eliminate his identity in the West, his next stop was Hanover, where he rented a room and submitted the standard registration form to the police. Then, however, he canceled the lease on the grounds of having to return to Italy. In reality, however, he drove from Hanover to the GDR with all his possessions.

Arriving in a very happy state of mind, Ernesto assured me that his parents would stick to our story. He also gave me a stack of personal documents, which I relayed to my colleagues in division VI. In their assessment, these papers would provide a solid basis for resettling a new Teichner in three or four years' time. His police registration in Hanover would serve as the link.

During the next months, I tried to fulfill my promise to help Ernesto establish a new life in the GDR. An MfS colleague in Dresden secured him both an apartment and a post as a scientific assistant in the real Dresden Technical University. A son, Roberto, was born just after his marriage to Elke, and a second child soon thereafter. In the end, the couple professed the highest esteem for the MfS, not realizing that it was only the value of Ernesto's personal documents that had made their happiness together possible.

I next had the difficult task of locating a new substitute. By deploying my entire domestic network, I managed to acquire numerous leads. Yet because so many stipulations were involved—from age and occupation to political and personal traits—all the candidates turned out be lacking in some respects.

Finally, the file of Klaus Berndt landed on my desk, and six months later I had secured his recruitment. A divorced physicist with no living relatives—and an SED member—he was exceptionally astute and most enthusiastic about intelligence work. After sending him on various assignments in the GDR as well as to Austria, Hungary, and Poland, I concluded that a better person could not have been found. Nevertheless, my own defection occurred before his final preparations were completed, and Berndt was never resettled in the FRG as the new Teichner.

5

After Axel's departure, I also acquired his old desk. Since I was now in the same room with Werner Hengst, there were frequent opportunities to discuss both theory and practice and draw from his wealth of experience.

Feeling quite at home in the department, I had become known as an ambitious young worker and began to receive more and more new assignments.

One day Christian placed four bulging dossiers and a large card index on my desk. According to him, all departmental members, along with the majority of other HVA officers, had the responsibility of accumulating information about a particular installation in the FRG. That meant collecting detailed material about each employee and using that data to make a recruitment or penetration.

After expounding at great length on the subject, Christian finally announced that as Axel's successor I possessed the so-called "installation file" for the nuclear research center in Karlsruhe.

"Henceforth," he said, "if anyone from the MfS or party leadership makes an inquiry about the center, then you must be ready with the answer. Since we don't have an agent there at the moment, it's hard to know exactly what's happening. But if it turns out that nuclear bombs are being secretly built and we remain uninformed, then it will be mostly your fault. You had best try to secure an agent there as quickly as possible." Contrary to what Christian told me, the department had already placed someone in the center, but not until three years later did I discover this fact.

Reading these files was another startling experience. The main card index contained a list of all those employees whose specific functions were known. A second index gave a more detailed breakdown on approximately half of these persons. Also surprising to me was the large number of names marked with only a letter of the alphabet, indicating that they had already been registered by another MfS unit. For example, a "W" meant that all information about that person had been transferred to the local intelligence authorities at Wismut, the joint Soviet-GDR uranium mining operation.* Written on many cards was simply the word "friend," which signified possession by the KGB.

In addition, there was information about past recruitment failures, as well as extensive data about the center itself. Among other things I found detailed structural and security plans, annual reports, identification cards, and numerous duplicate keys.

Once I had examined this material, Christian asked me to have a "target information report" prepared by the following year. That entailed summarizing all current data about the center and making an intelligence assessment. I also had to submit a list of those executives and workers who were best informed about the center's operation. Christian noted that the "special staff unit" wanted a short sketch of each of these persons.

As far as I knew, this unit handled only the military training of MfS

---

* A fuller discussion of the Wismut operation appears on page 171.

workers. Christian became impatient at my lack of response. "Don't be so naïve," he said. "Do you think the special staff unit has no specific functions during an emergency? In fact its main job is to prepare the HVA for a direct military confrontation with the enemy. Do you really think that in a crunch you'd be sitting comfortably at your desk and summoning your agents in the normal manner?"

Naturally I knew that headquarters would be evacuated in the event of war and most employees placed behind enemy lines as a diversionary tactic. Still, it was still hard to see any connection with the Karlsruhe center.

Christian answered my question with another question. "Are you convinced of the ultimate victory of socialism?"

"Of course," I replied.

"Then it's quite clear that we will be marching into Karlsruhe one day and must know which persons to place first under our control. Wouldn't you agree?"

All my previous exposures to SED hypocrisy regarding West Germany seemed to pale in comparison to this remark. While officially preaching a doctrine of coexistence, the GDR had in fact developed aggressive plans that included a military occupation of the FRG. Among those West Germans to be taken into "safekeeping" were not just military personnel and politicians but also journalists, scientists, engineers, and nearly anyone entrusted with classified material. Especially for the Soviet Union, the loss of so many important German scientists after the Second World War remained a fresh memory and was not to occur again.

My consternation only increased when I later discovered the so-called VSH card index. When none of my immediate colleagues could give me a satisfactory explanation, I turned to Rolf Schilde, a good acquaintance who handled security matters at the Dresden Technical University.

Schilde first made some derogatory remarks about that "high and mighty East Berlin intelligence bunch" who had no idea of the dirty work occurring at the grass-roots level. Then he explained, "The VSH card index contains all the dubious characters that we'll have to lock up as a precaution in the event of a grave political crisis."

I pressed him for more details. VSH stood for "preventive security information" and listed anyone with a proven or "justifiably suspected" dislike of the GDR regime. Also included were members of specific sects, political criminals, nonvoters, rebellious young people, citizens with strong ties to the West, and even ordinary criminals. Because this information would allow the MfS to respond quickly to a domestic or foreign crisis, it seemed hard to imagine events occurring in the GDR as they had in Czechoslovakia in 1968 and later in Poland.

Christian himself once made a remark about the GDR's emergency plan. "If any threat to socialism appears, we certainly won't pull any punches. A few enemies of the state will have no problem disappearing in the vastness of Siberia! Not only must we know who our enemy is, but what to do with him in a crisis. Our enemy is found not just on our Western border but in our own homeland as well."

Although such disclosures only increased my desire to leave the GDR, there were more immediate matters demanding my attention. I managed to compile a list of all the leading executives, scientists, and security officials at the Karlsruhe center—a total of nearly a hundred names. I also completed my target information report. In its conclusion, I confirmed the capacity of the center to manufacture nuclear weapons, even though no actual production was occurring. My inevitable recommendation was that the HVA make a concerted effort to penetrate this important and potentially dangerous enemy facility. At the same time, my departmental colleagues were compiling similar reports on such installations as the nuclear research station in Jülich, the Federal Ministry of Research and Technology, and Interatom in Bensberg.

6

In this period, I also began to send my domestic agents on their first Western assignments. For the HVA, such trips by so-called "travel personnel" were quite routine and fulfilled a variety of purposes. As couriers and instructors, these persons often maintained connections with other agents stationed in the West. Besides making their own observations and investigations, they were involved in the initiation of new contacts and the later recruitment of agents. As noted earlier, a ranking HVA officer might even have given them a shopping list of goods not available in the GDR.

The first such trip I organized on my own involved Martin from Halle. Like any agent, he had to receive some intensive political preparation before his first encounter with Western life. There was also a discussion of the risks involved, although I always tried not to sound overly ominous. Standard procedure further specified that the first trip be no more than a day visit to West Berlin.

In this instance, I wanted Martin to become acquainted not only with West Berlin habits and attitudes but also with the operation of the public transport system, specifically with the layout and control procedures at Tempelhof Airport, which, as the sole air entry and exit point to the city, was used by the majority of our agents to enter the FRG. Should he be questioned by authorities, he was to pose as a literary scholar from the University of Halle on an academic assignment to the Free University of Berlin.

After submitting my plan for approval, I was summoned to Vogel's office. "Are you convinced that this man will come back?" he asked. "Have you found any personal difficulties that might make him decide to stay in the West?"

"There are none to my knowledge," I assured him.

"Are you certain that his impeccable political attitude is not just a facade?" I became more and more uncomfortable. Whom could one ever feel that degree of certitude about? I thought about how both my coworkers and superiors considered me at least a reliable, well-adapted party member, even though it was a total pretense on my part. Nevertheless, having found Martin's family situation perfectly in order, I answered affirmatively.

"All right, then I'll approve the trip," Vogel stated. "But if the man emigrates illegally, you will be held responsible and sent back to Linke to look after the physicists."

This was admittedly a serious possibility, but then all case officers had to run such risks and the number of defections remained relatively few. Division VI/K next issued a one-day exit permit for West Berlin along with a GDR passport in the agent's real name. From Vogel's secretary, I received forty West German marks, which seemed sufficient to cover Martin's expenses and any unexpected costs.

Until then, I had not told Martin explicitly that he was working for the HVA, even though it could have been surmised from his instructions and assignments. I had merely phoned him to request that he come to East Berlin for two days. As a university assistant, he had no difficulty leaving his institute for this short period. I put him up at my new safe house.

"Tomorrow you will travel to West Berlin on our behalf," I told him candidly. "It's time that you knew what my real job is. I am an MfS intelligence officer working against the FRG."

Martin appeared shocked, but regaining some of his composure, he asked, "Am I supposed to go over there as a scout?"

"Of course," I answered condescendingly. "Or do you think we acquire secret information from the West without going there ourselves?"

Martin beamed. In fact, he seemed so pleased that I felt uneasy. Had I been mistaken about him? Would he forever disappear once in West Berlin? No, I thought to myself, he's only expressing his feelings about being regarded as a respected intelligence collector rather than a little Stasi informer. With no further qualms, I proceeded to give my eager agent several informational brochures about West Berlin and the Friedrichstrasse station that had been prepared by division VI.

The next morning he received his passport and money along with instructions to return punctually to the safe house at 6:00 P.M. All day long, however, I felt quite edgy. Werner tried to ease my anxiety, maintaining that if Martin had been cleared by the vetting process, he would certainly return. "By the way," he recalled, "when you were my agent and I wanted to send you to West Berlin, I received instructions from above that prospective candidates for full-time employment were not allowed to travel."

Already at 5:30 P.M. I was waiting at the safe house for Martin to return.

As 6:00 came, then 6:30, then 7:00, my anxiety grew by the minute. I began to doubt his reliability again—or perhaps he had been detected and arrested as an MfS agent. Finally, at 7:30, the bell rang, and my agonizing wait came to an end. There stood Martin, exhausted but happy.

Before I could say a word, he exclaimed, "Have you any idea what you got me into? The airport was huge, the university library hard to find, and I had to spend the whole day just rushing around. To top it off, it took ages to get back over the GDR border."

From his descriptive report about West Berlin, my own curiosity was whetted, for even this loyal party member could not completely disguise his positive impressions of this "decadent" city.

In the following years, my feelings of insecurity always returned whenever a novice agent of mine made his first trip to the West. Fortunately, however, none of these persons were ever arrested or attempted to defect. For me at least, it seemed that the MfS had overstated the attendant risks.

By the time I had completed my own network, roughly four people were dispatched on various errands each month. Considering that my case was a bit above average, it could be estimated that approximately 50,000 trips were made annually on behalf on the MfS. Although no more than twenty to thirty registered arrests ever resulted from that number, they always caused great agitation in the HVA. It meant not only a lost agent but a potential gain for enemy counterespionage, including the elimination of a valuable Western source. Yet, above all, the arrest of an agent was regarded as a political defeat, dealt not to the individual but to the system. That did not exclude the fact that some arrests, as in the spectacular Guillaume affair, might attest more to the success of the system.*

Although rarely having serious consequences, unlucky events involving agents sent to the West occurred on a fairly frequent basis. In some cases, these agents have been mistaken for drug smugglers, thieves, or burglars. More than once the problems were caused by the "double papers" that we had supplied ourselves. This practice involved secretly photocopying the documents of actual West Berlin and West German citizens at GDR entry stations and then forging identity papers for our agents.

Rarely were these documents ever called into question. In fact, during several West German espionage trials, experts attested to the genuineness of our products while raising doubts about the real documents. The problem was that we could never be certain that the original person had not, for

---

* After being resettled with his wife in the FRG, Günter Guillaume rose though a series of positions in the Social Democratic Party to become the personal secretary of Chancellor Willy Brandt. In 1974, Brandt had to resign from office when Guillaume's MfS affiliation became known. Following his return to the GDR as part of a 1981 spy exchange, Guillaume was promoted to the rank of colonel and awarded an honorary doctorate in law.

example, skipped an alimony payment and was wanted by authorities. Despite all the precautions taken in the preparation of these forged papers, the MfS might have simply lacked the latest FRG police records.

The cover of a former colleague, Hartmut Ritter, was almost blown for another reason. While still an agent, he was sent to West Berlin on an alleged bibliographical assignment for the University of Leipzig. His real task was to verify an address and discreetly ascertain if the person in question was at home. After choosing a children's playground from which he could observe the windows of the person's apartment, he sat down on the edge of the sandbox and pretended to play with the children. As a teacher who was quite fond of children, he had little inkling that his behavior might appear abnormal. Within half an hour, however, a police patrol arrived and took him into custody.

At the precinct, he indignantly denied the charge of "indecent behavior with children" and was subjected to a thorough cross-examination. When asked why someone on a scholarly errand had ended up at a children's playground, the inexperienced Ritter promptly revealed his lack of skill in dissimulation. Instead of saying that he was only taking a rest after having lost his way, he contrived some flimsy reasons that made the police immediately suspect the hand of the MfS. In spite of his many contradictory statements, Ritter continued to deny any connection to the security forces. The next day, despite their complete conviction that he was an MfS agent, the police had to release him for lack of evidence on any punishable charge.

6

A Tour de Force

1

On the last day of 1973, I again took stock of my situation. On one hand, having recruited one West agent and taken over the responsibility for another one, I had made a good start in my new job. Since my own domestic network had also increased considerably, I was viewed as a person on the rise. On the other hand, my personal abhorrence of the East German regime had grown more intense and was accompanied by deeply conflicting emotions. Despite my increasing doubts as to how long this schizophrenia could be endured, I kept postponing a definite resolution. There had also been no further contact with the BND since the first meeting nearly two years ago in Leipzig. Even though it had nearly faded into my subconsciousness, I still wore the "totem," which at times gave me the almost physical sensation of being watched by the other side. Later I discovered that was indeed the case.

The dawn of the new year brought full-scale preparations for the fall celebration of the GDR's founding. Because the MfS would be celebrating its own twenty-fifth birthday the following February, there was all the more reason to proclaim a massive competition within the HVA. To be sure, every possible facet of life in East Germany had been subjected to Lenin's notion of "the consciousness-building power of socialist competition." Whereas its overuse had long ago made it a meaningless concept in industry and agriculture, the MfS acted as if it still had continuing relevance. Nearly half of all our party events had the topic of socialistic competition on the agenda. That meant each of us had to make a "personal commitment" or face later reprisals.

However self-deluded we knew this practice to be, no one ever conceded it openly. A competent operational officer would be attempting his utmost in any event, while those lazy comrades never permitted any form of competition to disturb their comfortable existence. The latter group was easily identifiable at party meetings because of its long-winded rhetoric. Like all other GDR institutions, the MfS based promotions on party loyalty, and it was precisely those persons with fewer operational successes who wanted to proclaim their "revolutionary" devotion.

One day, Christian called me to his office to discuss a competition commitment. Since his recent promotion to major, he seemed more consumed by ambition than ever. "So, Comrade Lieutenant," he greeted me, "what birthday gift will you be giving to the republic on October seventh?"

I already knew from my colleagues that Christian was accepting normal assignments as a pledge. Besides, my recruitment of Ernesto was hardly more than a month old, and I was also at a loss to offer anything new. When I then presented a strong case for the resettlement of Ernesto and his wife in the West as my "personal commitment," Christian quickly disagreed. "That's the kind of thing you can do in your sleep! I've got something else for you. He's been a hard nut to crack for years. If you could recruit him, that would be really be a coup."

Two rather faded-looking files lay before Christian. Knowing that old files usually contained the most interesting cases, I could not suppress my curiosity and took the bait. He then told me to study the file of a particular GDR citizen, who in turn could lead to the real person of interest in the West. The case involved people in high academic circles, and Christian thought that I was best qualified for dealing with "such gentlemen."

Opening the file designated by the codename "Bodo," I was particularly interested by the first page, which listed all the MfS workers who had had dealings with the man. At the top stood the name of Reinhard Linke, whose involvement with the MfS as the secretary of the Physics Society was already well known to me. In actuality "Bodo" was Herbert Friedrich, a forty-year-old physicist who directed a working group in the Central Institute of Electron Physics, a division of the GDR Academy of Sciences. The institute itself was interlaced with MfS personnel and included the director, the head of the international division, and one of my own later recruited agents.

Friedrich, who also served as the secretary of the National Committee of Physics, was recognizable as a frequent visitor to the Physics Society. We had also had a long discussion about scientific politics once at an official congress. Of average height, stockily built with dark hair turning gray, and a prematurely lined face, he had impressed me by his objectivity and knowledge of his subject. Although I initially doubted whether he was suited for intelligence work, my assumption was to be proven wrong.

In 1965, Friedrich had been recruited by Linke in characteristic style. After mentioning to some colleagues that his neighbor was apparently having incestuous relations with his daughter, the young physicist had been approached by Linke. By telling Friedrich that this was a case for the MfS as the "guardian of socialist morals," Linke managed to extract a full account of the affair. Their subsequent meetings, detailing the development of the incestuous relationship, continued every month for the next half year. Still, I was puzzled by the fact that Bodo had learned everything from the aberrant father himself when under the influence of alcohol. If Bodo also took part in these drinking bouts, I wondered, could it be that he was an alcoholic as well? In any event, the file did not contain anything remarkable after his recruitment, probably owing to Linke's own negligent manner, and once Linke had been fired from the department, contact with Bodo ceased.

The second file was as suspenseful as the first had been banal. To my astonishment, it began in 1948, two years before the MfS's official establishment. Despite the absence of any official letterheads, it seemed clear that the KGB had been directly involved. What I found so remarkable was the cloak of secrecy that the KGB still maintained toward us, their so-called "junior partner." At the time, they were represented in our sector by a colonel whose main duty involved sifting through all the information given to him by our ranking officer. Considering the number of requests for photocopies, it seemed that there was hardly anything not of interest to the Soviets.

How a KGB agent is actually cultivated became clearer as I began to read about Professor Karl Hauffe. Born in Posen in 1913, he was an esteemed old-style German academic. After receiving a doctorate in chemistry, Hauffe had continued to pursue his scientific studies until, like most of his generation, he was drafted into the wartime army. In 1948 he received a lectureship in Berlin and was later made full professor at the University of Greifswald. One of his early teachers and sponsors was Professor Robert Rompe.

The name practically jumped from the page. This Leningrad-born scientist, known as the GDR's "high priest of physics," was not only chairman of the Physics Society but also a member of the SED Central Committee. Moreover, I had frequently come across his name in various departmental files. It was Rompe, for example, who had arranged for the agent "Sperber" to go to the Frenchman "Ludwig" at the time of his resettlement in the West. In fact, he had somehow figured in every important case that I had seen thus far.

Looking up at my colleague, Werner, who was sorting through some papers, I asked what Rompe's exact role was in our department. As was his custom whenever I asked a particularly searching question, Werner looked at me for a long time before responding, trying to decide whether I was adult enough to warrant an answer. Should he feel that it was premature for me to know, then he simply went back to his work and pretended not to have heard my question. This time, however, I received an explanation.

"Robert—or codename 'Frank'—is probably the most valuable agent working for the sector, and is handled by Willi Neumann personally. He's often helped resettle our people by asking Western scientists to take in a penniless East German refugee. He's also known as an independent spirit—a professed communist and member of the Central Committee and, at the same time, a teacher concerned about his students even when they've fled the GDR. At any rate, that's how his Western colleagues view him, which is most fortunate for us. Apart from the cases I know, it's hard to say for certain how many agents from our sector he has succeeded in placing." My own later experiences confirmed Werner's account.

I pressed him to continue. "According to the file it appears that he worked for the 'friends.'"

After a moment's reflection, Werner said patronizingly, "So you noticed that too. There is a long tradition of scientific-technical intelligence in the KGB, and Robert is one of the oldest East German friends of the Soviet Union. Why do you think he belongs to the Central Committee? There are doubtless other physicists in the GDR who are both decent scientists and reliable communists. But our Soviet comrades have special confidence in Rompe, and they must have their reasons."

It would have been most intriguing to know all about Rompe's secret activities, beginning with his work for the KGB in the 1930s. Certainly the exploits of Soviet espionage in scientific and technical fields had had an early and successful start. Once the head of the sector told me how Lenin, during those uncertain days immediately after the October Revolution, had personally dispatched Peter Kapitsa, a highly talented young physicist, to the world-famous British physicist Ernest Rutherford to learn as much as possible. Upon his return to the USSR around 1929, Kapitsa possessed enough knowledge to lay the foundation for the Soviet nuclear physics. In fact, before his departure, Rutherford had also given him a complete set of laboratory equipment as a token of his strong affection.

Gradually it dawned on me that Rompe was the person who had lured my new target person into the KGB web. According to the file, Hauffe, who had gained a reputation as an important chemist, felt constricted in the small university town and had pushed strongly for an appointment in East Berlin. As a key official in the Ministry of Higher Education at the time, Rompe not only helped secure his protégé's request but also passed his name on to the KGB. Suddenly, after his new appointment in 1952, Hauffe and his wife, one of his earlier laboratory technicians, mysteriously fled to the West and ended up at a research institute in Oslo. Although the reasons for their presumed escape were missing from the file, he was later contacted by KGB agents while directing research at a well-known chemical firm. For a long time he must have been useful to the ailing Soviet economy.

In 1962 Hauffe was abruptly dismissed from his well-paid job. Although the file contained no further details, it seems possible that the board of directors had become suspicious of his activities and wanted to preserve the firm's reputation by avoiding an espionage trial. After a long search, Hauffe received the directorship of an institute at the University of Göttingen. The KGB surfaced again after a hiatus, but the former agent apparently wanted a clean break and refused to return for talks in the East. At this point, the Soviets appear to have given both him and Rompe to the MfS, thus explaining why his file was in East Berlin.

Attempting a different approach, the MfS immediately sent a letter by messenger from Rompe to Hauffe. The text included a sentimental evocation of old times along with an invitation to East Berlin, which Hauffe declined point-blank to the waiting courier. Afterward nothing more occurred other than a few innocuous letters from Rompe and, in reply, some Christmas and birthday cards from Hauffe. The file lay dormant in the HVA archives until 1972, when Hauffe's plan to attend a conference in Prague became known and Christian was assigned to the case. In the end, however, Hauffe canceled his trip. Another attempt by Rompe to entice his protégé to Bucharest similarly ended without success.

At a loss as to how to proceed, Christian had now given me this mixed-up file as my "personal commitment" for the GDR's twenty-fifth anniversary. Having seen how both the KGB and the HVA had struggled with this case for the past ten years, I could well understand why Christian regarded its successful resolution as a real coup. My own chances seemed slim. I wondered, for example, what kind of cooperation I would receive from such an apparently uncomplicated person as "Bodo." The only opening he provided was his close association with Rompe. But it seemed as if Hauffe had completely severed his friendship with Rompe, perhaps even blaming his former mentor for the KGB's intrusiveness and his various mishaps.

Still, the case excited me. Even though the KGB had given us only a fragmentary version of the early history of the case, presumably preferring not to reveal all its cards, this nevertheless had the earmarks of a first-class Soviet operation. Of the few KGB assessments remaining in the file, one line caught my attention because of its remarkable candor: "Hauffe covets money. He gladly accepts financial payments." This fact, I thought, might well provide the means for a contact. Avarice, after all, is a trait that usually increases rather than diminishes over time.

Christian agreed with me that money was the most expeditious means of luring Hauffe, and together we worked out a plan. Bodo was to approach Hauffe with a proposal for a joint project whereby he could earn a great deal of money. It also seemed unlikely to us that Hauffe, in light of his earlier espionage involvement, would turn Bodo over to the police. Before dispatching Bodo, however, I wanted to meet him in person. On the telephone, I introduced myself as "Schilling," a colleague of Linke and Christian, and a meeting was arranged.

2

We met at the "Mokka-Eck." Located near the Alexanderplatz and opposite the East Berlin police headquarters, this café was known for the quality of its ice cream and had remained very popular despite its reputation as a notorious Stasi hangout. For MfS case officers, it was mostly the attractive waitresses that had made it a favorite meeting spot.

Bodo was already sitting at a corner table but failed to recognize me, even though only two years had passed since our last meeting at the Physics Institute. So much the better, I thought, for then he won't know my real name. According to MfS regulations, agents could identify their case officers only by a surname or a pseudonym.

Although I was nearly fifteen years his junior, Bodo accepted me right away, and we talked easily about physics, the institute, and even some politics. He was, as his file had indicated, a genuine gossip. Only later, however, did I realize his skill at playing naïve and asking the most probing questions with an air of utmost sincerity. At this meeting, Bodo remained quite reticent, and when I directly inquired about the date of his next official journey to the West, his reaction was one of instant fear.

"Will I have to do something for all of you there?" he asked in an uncertain voice.

Cursing Christian and the whole case under my breath, I wondered what on earth could be done with such a frightened person. When I brusquely told him just to answer my question, he hesitated a moment, and then said, "In March there's a Unesco conference in Holland, and I've been invited as the GDR representative. I really ought to attend it, but then who knows whether that will be possible."

This seemed a stroke of luck for me, as he could easily visit Hauffe in Göttingen on the return trip without making a long detour. "Don't worry," I replied, "you'll be able to attend the Unesco conference."

Nothing, however, was mentioned about the real point of the trip, or even the stopover in Göttingen. Moreover, I had promised far more than I should have, since official approval of Bodo's conference first had to come from the Academy of Sciences. But it took only one phone call from Christian to obtain permission, and when I returned to his office, he merely said, "Bodo goes." Sometimes things could be that simple in the GDR.

At our next meeting, when I asked Bodo if he knew Hauffe, he said, "Only in passing."

"We'd like you to visit him on your Holland trip, preferably after the conference."

Not surprisingly, he attempted to find various excuses, complaining about the length of the detour, the irregularity of an official journey including two capitalistic countries, and the amount of risk involved. After patiently listening for a while, I finally cut him off. "You will go visit Professor Hauffe. You will give him greetings from Rompe and extend his invitation to come to the GDR. You will also tell him that Rompe is anxious to discuss a lucrative joint research project, indicating that it involves highly stable materials, which is one of his specialties."

Handing Bodo some extra money, I wished him a pleasant trip. Although he had many personal liabilities—a weak and fatalistic personality, an overfondness for alcohol, and, as I had recently discovered, a shamelessly cheating wife—I also knew that his reputation as a physicist could easily secure him a job in the West.

Fortunately he returned as planned. I gave him a friendly greeting and asked him about his impressions of the "wicked West." With a grimace, he said, "Do you know something? A few of those evil things over here would do us a lot of good! I saved quite a bit of the money you gave me and bought myself a handyman's tool set from Black and Decker. I hope that's O.K.?"

"That all depends upon what happened with Hauffe."

"One thing at a time," Bodo said. He then opened his bulging briefcase, which contained a pile of the latest research reports on the use of solar energy. Some of them, he explained, were gifts at the conference, while the others had been taken from a suitcase accidentally left behind by a departing American. I was quite taken aback. Even though I was required to reprimand him for having taken a risk beyond his official instructions, our evaluations of his booty turned out to be highly positive.

"How did it go with Hauffe?" I impatiently asked. He then began to talk about the hospitality of the professor, who had taken him on an interesting personal tour of the institute. Knowing that he purposely took pleasure in keeping me in suspense, I said abruptly, "Tell me right now how the professor reacted to the invitation."

"Well, he was very pleased and sends his greetings to Rompe. He wants to come over in May. He also said that he might have some ideas himself for the project."

From Bodo's manner alone, it was clear that his mission had been a success. After extending my generous praise, I reported back to Christian to discuss our next step. At his last meeting with Neumann, Rompe had agreed to welcome his protégé, but any further recruitment attempts were out of the question. Besides emphasizing that his salary was not paid by the MfS, he wanted to avoid any compromising situation, should something go awry. That meant that we would have to handle Hauffe ourselves.

Christian agreed to my suggestion of preparing an "advisory contract" for Hauffe. Bodo's excellent report about the professor's institute helped me better know the nature of his research and the materials involved. To add to the precision of my draft, I turned to the team of analysts run by the sector's evaluation section, who also concluded that Hauffe's research subject had great relevance to the GDR economy. In addition, the professor had informed Bodo of his contacts with leading aircraft and nuclear industries. In my final draft, drawing upon Bodo's reconnaissance efforts and the results of our evaluators, I was thus able to compile a complete list of topics from Hauffe's scientific repertoire relevant to us. I also included the important clause noting Hauffe's share in the profits owing to his "advisory function." The draft received Neumann's endorsement.

Christian, who wanted to participate in the discussions with Hauffe, agreed that we should both present ourselves as employees of the Ministry of Science and Technology. Such a cover would explain our interest in acquiring research reports and technological documents. In the event that Hauffe still harbored a grudge against the KGB, we wanted to avoid any mention of his previous espionage work. Even though our main aim was to appear as representatives of a ministry concerned solely with science, we also hoped that Hauffe would quickly grasp with whom he was really dealing and what was expected of him.

Rompe conveyed to Neumann that he would do nothing more than "legitimize" us to the professor.

3

When the designated day arrived, Bodo called to say that Rompe had just received Hauffe. At midday he called again. "Rompe told his guest about two men from the Ministry of Science and Technology wishing to speak to him, and he's agreed to have lunch with you. Any objections if I come too?"

I checked it out with Christian. "He just wants a free meal, but it's not a bad idea to have a close acquaintance of Rompe with us." I told Bodo that we would collect him and Hauffe at Rompe's institute.

Parking the car some distance from the building, Christian explained, "Several employees here know who I am." This was quite true, for the Central Institute of Electron Physics constituted a branch office not only for us but for other units of the sector as well.

After the two men got into the car, we were introduced as Messrs. Schubert and Schilling from the Ministry of Science and Technology. Hauffe reacted coolly. A tall, slender man with well-groomed, graying hair, he wore gold-rimmed glasses and had an interesting face. He also had such an unapproachable manner that any recruitment attempt seemed almost out of the question. Had we misinterpreted his reaction to Bodo's invitation? Or had mistakes been made at the very outset, perhaps by the Soviets? In any case, it seemed practically inconceivable that such a traditional German academic would have ever worked for a roughneck outfit like the KGB. I foresaw disaster. Hardly a word was spoken during the drive, as

Christian remained preoccupied with giving directions to our ever-confused driver.

I had chosen the Ermelerhaus for lunch. Overlooking the Spree River, this former bourgeois residence had undergone an elaborate restoration to become the GDR's most conspicuous international restaurant. We were greeted by a waiter in tails, who showed us to the almost empty Peacock Room. I was most impressed by my first look at the restaurant's elegant interior and by the gracious and attentive service. All of our calculations seemed right, except for the target person. Christian's face indicated that he had drawn a similar conclusion about Hauffe.

As we studied the menu, the professor remarked admiringly, "This is the old pre-war Berlin I knew and loved." Such a comment left both Christian and me baffled for a response. Should we try somehow to connect what he had said with the achievements of socialism? That would hardly have worked. My discomfort grew as Christian concentrated desperately on the menu. Hauffe, as impenetrable as ever, was obviously a major mistake on our part.

The only person oblivious to the tense atmosphere was Bodo, who blithely proceeded through the menu making comments on each dish. Hauffe then said, "The menu is quite excellent, gentlemen. I'll have the turtle soup and pork tenderloin." Christian and I followed his lead, while Bodo opted for a hearty Berlin-style pork knuckle.

The waiter then inquired, "What would you like to drink? Perhaps an aperitif before the soup?"

As the waiter began to recite the list of almost exclusively Western wines, Hauffe interrupted, "I would like a beer." He turned to us and said almost apologetically, "It reminds me of the old times in Berlin." Bodo agreed that a beer would also taste best with his pork knuckle. When the waiter then informed him that beer was not normally served, Hauffe replied sardonically, "Surely if a Berlin-style pork knuckle is on your menu, you don't expect my colleague to order a Moselle wine with it."

Leaving the waiter with little choice but to comply, Hauffe had handily shown how much remained of that East German provincialism that the leadership had tried so hard to eliminate. Still, his request for a beer and his reference to Bodo as a colleague helped to break the ice.

Hauffe opened the discussion. "Rompe said that you are members of the Ministry of Science and Technology and wanted to talk with me. How can I help you?"

Fortunately, he looked directly at Christian, as I still felt incapable of handling the situation. Regaining some of his poise, Christian replied, "Professor, I want to express my great pleasure at seeing you in your earlier domain after so many years. We have a problem to discuss with you, but it is perhaps best left until after our meal."

Although this seemed a shrewd move and gave us more time to loosen up the situation, Hauffe maintained his distant air. When the table had been cleared, Christian came right to the point. "Professor, you no doubt know that we are lagging behind in the development of certain materials. Let's not go into the reasons why, but concentrate instead on how we can improve this situation. Given your experience and insight, we thought that you might assist us in an advisory capacity, for which you would naturally receive adequate compensation."

This blatant offer did not produce a flicker of emotion. "I am not entirely familiar with you or your system," Hauffe answered reticently. "To avoid any misunderstanding on my part, you might kindly explain the aims of your ministry and its role in the East German economy. That presumably is why we are meeting."

This clever reply put Christian on the defensive. After he explained the various functions of the ministry and gave a few specific examples, I timidly began to enter the conversation. Eventually Hauffe returned to Christian's proposal. "Gentlemen, you obviously do not know the conditions in the FRG. We have an open exchange of opinions and information. If you feel that I can help you in any way, then send Dr. Friedrich to me and I will answer all his questions, naturally without charge. That is the least I can do for my old friend Rompe. Of course, you understand that I also advise a number of West German firms and, for reasons of loyalty and outside competition, cannot talk freely about all I know."

Everyone knew this amounted to a refusal. Thinking perhaps that Hauffe had not comprehended the real motive behind our offer, I tried to press further, but Christian broke in. "That is most kind of you to give Dr. Friedrich a bit of help, and I am very grateful. We will certainly be in contact at the appropriate time." I quickly called the waiter to bring this frosty meeting to a close.

Christian and Bodo preferred to bid farewell at the restaurant, and I was left to escort the professor back to his car. Once we were alone with only the driver, he spontaneously began to reminisce. "Do you realize, Schilling, that I regret to this day not having stayed in Berlin?" I tried to hide my surprise at this sudden break in his facade. That he was also addressing someone he probably considered a lowly bureaucrat confused me even further. To be on the safe side, I remained silent.

"I'm not really in very much of a hurry," he continued. "Let's find a nice place somewhere and have a beer." Little did he realize that, despite the large number of establishments in East Berlin, most of them had long ago lost their congenial atmosphere through neglect and ill-paid personnel. Then I remembered a newly opened beer cellar downtown, which had been specifically designed to give visiting foreign officials a chance to rub elbows with a carefully chosen group of merry working-class Berliners.

Soon Hauffe and I were immersed in a discussion about current issues in physics. Still I felt a certain annoyance as he repeatedly dropped the names of specific Western installations with which he had connections. Was he simply showing off after having refused our offer? Finally I said, "Professor, what you tell me is enormously interesting. I'm sure that your vast knowledge and impressive connections could provide the basis of a mutually advantageous business arrangement. You should give our offer another consideration." His lack of response only made me feel angry with myself for not having left an obviously hopeless situation alone.

When he next began to inquire about my connection to Bodo, I felt suspicious. Apart from his report on Hauffe's institute and his assistance in arranging this meeting, I denied having any other connection with the man. Seemingly satisfied with my reply, Hauffe turned the conversation to politics. "You know, Schilling, I believe that the old Prussian virtues of discipline, order, and industriousness are alive and well in the GDR today. It's not like the West, where every lazy rascal is demanding all sorts of rights and protection; where the students would rather strike than work; where foreigners of every description are overrunning the local population; where a spineless government pursues spineless policies; and where everything that once stood behind the good name of Germany is degenerating more and more. Germany's real future lies here in the East."

As he continued in this vein, I again felt taken completely by surprise. "Professor," I cautiously replied, "certainly much of what you say is true, even if I can't agree with everything." His dubious compliment might actually provide the opening we had been seeking, and I tried to exploit it to the fullest. Initially, it seemed to me quite farfetched to consider the GDR as the historical heir of Frederick the Great's Prussia, but then again, there had been a concerted official campaign to inject certain carefully chosen aspects of the Prussian past into the GDR's "national consciousness." His line of reasoning was not without some merit and became easier to follow.

When Hauffe finally dropped the subject, the conversation took another unexpected twist. "Schilling, I have decided to accept your offer after all. You understand, of course, that it should remain as confidential as possible. If any ties to an East German ministry ever became known, my industrial connections would be seriously jeopardized. I suggest excluding Dr. Friedrich from any further talks, lest he make an indiscreet remark on one of his Western trips."

Now everything seemed clear as daylight. His excessive punctiliousness, his proud bearing, and his indignant refusal of our offer had all been ploys to convince Bodo that the whole enterprise was a failure. I also understood why he suddenly wanted to have a beer with me and probe my own scientific background. In all likelihood, he had desired an agreement with us before arriving in Berlin and had merely constructed this elaborate political pretext.

Even so, I was hardly prepared for what happened next. He opened his briefcase and pulled out a stack of scientific papers. Seeing immediately that they contained valuable information, I debated with myself whether to give him the 1,000 West German marks that were in my pocket. Incidentally, my decision to take some extra money along had prompted several mocking remarks from Christian.

Finally, I handed Hauffe the envelope. "Naturally, Professor, these papers will have to be evaluated by our own experts to establish their value, but this should be a fair amount."

Hauffe's greed had certainly not been underestimated by the Soviets, for hardly had the envelope reached the table before he placed it in his briefcase. "What sort of documents are you interested in?" he inquired. As I began to name the topics that had been prepared in advance, he cut in and said with a knowing smile, "Don't bother, I think I know what you'll want."

Everything now seemed in order, but I thought one more precaution necessary. "No doubt you will understand if I ask for a receipt for the money. Without some proof, my superiors might think that I had spent it in an Intershop on myself."

He paused a moment, obviously knowing that his signature meant a definite commitment on his part. In addition, since I could add the recipient's name later, he was demonstrating his personal trust in me, regardless of my own governmental affiliation.

As he got into his BMW sedan, I asked him when we would meet again in East Berlin. His answer of about four weeks made it even sooner than I had hoped. After we agreed on a date and place, he added, "Before I forget, would you also be kind enough to arrange a meeting for me then with Professor Rompe? There are still some points to discuss." Obviously wasting no time to devise a cover story for his next trip, this man, I thought to myself, is a thorough professional. We departed in a cordial, almost affectionate manner.

4

On the way back to headquarters, I reassessed the situation. Since the necessary exchange of information and money had taken place, my second official Western recruitment seemed almost in the bag. Admittedly, some doubts lingered as to whether Hauffe knew, or even wanted to know, my own identity, but then he had taken several steps to keep his activity concealed. Most important, however, we had agreed on a modus operandi for the future. Arriving at the department just before quitting time, I was anxious to tell Christian the news about Hauffe.

"Well, well, look who's here, it's Comrade Stiller!" he said with biting sarcasm. "He drags me along to a meeting with a man he wants to recruit, but ends up saying nothing, leaving me to talk my head off to someone who treats us as condescendingly as his own students." My smiling colleagues were taking malicious pleasure not only at my own dressing-down but also at a seeming failure of the ambitious departmental chief.

I purposely tried to look guilty and stammered sheepishly, "Christian, I don't have the one thousand marks any more."

Drawing a deep breath, he was poised for a new attack. "What have you done with it?"

"Well, I gave it to Hauffe."

"How dare you start making light of this matter after getting me so involved! Instead you ought to be asking yourself what you did wrong." He then vented his emotions, showing that remarkable skill, so indispensable for advancement in the MfS, of turning black into white, and white into black. He ignored, for example, the fact that he had rated the chances of Hauffe's recruitment in East Berlin as "excellent" and wanted to attend the initial meeting himself. Nevertheless, it seemed better to stick to what had actually transpired, since any reminder of his earlier statements could only incur his long-lasting hostility, regardless of my eventual success with the professor.

"No," I said, pulling the receipt from my pocket, "this is no joke. Here is what I got for the money."

His scorn and anger suddenly vanishing, Christian seemed at a complete loss for words. Handing him the pile of documents, I relished the situation I had hoped to bring about. "He also gave me these along with best regards to Comrade Mielke."

Now it was Christian's turn to look sheepish—but it was no act. Knowing that he had gone too far in front of my colleagues, he tried to save face by ordering me to his office. My news caused him to struggle visibly with two conflicting emotions. Fortunately, his delight over a successful recruitment, which would help to advance his own career, outweighed any feelings of revenge for having been so purposely misled.

Quickly readjusting his attitude toward me, he reached for the phone to call the divisional head. "Horst, I just wanted to you to know that Comrade Stiller has fulfilled his twenty-fifth-anniversary 'competition commitment' ahead of time. Hauffe is as good as recruited." This contrived understatement was specifically intended to impress his superior.

He then turned to me and asked in a collegial tone, "Would you mind much staying behind to write your report now? Vogel has scheduled a meeting of departmental heads tomorrow morning, and I would really like to be one up on the others. For quite a while, we've been under fire for living solely off our reserves of old agents."

For Christian to admit that such intrigues and careerist infighting took place behind the scenes was a rare confession, even though I had seen much earlier how some colleagues would unscrupulously seize upon a moment of inattentiveness. I did Christian the favor of writing my report right away. Nevertheless, because of the embarrassing scene before the departmental staff, I still feared some lingering resentment and decided to omit the fact of his absence during the decisive moment of Hauffe's recruitment.

Four weeks later, punctually as promised, Hauffe—whom we had now designated with the codename "Fellow"—arrived with a briefcase full of documents. We returned to the Ermelerhaus, which he had so enjoyed, and discussed some further possibilities. From the way that he told me how other papers could be secured and what their individual significance would be, it was clear that Fellow was no newcomer to the espionage game. Our complementary relationship seemed to bode well for the future.

Fellow then began another political testimonial. "You know, Schilling, what I always tell my students is honesty, honesty, and again honesty. That is the unique characteristic that accounts for Germany's greatness." Although I felt repelled by such blatant hypocrisy, he was evidently trying to reaffirm his earlier linkage of the GDR with glories of old Prussia. This time, however, I wholeheartedly agreed with him, having received permission beforehand to deviate from Marxist doctrine and endorse any political position the professor might take. According to Christian, when the acquisition of information was at stake, "we'd even make a pact with the devil, or worse, with God himself."

Fellow seemed pleased by my offer to double his payments. Thinking that our relationship ought to be placed on a more professional basis, I stated, "You know, Professor, perhaps it might be better for you not to sign the receipt with your own name. You know how the tax people always like to check everything, including things that are not their own business."

With a sigh of relief, he agreed, and signed the name "Oswald" on the paper. Then, apparently wanting some further assurance, he requested a visa and hotel room for the evening. "Surely your office can make arrangements so that I won't have to spend the night in West Berlin."

His reference to "your office" immediately removed any remaining ambiguity between us. After I agreed to his request, he offered his hearty congratulations on the Guillaume affair. "Placing such an influential agent so close to the West German chancellor," he said, "proves to me that your 'office' fully deserves its reputation for quality work." I grinned as if personally flattered.

Besides revealing his full awareness of MfS involvement, his remark only confirmed what the HVA had earlier found to be true. Instead of producing fear among our remaining agents in West Germany, the arrest of Günter Guillaume in late April 1974 had actually advanced the reputation of the HVA. As a result, many dormant agents became active again and the cooperation of some dubious contact persons was secured.

Whether there were other East Germans similarly positioned in the FRG was a question often posed but of course never officially answered. An HVA colleague specifically assigned to the West German Social Democratic Party later told me that most important positions in this area were fully active at the time, even though no details could be divulged. Nevertheless, there were others in the MfS leadership who felt decidedly less positive about Guillaume's arrest. As later confirmed to me by an acquaintance working in the foreign ministry, Guillaume's information had been of utmost importance in negotiating key treaties concluded with the FRG. By knowing the West German negotiating positions in advance, the GDR leadership was able to obtain maximum gains with minimal concessions. Besides stopping this flow of top-level information, the exposure of Guillaume quickly resulted in a much less accommodating government under Helmut Schmidt.

As far as Fellow was concerned, our association functioned smoothly for some time. At intervals of two or three months, he brought some extensive scientific material to us and received a payment of about 2,500 West German marks. Later, when I could better ascertain what material was available to him, notably in the area of military technology, it often seemed that he was holding something back from me. When reminded that some promised documents had not been delivered, he tried to change the subject. I could find no good explanation for this behavior, especially since his desire for making easy money had showed no signs of abatement. Initially thinking that perhaps his fear of exposure outweighed all other considerations, I was surprised when, about a year later, Fellow requested an honorary doctorate from Humboldt University. Presumably he wanted to extract as much from us as possible without running any further risks.

Contrary to my expectations, Christian gave his approval for the degree, stipulating in his sardonic manner that the professor deliver several good pieces of information so as to give the degree "a more scholarly justification." Although the ceremony was planned for 1978 on his sixty-fifth birthday, a change in my life was to prevent the professor from returning to receive this honor.

Before that happened, however, Fellow had devised another means of using us to his advantage. Expressing his anxiety at repeatedly crossing the intra-German border with a bundle of documents, he proposed transferring our meetings to Romania, Hungary, or Poland. Since airport inspectors were usually far more rigorous, I did not follow his logic completely, but the thought of such a journey was very tempting to me. I was also able to overcome Christian's initial reluctance by stating that the professor would miss the next East Berlin meeting because of a commitment in Budapest. Christian, now having advanced to deputy head of our division, merely stipulated that he make the trip as well. Like most citizens of the GDR, he was drawn to the prospect of leaving our own "socialist paradise" for several days, even if it meant just visiting another East bloc country. Fortunately, as it turned out, Christian had to cancel his plans, thus allowing me to spend several enjoyable and informative days with Fellow in Hungary.

5

In May 1974, my family and I were assigned to a new two-bedroom apartment in an MfS apartment house in the Sterndamm. When handing me the official papers, Christian noted that many other successful HVA officers, including himself, had previously lived there. "Now," he said with a touch of irony, "you can become acquainted with the wide range of recreational activities available in an MfS housing block."

Having lived anonymously in a working-class district up to now, I had enjoyed a considerable degree of freedom within my own four walls, which even included watching some occasional West German television. The thought of the Sterndamm apartment house filled me with apprehension, for the residents maintained a sharp vigilance on each other and there was also the pressure to participate in the local party organization. In addition, one of my upstairs neighbors was Olaf Junghanns, an unpleasant, dogmatic colleague in the department who would be likely to report every future marital tiff to my superiors.

My fears, however, proved unfounded, at least regarding the general atmosphere. Hardly had the furniture arrived before our new neighbors came over for a welcoming toast that lasted nearly the whole day. Olaf also turned out to be a good and compassionate friend, even though his absolute adherence to the daily party newspaper meant the avoidance of all political discussions. Whereas the apartment on the left stood temporarily empty— the couple had been assigned to the GDR embassy in Beijing for three years—Hermann Linder, a member of the MfS military counterespionage division, lived to the right with his family. Since his wife was notorious for eavesdropping on neighbors by putting her ear to a saucepan held against the wall, I had to exercise caution.

Still, the next five years were generally convivial, due primarily to the heavy drinking that took place in the apartment house. It was also here that I acquired my first car, a Trabant, used but in good condition. In fact, my driving license was issued by an MfS automotive expert who was routinely drunk and needed a "test drive" to the nearest liquor store.

Taking advantage of a well-equipped lakeside "dacha" maintained by our division, I had made plans for a two-week vacation in early July 1974 with my family. My main desire was to do some fishing and sailing and also watch the World Cup soccer championships on television. In mid-June, however, I was unexpectedly summoned by the divisional head. Although unaware of any infraction on my part, I knew that Vogel preferred to handle all breaches of conduct personally. Christian's presence in the room only added to my discomfort.

After I was silently motioned over to his desk and given a careful scrutiny, Vogel shook my hand and offered me a chair. To my further surprise, he addressed me in the familiar form. "What will you be doing on July eleventh?"

When I told him about my vacation plans, including following the GDR team in the World Cup games, he replied, "Then everything is settled. You may go."

Concerned that I might have missed something, I assured my superiors that the dacha was only a short distance away and it would be easy to return should anything important arise.

"Good," Vogel said. "On July eleventh you'll go to Federal Republic to see our team play in one of the championship games." In order not to arouse the suspicion of my two superiors, I tried to suppress my strong feelings of pleasure, albeit with considerable difficulty. Vogel told me to consider the trip a reward, doubtlessly for Fellow's recruitment, and not to mix business with pleasure while in the FRG.

When I went to the staff division for a more detailed briefing, my exhilaration was quickly deflated by an officer's reminder that the trip would be possible only if the GDR team survived the first round of matches. Besides having overlooked that fact in my excitement, I also had a fairly low opinion of the GDR team. Still, they might be lucky and enable me to see a part of Germany for which I felt a growing sympathy, despite all my efforts against it.

After obtaining a passport photo from the personnel department, I filled out the same application form required for agents going on active duty and used the name Werner Schilling. Vogel had stressed the importance of keeping my journey secret, even among my colleagues.

Never were my fingers so tightly crossed for the GDR team as during the first two qualification games. Our trainer had obviously done his work well, as the team advanced to the group finals against the West Germans.

Returning to headquarters from my vacation retreat, I joined five other HVA officers who had been selected for the trip to receive our final instructions. "If asked, simply say that you belong to the Sporting Facilities Authority in East Berlin," we were told. "Stay together in groups, and take no notice of other tourists. Out of every six visitors from the GDR, at least three will be counterespionage agents to make sure that no one gets any funny ideas. They have been specifically briefed and will submit reports afterward. So all you need to do is enjoy yourselves. It doesn't really matter how our team fares against other countries, but they must do everything possible to beat West Germany. After all, it's a question of politics."

Finally, on July 11, I was able to cross the GDR border for the first time in a westerly direction. It made me feel like a completely different person, if only for a day. As it turned out, the GDR team correctly understood its "political duty" and beat the West Germans by one to zero, thus allowing it to enter a group with Argentina, Brazil and Holland.

After arriving in Gelsenkirchen, we had an hour's time to tour the downtown area in our designated groups. Despite the shops filled to overflowing with all kinds of merchandise and the town's bustling activity, I had become preoccupied with a sudden thought: Why not defect now? My own repugnance toward our "Workers' and Farmers' State" had seemingly reached its limit. Even the train trip—filled with multiple control points, identity checks, border searches, and secret informers—had been a vivid reminder of the state's complete monopoly of power. When a West German border official innocently asked whether any foreigners were on board, one of the accompanying train guards coldly answered: "We're all foreigners."

Although I felt strongly tempted to approach the nearest policeman and simply request permission to remain in the FRG, I knew that my mother was still in Leuna and my family in East Berlin. In addition, my long-standing intention was not to defect empty-handed. Indeed, rather than relying exclusively on my memory, I could now begin to take advantage of my official position to make a more substantial offer to the other side. Despite my growing conviction that I would be approached again—my "totem" remained always with me—the long wait produced some anxious moments. Had it not been for the constant presence of my colleagues, I would have tried to reestablish contact with the Western agents.

The remainder of the day was quite uneventful, including the three-all tie against Argentina. When an observant colleague commented about my withdrawn mood, I blamed an upset stomach from lunch at the Hans-Sachs-Haus. Nevertheless, he kept me constantly in his sight for the next several hours, and only after we passed over the border did he put any credence in my story.

While feigning sleep as my colleagues played cards, I was actually pondering how next to proceed. In order to work actively against the SED regime, I knew that my family relations would have to be severed. Moreover, if discovered by GDR authorities, I would inevitably be sentenced to death by a firing squad. Although the BND appeared to be my only conceivable partner, I knew of no way to reestablish contact. I simply had to trust the judgment of the West Germans and wait for their next move. Still, all the important information that came my way concerning agents, operational techniques, and special operations could be secretly collected. At the same time, it was important to demonstrate increased loyalty and devotion to advance my career and thereby gain access to more confidential material. A firmer footing within the MfS would also reduce some of the risks involved in working for the other side.

7

My New Goal

1

Returning to work from vacation, I felt reinvigorated by these new thoughts. My first concern, however, was to learn for certain whether my wife could tolerate a less orthodox attitude toward the GDR. To my dismay, her political indoctrination was so advanced that she reacted with absolute disapproval to several mild statements of mine. Afterward she even remarked to Olaf that more attention should be given to the political correctness of our party group. Fortunately for me, he thought her comment was directed at his lack of zeal as group leader and not at my behavior. In any event, I realized that my married life could no longer be a consideration in making future plans.

One immediate step was to display an even stronger sense of ideological commitment. At divisional party meetings, and during informal conversations with my colleagues, I was always quick to reinforce the official line. Around that time, a new political campaign had been sparked by a speech of Margot Honecker, the minister of education and wife of the GDR leader. Fearful that the policy of détente would lead to weakened class consciousness among young people, she had demanded that teachers develop a more strongly defined "picture of the enemy" and emphasize that any notion of normalized relations was merely a foreign policy ploy. Utilizing this intensified atmosphere to my advantage, I became known in our routine rituals as a hawkish voice of fanaticism and uncompromising toughness.

Since success in the MfS was highly ephemeral, I returned to my operational work with increased determination. With two Western recruit-

119

ments under my belt, it seemed time to concentrate again on my domestic network. Although I had managed to obtain many tips, all the persons who had the proper political credentials turned out to be already taken. By no means, however, was this activity without its rewards, for I continued to disobey MfS regulations and maintain a secret list of all persons found to be registered.

One day, to my considerable surprise, I discovered that Rudolf Hermann, the director of the physics department at Humboldt University, was not indicated by division XII as taken. Naturally, I had him put under my name and decided to make direct contact the following morning. After my experience with Fellow, I felt far fewer inhibitions vis-à-vis academic celebrities.

Arriving at his office, I ignored his secretary's request to identify myself, knocked on his door, and then entered. Despite his initial displeasure over my unannounced visit, the sight of my official identity card abruptly changed his mood. He obviously had respect for the MfS, which was a good omen for me.

For someone holding such an important position, he seemed quite young. A person of average height and somewhat stout, he had a round face with carefully parted black hair and wore gold-rimmed glasses. His manner was courteous, and I found him very likeable. Nevertheless, Hermann answered all my questions about his colleagues in a decidedly hesitant manner. When I finally inquired the reason for his reluctance, he stated that a connection to the MfS had already been established and a warning made to be on guard with any other security personnel. After learning from him that one of the persons involved was named Wertke, I promised to investigate the matter and return.

The name was familiar to me as the head of a counterintelligence department in the East Berlin district office that had been charged with maintaining surveillance over part of Humboldt University. It was puzzling, however, why Wertke had been in contact with someone not registered in his name. Back at my office, thinking that division XII had perhaps made a clerical error, I decided to telephone Wertke.

An argument quickly ensued, each of us claiming the physics professor as our own. Even though it appeared that my position was the weaker, I went to division XII personally to make absolutely certain.

As it happened, Hermann was registered to both of us. The reason for this duplication was the entry of two different dates of birth for the professor. From the police registration files, I then ascertained that I was the lucky person with the correct date.

To put the matter to rest, I proceeded directly to Wertke's office. Wertke, who had already taken a dislike to me because of my intensified recruitment efforts in the university's physics department, saw no point in even discussing the question.

"The man belongs to me," he said, "and that's the end of it."

I smiled and pointed out that he had the wrong birthdate. "You see, the real Hermann belongs to me. Why don't you look for someone who was born on November sixth and have fun with him? Let me have his file now, and I'll forget that you've been breaking the rules by contacting my man."

Wertke turned crimson. "We'll see about that!" he barked.

I was left standing in the corridor while he went to consult with his divisional head. Upon his return, Wertke silently handed me the file and wrote out a transfer order. The bureaucracy had helped bring about my victory, and I grinned with a touch of spite.

Wertke, however, swore revenge. "Now you'll see how difficult any cooperation from us will be. I'll make sure of that."

"My dear comrade," I said calmly, "it's altogether understandable that your disappointment would cause you to voice such threats. As it happens, I have enough recruits already in the physics department. If you try to make trouble for me, then I'll make even more for you."

Incidentally, this was not sheer bluff on my part. By then, I had three important leads that all became later recruitments. In fact, I helped train one of them to become a regular member of the MfS. As for Hermann, the actual recruitment was nothing more than a formality. Since he had already been thoroughly investigated by Wertke's unit, I had only to prepare the contract for his signature. Working under the codename "Kaehler," he turned out to be one of my best domestic agents.

2

With the twenty-fifth anniversary of the GDR's founding came lavish festivities in the MfS. A series of promotions also occurred. Werner Hengst became a major, Vogel a colonel, and Weiberg a brigadier general. As my own status had been strengthened by the recruitment of Fellow, Christian indicated a possible promotion to first lieutenant at the MfS anniversary ceremony the following February.

Before then, however, there was some business in Dresden that required my attention. As all MfS officers had the privilege of unlimited first-class travel on the East German railroad, I went to the HVA office to acquire the necessary card. But once on the train, I could not find the card again and had to return to East Berlin. Even though its value was placed at 8,000 marks, the real offense was the fact of having lost it. A very serious conversation with Vogel soon followed.

"What is the point of your good record if we can't be certain that a list of your agents might not be accidentally left somewhere?" he asked.

Despite feeling annoyed with myself for such carelessness, I began to ponder what would happen if a similar object had been deliberately lost.

"In view of your good work," Vogel concluded, "I've decided to suspend any punishment and just let you wait a while longer for your promotion."

By the way, when I finally found the card in the lining of an old winter coat, it was several years later, and my defection was imminent. It seemed better just to destroy the card.

Nevertheless, I remembered this episode about a year later when trying to acquire some important confidential information from the HVA. By then, I had also established a direct relationship with the BND. As the HVA switchboard had to be staffed around the clock, a rotating system known as the "extra-duty responsibility" had been instituted. Once every three months, each operational member had to spend either a night or a Sunday answering incoming calls and directing them to the relevant person at home. The switchboard room also contained a large file with the names, addresses, and telephone numbers of practically the entire HVA staff. For reasons of security, two persons were always on duty together.

On one occasion, when my turn came for an evening at the switchboard, my companion happened to be a new HVA member. Although the apparatus was not especially complicated, he had considerable difficulty understanding the procedure, and I suggested that he take a rest around 10 P.M. This was officially permitted as long as the switchboard remained quiet. In fact, there were two couches for that purpose, one in the outside corridor, the other in the office.

Since the duty officer would not be making his rounds until the next morning, it was an ideal opportunity to copy names from the large file. After making certain that my companion was fast asleep, I started to work. In case anyone happened to enter unexpectedly, I had placed a novel in front of me to conceal my notebook and give the appearance of casual reading. At one point, the regular night watchman came by and complained about a window that had been opened in violation of the rules, but nothing else attracted his attention. Concerned, however, that he might wonder why the light was constantly burning on such a quiet night, I stopped around 2 A.M. Even so, I had managed to copy the bulk of the names from the file.

There was, of course, the question of where to store such material until it could be delivered to the BND. Immediately after acquiring my safe house from Axel, I had discovered that a second ceiling of plastic tiles had been built over the kitchenette. Between these tiles and the original ceiling was just enough room to insert various documents and small objects. As I was the only person officially using this safe house, the risk of detection seemed minimal.

It also turned out that this was my last opportunity to examine the large staff file. A year later, the extra-duty responsibility was abolished, and the task of manning the off-hours switchboard fell to the duty officer himself.

3

Because of the added responsibilities brought by his promotion, Christian was forced to distribute some of his own agents to the rest of us. One day he announced that I was to become the case officer for one of the most important agents of the department. As with all the cases that had been previously transferred to me, Christian first delivered a lengthy background report.

Already the recipient of the Friedrich-Engels Award First Class, my new man had made several notable contributions to the economy and national defense of the GDR. He had also been handled by Axel before his departure from the department.

"You'll find that he's extraordinarily sensitive," Christian noted, "and doesn't like having his case officer changed. He's been very successful in the FRG, but he also has a lot at stake. If you make a mistake with him, you'll be given the boot for sure."

Although his next visit was not until the end of the year, Christian wanted me to study his file now. Having in the meantime gained the necessary experience, I was also to prepare his instructor for a forthcoming trip.

The multi-volume file was marked with the codename "Sturm," in reality Gerhard Arnold. Born in 1935 in the Erzgebirge, he had humble but supportive parents who helped him to study electrical engineering in Dresden. Nevertheless, he proved a mediocre student and remained relatively uninvolved in politics.

Yet it was during this period that he came to the attention of the MfS, albeit quite by chance. Assigned to the Leipzig trade fair, Roland Herrmann had been checking out a West German visitor who happened to have a sister living in Leipzig. She was a medical student and also the fiancée of Arnold. Herrmann had tried to gain the girl's assistance to arrange a meeting with her brother, but almost immediately she escaped to the West herself. The year was 1959—the height of the massive intellectual exodus from the GDR—and Herrmann assumed that Arnold would leave as well.

But to the surprise of the MfS, he remained, finishing his studies and going to work for a company in Leipzig. Herrmann then placed a postal check on Arnold's correspondence with his fiancée to discover the reasons for his unexpected behavior. These letters revealed that it was his reluctance to leave his parents in the GDR that had made him stay behind. Noticing too that Arnold was yearning for his fiancée and that his own departure was just a matter of time, Herrmann devised a plan to assist the young engineer to emigrate.

When approached by Herrmann, Arnold was in a depressed state and quite vulnerable to a recruitment offer. Herrmann, however, avoided any mention of his fiancée and first asked about several former fellow students suspected of planning an escape to the West. Because of Arnold's candid and cooperative response, a second meeting was held. Herrmann then made a proposal that would purportedly work to the advantage of all concerned. If he were willing to execute assignments on behalf of the MfS, Arnold could join his fiancée in the FRG and also retain the right to visit his parents at any time. His assent came with little hesitation.

With his new name, "Sturm," he eventually settled in Munich, married his fiancée, and secured a position at IBM. Not only did he rise rapidly in the company, but his first reports, despite the absence of any prior intelligence training, were excellent. Pleased with his information about new computer research, the MfS proceeded to make his induction into the party a quite ceremonious occasion.

Nevertheless, several complications remained. Ever mindful that Sturm's wife had left the GDR illegally, Herrmann knew that his agent's activity had to be cloaked in strictest secrecy. Further, since his responsibilities at IBM precluded frequent trips to the GDR, an instructor had been deployed to maintain regular contact. The person chosen for this role was Walter Kremp, a GDR agricultural specialist working under the rather obvious codename "Farmer."

Fortunately, a smooth working relationship soon developed between the two men. Approximately four to six times a year, Farmer went to Munich, picked up a stack of company papers from Sturm, and then returned to the GDR. Although lacking much political motivation, Sturm still felt strong ties to his homeland in the Erzgebirge, which were successfully exploited by his instructor. For the HVA, only minimal expenditures were necessary. As a resettled agent, Sturm was reimbursed only for his expenses, and with easy access to all the desired material, he had little need for any special equipment. The only other outlay involved the travel costs incurred by Farmer.

In 1969, when the importance of data processing was finally realized by the GDR leadership, Sturm's efforts became all the more significant. To be sure, once the stubborn and increasingly senile Walter Ulbricht took up the cause himself, the term acquired almost mystical connotations, and data processing centers sprang up everywhere between the Elbe and the Oder rivers. Sturm's copious and valuable information—a single delivery in 1971 was estimated by GDR industrial experts at 55 million marks—proved essential for both the army and the economy as a whole. Along with an agent handled by division XIV of the HVA, Sturm might well be regarded as the founder of data processing in the GDR.

For several years, despite three different case officers, Sturm continued to work under the skillful guidance of Farmer. Their meeting place in Munich was once changed as a precaution, but still nobody appeared to notice that the two men met regularly outside the Town Hall bookstore and exchanged a bulging briefcase. While returning to East Berlin only when exceptional material had to be delivered, Sturm visited his parents in the Erzgebirge quite frequently. On those occasions, however, he expressly wanted no contact with the MfS.

In 1973, it was decided that Farmer should be replaced as Sturm's instructor. As Farmer was about to be named to a ranking position in the Ministry of Agriculture, he could no longer risk using a false passport and making these "avocational" trips to Munich. Moreover, from the HVA's perspective, the relationship between the two men had grown dangerously close. Besides knowing each other's real names and addresses, they had been making direct telephone calls whenever a meeting had to be delayed or canceled. They had even visited some of the local Munich brothels together. Naturally Sturm reacted negatively to the announcement of a new instructor, but the HVA was adamant.

Also in the same year, Sturm decided to leave IBM and start two new companies of his own. In this instance the HVA seemed more amenable, provided Sturm could maintain his contact to IBM and continue to deliver material of the same quality. He agreed, and the two companies—one in Munich, the other in Hanover—soon commenced operations. For the time being, he also decided to make his residence in Hanover.

Closing the file, I felt quite impressed by Sturm's curious combination of capitalist enterprise and socialist allegiance. My immediate concern, however, was the preparation of his instructor for the next trip to Hanover. Our first encounter was to take place in a high-rise complex located on the Leninplatz and completely laced with MfS safe houses. Specifically, we met in an apartment that had been frequented by Sturm and his instructor for the past months. Wanting to deliver the final instructions himself, Christian had also accompanied me.

The instructor was Heinz Hiess, or codename "Rechner." An engineer by training, he worked for the data-processing combine "Robotron" in Dresden. Of average height, he had a sloping forehead and blond hair combed straight back. As he began to speak, however, I was horrified by his unmistakable Saxon accent and his typical East German provincial manner. This man, I thought to myself, could never travel through the FRG without attracting attention. Sturm's dissatisfaction with him now seemed all too understandable.

Nevertheless, he had made ten successful trips thus far, and few changes in the routine seemed necessary. Acting on Christian's instructions, I had simply copied his last itinerary and changed the dates. At the meeting, Christian handed Rechner a forged West German identity card and a three-page list of the requested IBM documents. He also asked him to convey his best regards to Sturm. I then gave Rechner 400 West German marks to cover his travel costs and 1,000 marks for Sturm's expenses. As an added precaution, all articles of Rechner's clothing were checked, and anything not of Western origin was put aside. Even so, the FRG border police had to be exceptionally naïve or lax in their procedures not to spot this man as an MfS agent.

From the Friedrichstrasse station, he took the subway to Tempelhof Airport and boarded a plane to Hanover. Upon arrival, he next proceeded to a prearranged location near the Town Hall. After giving a special signal to indicate that neither one of them had been followed, Rechner and Sturm exchanged greetings and arranged to meet an hour later at a nearby restaurant. This brief interval between the initial contact and the actual meeting was standard HVA procedure, designed as a further check against any enemy surveillance.

Over a fast beer, Rechner relayed the money and the new list of requested IBM material. No mention, however, was made about the change of case officers that had just occurred. In return, he received from Sturm two large plastic bags of documents along with the assurance that all was going well. Because of the sensitive nature of the material, Rechner returned to East Berlin by train, using a transit visa to Sweden to facilitate the GDR border crossing. I met him near the Friedrichstrasse station late in the evening, and we returned to the safe house together.

After a quick report, Rechner gave me the documents, the identity card, and the transit visa. In order to prevent a search for a presumed West German still at large in the GDR, it was important to return the transit visa immediately to division VI/K. He spent the evening at the safe house and was compensated the following day for his return trip to Dresden. Because of his four young children, I made it a generous amount. It also happened that his immediate superior at Robotron worked for the MfS and could thus provide an excuse for his two-day absence from work.

My only remaining task was to prepare a so-called accompanying material list and send everything to division V of our sector for a scientific-technical evaluation. Four weeks later, I learned the grades that each document had received. An "I" was the highest designation possible and connoted a minimum value of 150,000 marks. That meant that the GDR would have had to pay this amount in hard currency either to develop the necessary research or to pay an intermediary source for the information, if, of course, it was purchasable in the first place.

As was normally the case, Sturm's material had been given the top marks of I and II. After I had placed all the various applications and reports in my file, it was just a matter of waiting three more months until Rechner's next trip to Hanover.

4

When I heard the radio report that Peter Lorenz, the chairman of the West Berlin Christian Democratic Union, had been kidnapped by the Red Army Faction, it seemed a deplorable act but not one with any repercussions on my work. The following day, however, headquarters seemed to be in a highly agitated state. By mid-morning, we were summoned by Gerhard Jauck, the divisional head, who announced an immediate cessation of all operational trips to the West.

The HVA promptly sent out scores of radio telegrams to cancel all previously arranged meetings, and those instructors waiting in GDR safe houses for instructions from their case officers were temporarily suspended. It turned out that the full-scale manhunt mounted in West Berlin for Lorenz

and his abductors had put our regular Western operations in severe
jeopardy.

As might be expected, we had some strong words for the kidnappers for
having so completely disrupted our work. Christian could not resist a
typical remark. "Why couldn't they have just wiped out Lorenz on the
spot? Then we'd be one enemy less, and our work could proceed as
normal."

The manhunt also began to expose some irregularities in the division
itself. In one instance, a very important Western source had come to an East
Berlin meeting the day before the Lorenz kidnapping. Because his access to
classified material had explicitly prohibited any travel to the East bloc, he
had used a forged FRG passport to make the trip. Yet when he attempted to
return to Frankfurt the following day, there was no way to avoid a thorough
security check at Tempelhof Airport. By the time the plane landed in
Frankfurt, his spurious passport had been confirmed, and the police were
waiting with handcuffs. An HVA internal investigation then revealed that
both the case officer and the departmental head had authorized his return
flight while fully cognizant of the manhunt underway. This error of
judgment was officially deemed a "political" failure, and the two men
received a reprimand.

Although some of the travel restrictions to West Berlin were slowly being
lifted, the Lorenz kidnapping resulted in several permanent changes in
HVA procedures. If an operation were to take place in the FRG, no fictitious
name could be used on any passport or identity card. There was the further
problem of how to cross the intra-German border. Owing to the relative
skill already shown by the Bavarian Border Police in spotting MfS agents, all
crossings in this region had been previously curtailed. Now all airline flights
into the FRG became off-limits for agents traveling with false papers. In
addition, because of the modern screening devices that had been installed,
the newly opened Berlin-Tegel Airport fell under the ban.

Because of the many complications that resulted from this communications rupture, the HVA moved swiftly to find a new solution. One possibility
involved the GDR's main airport in Berlin-Schönefeld. As it had regular
flights not only to Moscow and other East bloc cities but also to Amsterdam,
Copenhagen, Vienna, Milan, and Stockholm, an instructor heading for a
meeting in the FRG could fly first to one of these West European cities. But
there were several drawbacks. Besides the long and expensive detour that
was involved, a minimum of two nights had to be spent at each stopover as a
security precaution. Since a simple trip could easily take as long as a week,
it became difficult to find instructors who could afford such a long absence
from their jobs.

Nevertheless, planes leaving Berlin-Schönefeld for Western destinations
were soon packed with HVA agents. Because of its easy access to the FRG as
well as other points in Austria, the most favored stopover was Vienna,

already a well-established hub of East-West espionage. Concerned, however, that a thorough security check might occur unexpectedly, the HVA leadership stipulated that no more than two persons with false papers could travel on the same plane. As it turned out, the Austrian officials proved quite harmless, and I sent many agents myself via this so-called "Alpine route."

One summer evening in 1975, Christian called me at home to announce Sturm's arrival in East Berlin. I was told to collect the documents that he had deposited at the Friedrichstrasse station and then to join both of them at the Restaurant Budapest. Evidently Sturm was in a hurry to return to Hanover the same day, for otherwise the meeting would have been held in the safe house. After securing the necessary forms and the key to the baggage locker, I drove directly to the station. Despite my desire to get to the restaurant as soon as possible, I obeyed the recent HVA directive and parked my car several blocks away. As we had been repeatedly told in departmental meetings, the possibility of enemy surveillance at the station could not be entirely excluded. Besides, this was not the way that I wanted to establish contact with Western intelligence.

By now, emptying the baggage locker had become a routine matter, and I was back at the car in ten minutes. Inside Sturm's briefcase were the two computerized magnetic tapes that had been requested at his last meeting. Because they contained information essential to the GDR industrial sector, I felt confident that two "I" evaluations would be forthcoming.

When I arrived at the restaurant, it took some searching before I found Sturm and Christian happily amused in the "Weinkeller." With an expansive gesture, Sturm beckoned me to join them.

"Aha!" he said with a grin. "So you're the pupil I'm to serve in the future."

I leaned over and whispered in his ear. "You're not serving me, but rather the fatherland of all good Germans, the Workers' and Farmers' State, the first socialist state on German soil, led by the glorious and experienced Socialist Unity Party. But don't tell anyone else. Just like everything else here, it's still a big secret."

Judging from his hearty laughter at this remark, I had apparently struck the right note and gained a measure of credibility. For my part, Sturm seemed quite appealing. With his black hair and darkly handsome features, he might easily have been taken for an Italian. He also had the intelligent and confident air of a successful young entrepreneur.

We talked a bit about his most passionate interests—the Erzgebirge, old porcelain, and hunting. This last topic prompted me to relate the latest MfS joke making the rounds. Whereas an ordinary GDR citizen told such a story at great risk, this was yet another area in which we enjoyed far more latitude.

It seemed that three groups of comrades—one from People's Police, one from the NVA, and one from the MfS—set out on a hunting expedition together. Each group thought itself superior as hunters and regarded the other two with jealousy. To decide who possessed the superior skills, they agreed to meet back in the clearing at day's end and compare their respective kills. When the final horn sounded, the NVA soldiers were able to produce a stag and the People's Policemen a roe deer. The MfS comrades, however, had failed to return, and a search was undertaken. When eventually found, they were in the process of beating a small rabbit and shouting, "Go on, admit that you're really a wild boar!"

From the way that Sturm responded to the story, I could sense my clear acceptance as his new case officer. Our conversation continued in this vein for quite a while, and only at the end did we get down to business. Because his new house near Munich had now been completed, he requested that the meetings return to the locale where they had originally begun. I had to explain, however, that the Lorenz kidnapping had made the Bavarian border patrol much more wary and that the meetings would be more safely held in Austria. If a Bavarian border guard happened to discover the material in his possession instead of Rechner's, then there would be much less explaining to do. Sturm reluctantly agreed and suggested making the Goldenen Dachl in Innsbruck the meeting place.

What he should acquire from his contacts at IBM had already been determined by our evaluators. Although Sturm normally managed to obtain nearly all the requested materials, a new complication had arisen in the meantime. It seemed that an agent handled by division XIV of the HVA had access to the same documents as Sturm. Yet because this person was directly employed by IBM, the material could often be delivered more rapidly. Christian and I thus implored Sturm to work with greater speed, pointing out that his documents arriving after those of the other agent would be worthless. With his promise to do what he could to expedite matters, the meeting came to an end.

As the least inebriated member of our group, I first drove Sturm to a spot near the border checkpoint and then took Christian to his home. En route, Christian began to muse in a way that made him seem almost human.

"For many years Sturm has been one of the department's most successful sources, asking only for his expenses and an occasional present in return. Why does he do all that for us? It's certainly not owing to any political belief, for the man's been a capitalist much too long. He acts simply out of love for his homeland in the Erzgebirge. If he ever discovered that his material also goes to the 'friends,' we'd probably never get another scrap of paper from him. At root is some sort of guilt complex for having left the Erzgebirge, but we'd never write that in a report. Ideological conviction sounds a lot better."

Afterward I thought over my own experiences thus far in the MfS. To secure a person's cooperation, there was hardly a human motivation—adventure, sex, greed, guilt, fear of exposure, or familial affection—that had not been exploited. Only rarely, however, had I seen anyone working because of an absolute devotion to socialism, even though this was the theme most constantly expounded in our regular meetings.

The following day, to help ensure Sturm's continuing success, I decided to visit Herbert Kulka in the evaluation unit. Besides receiving all incoming information, he was charged with issuing new assignments. After giving him a bottle of excellent French cognac and then talking as cleverly as possible for the next half hour, I managed to obtain his promise to delay slightly the next list of requests to the rival agent working for division XIV.

Not long after Sturm had started making regular visits to Innsbruck, I requested that he return to East Berlin for a meeting. After first refusing to see any necessity for this trip, he finally agreed to come. Since he had just celebrated his fortieth birthday, I made arrangements with the departmental secretary to have an elaborate cold buffet ready at the safe house. With ample funds at our disposal, all the items were purchased at one of the "Exquisit" shops—a new chain that had been established not only to satisfy the people's desire for certain Western luxury goods, at vastly inflated prices, but also to reap some profits from the black market.

On the evening of Sturm's arrival, both Christian and Vogel were in attendance, and it soon became a very festive occasion. Most significantly, Sturm was cited for his "contributions in the protection and promotion of socialism" and given the GDR Medal of Service, the state's highest distinction after the Friedrich-Engels Award. Despite his avowedly nonpolitical motivation, he seemed quite impressed by the medal. I thought it absurd to bestow something that could not be openly worn, unless, of course, Sturm decided to retire in the GDR. Vogel, however, had another purpose in mind.

After a short review of the international situation, he concluded that the GDR needed to make greater strides in the military sphere to offset "certain warmongering imperialistic groups." More specifically, Vogel presented a plan that would involve Sturm's computer business with leading West German defense contractors. One could start in a small way, Vogel noted, and wait for the right opportunity to secure additional information. Sturm first gave us a skeptical look, but with the new medal in the lapel of his elegant jacket, he promised to make some preliminary investigations. By this point, he realized why the HVA had so readily accepted his earlier decision to found an independent company. With a new agent in a position to obtain the same information from IBM, Sturm's own firm could be enlisted in the service of the GDR.

5

Even though the following year brought no new Western recruitments, there was plenty to do just handling the agents under my supervision. All of them were performing quite well, with the notable exception of Sperber in Paris. To help rectify that situation, he had been invited to East Berlin to receive a new award in commemoration of the GDR's twenty-fifth anniversary.

That Willi Neumann was to bestow this honor personally on Sperber made me feel very apprehensive. Only a few months earlier Christian had warned me, "Whenever Willi comes along, you know something will be broken. Sometimes it's just a dish or two, but it can also be the agent himself."

Simply getting the overweight Willi up the stairs to my fifth-floor safe house meant a long pause on every landing. When we finally reached the apartment, he took a deep gasp and fell exhausted into a chair. It then took an oversized cognac to put some life back into him.

I had prepared a dinner for the three of us, which Willi had no trouble in devouring. During dessert, when he accidentally sprayed whipped cream all over himself and his immediate surroundings, Sperber could not resist an ironic remark: "Ah, Comrade Willi, I'm glad to see you're the same as ever." It obviously did little to alter his grumpy mood.

Christian soon arrived with the medal, and Willi carried out the standard ceremony. At its conclusion, however, he began to vent his anger, asking Sperber why he was still living in France and had not taken steps to relocate in the FRG or the United States.

None of the agent's rationalizations carried any weight. When Sperber noted that his spouse was unwilling to leave France, Willi replied hostilely, "Oh, that's most unfortunate to be so susceptible to blackmail by your own wife. We'll have to see about that." After a brief farewell, he left the meeting.

Christian was more specific. "Rolf, if no solution is found, we'll have to ask you to return to the GDR. We've had very bad experiences in France, and the leadership is highly sensitive in this regard."

From Sperber's shocked reaction, it was quite clear how he felt about living again in the GDR. Before leaving, he gave his promise to disappear from Paris, if only for a short period.

Back at headquarters, Christian explained to me that most of the information Sperber acquired was actually of little use to the GDR. "Since we're not involved in laser weaponry research or in the business of building nuclear fusion reactors, the evaluators will continue to give us only mediocre marks on his material. Our friends from the KGB, on the other hand, find this information extremely valuable. Neumann, however, is thinking only about his approaching retirement and wants to be certain that Sperber doesn't interfere with his pension."

When my report of the last meeting with Sperber was returned, I was stunned to see a comment written at the top in red ink: "Preparations to be made for a return to the GDR." Besides losing a good source, I would have all the trouble of trying to arrange his reintegration.

Although it would have been easier merely to ignore the order for the time being, I decided on a different course of action. Knowing that

Christian had a good relationship with the new KGB liaison officer, Captain First Class Igor Ovsyannikov, I wrote a lengthy memorandum stressing the importance of Sperber's information for the friends. I then gave it to Christian, who lauded my initiative for trying to save a good Western source and assured me of his support should there be any repercussions from not following the order. He also wanted to see "what Igor could do."

Quite by accident, Neumann happened to hear about Sperber's next visit to East Berlin and immediately demanded my report of the meeting. Unfortunately, since the document was with the divisional head, I had no opportunity to doctor it before Neumann's perusal. When it came back to me, Neumann had written: "Comrade Stiller, is this how you obey my orders? Arrange the return forthwith."

I continued to stall. Christian, who had already begun to doubt our ability to hold out much longer, now withdrew his support. "I know nothing about it," he said. "As your superior, I expect you to follow orders from above."

Finally the whole affair came to the attention of Vogel, who had recently become the new head of the sector. Despite his reluctance to have a West agent pulled from the field, he felt, as a matter of principle, that a stated order should be followed. Vogel also wanted to avoid a showdown with Neumann, ostensibly his inferior, so soon after assuming this new position. Nevertheless, Vogel agreed to a postponement on the condition that Sperber refrain from any further operations.

During his next visit, I sternly warned Sperber not to return to East Berlin for at least another six months. Since we were meeting alone, I also added a note of encouragement, emphasizing that he would be welcomed back in the fall. Given his chronic financial problems—he was wearing the same threadbare winter coat and brown corduroy suit—this precaution was probably superfluous. That another padded expense account could be submitted for his trip would be motivation enough to return.

Just when I began to resign myself to the inevitable recall of Sperber, a letter arrived from the KGB affirming the importance of certain documents and "requesting" that the collection channel be maintained at all costs. Apparently Christian's connection to Ovsyannikov had worked after all, and Vogel now agreed that the agent could remain in France. To minimize the risk, however, Sperber was barred from further meetings in the GDR and had to destroy all the technical equipment that might be used as evidence in the event of an arrest.

When Christian recommended appointing an instructor in these circumstances, I demurred. "That won't be enough. Given his eccentric political beliefs, a personal meeting at least once a year is necessary, for otherwise he will end up completely in Mao's camp." We also knew that he had been studying Chinese for quite a while.

"If he's not allowed to return to the GDR any longer, we'll have to meet him in a third country," Christian replied. "Because the information is so valuable to the friends, surely Comrade Wolf will let us go to Austria for a meeting."

Normally members of the headquarters staff were not allowed to attend meetings with their agents outside the East bloc. But Christian seemed quite serious about this trip, and my hopes soared. Even though I would not be traveling alone, there was still the possibility of making contact with the BND or, if necessary, another Western service.

Upon learning that he was no longer in danger of being recalled, Sperber expressed considerable relief. Without inquiring as to the reason for this decision—long experience had taught him that such questions were never answered—he pledged that his wife would know nothing more about his dealings with us. Presumably irreconcilable political differences had caused him to break with the MfS, and would also explain why his trips back to the GDR had ceased.

He requested, however, a final visit with his parents in Rostock. Because time was pressing, I accompanied him in the car and conducted our obligatory political discussion en route. Not surprisingly, he once again subjected the GDR and the Soviet Union to a harsh critique. I had decided to limit his good-bye to an hour. From his silence during the return trip, it was clear that his periodic visits with his parents would be terminated with great difficulty.

As we approached East Berlin, I carefully restated the new working rules. Knowing that I was the person primarily responsible for his reprieve, Sperber promised to make every effort to find work outside France. When I asked him to come to a meeting in Salzburg in four months' time, he wanted to know who his counterpart from the HVA would be.

Even though Christian had already received approval for our trip, Sperber was definitely not to be informed. "Just stick to the contact plan and let yourself be surprised," I replied laconically. If he managed to guess correctly, it was not because of any hint from me.

6

In March 1975, I found myself on a flight to Moscow together with six colleagues from the sector. At the invitation of the KGB, we were to attend an industrial fair and try to cultivate contacts among the West German exhibitors. Christian put it somewhat differently. "Just consider the whole thing more a tourist trip to learn the land of Lenin firsthand. Besides, it's a disgrace that you haven't been there already."

A flight in the other direction would have been far preferable, but still my curiosity was piqued. Looking out of the cabin window, I saw a thick mantle of snow and no sign of habitation in the vast Russian expanse. When we landed at Sheremetyevo Airport, it was disappointing to find nothing more than an ugly, moderate-sized building at the edge of the runway— hardly the appropriate point of entry to the capital of world communism.

An endlessly long wait at the passport control ensued. Judging from his slow inspection of each page, it appeared that the very young border soldier was barely literate. Although our special service passports were written in both German and Russian, he occasionally had to turn for advice to a higher-ranking soldier. Knowing how closely the organization of the MfS was based on that of the friends, I had no doubt that he belonged to the KGB. The unique smell of the building—a mixture of heavy perfume and garlic—recalled my schooldays in Merseburg and the house where the Soviet officers had been stationed.

"Didi" Ullrich, the head of department two and the leader of our delegation, was greeted by a burly officer wearing a fur hat. He introduced himself as Colonel Ivanov, an obvious pseudonym since every third Russian we encountered seemed to bear the same name. In all likelihood, however, he did hold the rank of colonel. It was a source of much envy among us that the average rank in the KGB remained noticeably higher than in the MfS.

Reminded of a Russian joke involving the name Ivanov, I took one of my colleagues aside and related the story to his great amusement. Since Werner Zeisler and I had been good friends for a long time, there was no particular risk involved. To be sure, at nearly fifty years of age, Zeisler, who now served as Vogel's personal consultant, was so case-hardened and worldly wise that questions of political ideology left him completely unmoved. If anyone happened to boast about the imminent victory of socialism, he simply smiled and went about his work. As Zeisler also enjoyed getting drunk each day, a reference to a bottle of schnaps in my story prompted him to go directly to the airport kiosk for his daily provisions.

After Ivanov loaded us into two ramshackle Volga limousines, we drove along Leningrad Avenue, past a series of dilapidated wooden huts. Upon passing through the memorial tank barrier that marked the point where the Red Army had stopped the Wehrmacht in December 1941, Ivanov noted in his broken German, "We have Comrade Sorge to thank for that." That this ideologically committed German spy had indeed played a critical role during the Second World War was a matter of historical record and had been drummed into us at the HVA school.*

As we entered the central district of Moscow, the uniform housing blocks on both sides of the street seemed even more monotonous than in East Berlin. There were also some older prewar buildings badly in need of renovation. Our destination was the Hotel Belgrade, located opposite the huge foreign ministry building on Smolensk Square. Built by Yugoslavian

---

* Of Richard Sorge's numerous exploits on behalf of the USSR, his successful penetration of the German embassy in Tokyo in the late 1930s remains the most historically significant. In 1964, he was declared a Hero of the Soviet Union; three years later the GDR launched an intensive public propaganda campaign of its own.

labor, the hotel was quite decent and featured the only bar in Moscow where one could pay in domestic currency.

After a good lunch, we boarded the subway for Red Square. The elegant marble-tiled stations formed an extraordinary contrast to everything seen thus far on our trip. So too, the heart of Moscow, with its wide avenues and impressive architecture, could have been another city. We paid a visit to the famous GUM department store, but the long lines of shoppers inside made us retreat quickly.

By late afternoon, we were enjoying the opulent, old-Russian atmosphere of the Restaurant Berlin. It was located not far from the main KGB headquarters on Dzerzhinskii Square and was restricted to foreign visitors. Although the prices on the menu were quite high, Vogel had approved plenty of "operational money" in advance for such purposes. All of us opted for the caviar, which was served in bowls and eaten with long spoons.

The bar had just opened for business when we returned to the hotel. Seeing an abundance of attractive young women, we anticipated a very pleasant evening ahead. But to our disappointment, all of them gave us the cold shoulder as soon as they learned that we were from the GDR. By contrast, the West Germans in the room received the sort of treatment reserved for royalty. Spotting us alone with our vodka and tomato juice, Ivanov imparted some consoling words. "Comrades, you must look at this dialectically. Tomorrow morning these women will be writing long and quite interesting reports about their encounters tonight. These comrades are truly worth their weight in gold, so don't think too badly of them."

The next day we were driven north of the city to the exhibition center at Ostankino. Having spared neither money nor effort in its construction, the Soviets clearly wanted to make as favorable an impression on foreign visitors as possible. We proceeded directly to the West German pavilion where a line of Soviet factory delegates, easily six miles in length, stretched far into the distance. Many of them, knowing that they would be standing outside for most of the day, had brought along folding chairs and packages of food. Fortunately, Ivanov had provided us with special passes.

Once inside the pavilion, I found that the surging masses of people obscured all the individual display booths. At one point, so amazed at hearing quadriphonic sound for the first time, everyone stopped moving, and I felt trapped. Making a contact under these conditions was obviously futile, and I joined my colleagues outside at a nearby kiosk. Just looking at the cloudy beverage called kvass, which they were drinking from disintegrating paper cups, made whatever thirst I had rapidly disappear. As we were about to leave, I noticed that a long line of people had also formed in the opposite direction. Their goal was a small booth where the recordings of a popular young West German singer could be purchased.

The following day, Zeisler, who had not participated in our expedition, persuaded me to return with him to the exhibition center. After taking a filthy taxi, we found the same huge mass of people attempting to visit the West German pavilion. Zeisler, however, quickly lost his patience and guided me to the edge of the crowd, and we ducked under the rope of one of the booths. Sparsely visited, it contained an attractive display of special measuring instruments made by a small south German firm.

Assuming that we were Soviet citizens who had broken the strict convention regulations, a representative of the firm immediately came over and started to question us. After explaining that the crowded conditions had left us no other alternative, we introduced ourselves as members of the GDR Academy of Sciences on an official trip to Moscow. I used the name Schilling, while Zeisler came up with a pseudonym on the spot. Two fairly sinister-looking Soviet officials had also noticed our illegal entry, but hearing us speak in German persuaded them to leave the matter alone.

Welcomed as fellow Germans by the representative, we were led into a small room and offered cognac. As the conversation turned to the crowded exhibition outside, he gave us his own well-founded explanation. "As citizens of a socialist state, you gentlemen must know better than I, but apparently the GDR has yet to acquire the same degree of fanaticism about Western products that is found here. There are delegations from every state industry in Moscow as well as from the rest of the Soviet Union. Naturally the party has selected only those loyal workers who will not be ideologically 'contaminated' by viewing Western products. Since all the time spent here is clocked as working time, they'll also keep returning every day until it's finally possible to get inside."

When I began to inquire about the firm's line of products, the man showed no hesitation in giving us quite detailed scientific explanations. He further noted that a former engineer at the rocket-testing facility in Peenemünde had founded the prosperous firm and that it was currently involved in the construction of submarines, tanks, and rockets. As the man continued to talk in a very open and obliging manner, an idea occurred to me, and I decided to bring the meeting to a quick close.

On the way out of the pavilion, Zeisler complained about having to leave while some cognac was still left in the bottle. I told him that there was a more effective way to proceed and then promised him a bottle of vodka from the next shop as compensation. That Zeisler asked no further questions about my plan showed his evident lack of professional interest.

As it happened, Professor "Singer" was in Moscow on official university business, and I had already made an appointment with him for that evening. Arriving punctually as ever, he first made some ironic remarks about conditions in the Soviet Union, especially the state of scientific research. I found nothing to contradict in what he said, and proceeded to explain my plan for ensnaring the south German exhibitor. Singer agreed to cooperate.

I had secured Zeisler's special pass for Singer to use, and we returned to the pavilion the following morning. With the crowds as dense as before, we relied on the same illegal maneuver to enter the booth. "Quite by chance I met Professor Stiller last night," I explained to the representative. "He's a physicist and very interested in your firm's products. I promised to introduce him to you." In this situation, it seemed better to use Singer's real name.

Once in the small room, Singer made a strong impression with his academic credentials and quickly took control of the conversation. As the two of them became absorbed in talking shop, I remained quietly in the background scrutinizing the personality of the south German. In my estimation, he was clearly a shrewd businessman and had the potential of becoming my first Western recruitment of the year. For now, however, the man was better left in Singer's capable hands. I knew that the professor's agreeable personality, immense knowledge, and sense of humor would all work decidedly in our favor. On the pretext of another appointment, I excused myself.

The next day Singer, whose own instincts had been sharply honed during his period in the West, telephoned me with an optimistic assessment. Not only had they dined together, but the south German had also accepted an invitation to come to Dresden. I then began to formulate my next step, deciding that a substantial sum of money would be the most effective offer for access to his firm's confidential material.

Upon my return to East Berlin, I immediately submitted an inquiry to division XII to determine his registration status. To my great disappointment, I learned that he had already been taken by Comrade Michel of the regional office in Dresden. A trip to see Michel in person and plead for the man's transfer to my jurisdiction proved of no avail. Contending that his own agent had established contact with the south German a long time ago, Michel could not be budged. I explained the situation to Christian, hoping that his superiors might be persuaded to intervene on my behalf. Unfortunately, that effort failed as well, and the south German remained out of our reach.

7

The following summer, one of my domestic agents, Gertraude Sumpf or codename "Karla," alerted me to an amorous affair with considerable potential. It involved two young students, Petra Fehr from the GDR and Heinrich Gewecke from the FRG. According to Karla, the girl's father, fearful of losing his high position in the GDR criminal investigation department, had demanded that the relationship be terminated. As the parents were divorced, the girl had turned to Karla for advice. Gewecke was a student of pedagogy in Brunswick and very sympathetic to the German Communist Party (DKP). A person with this background was hardly an ideal candidate for recruitment, but some use for him could always be found. Christian agreed with my assessment, and I decided to pay a visit to the girl.

Her modern apartment in the Karl-Marx-Allee revealed the sort of advantages that her family background could confer. I came straight to the point and introduced myself as a member of the MfS. Presumably her father had been required to report her relationship to Gewecke, and it was my duty to make certain that he had no ties to enemy intelligence. A good comrade from all reports, the girl had no difficulty seeing the logic of my investigation.

Unknown to her, however, was the fact that her father also worked for the MfS. Although outwardly the head of the East Berlin homicide squad, he was in reality a so-called "officer in special deployment." In fact, most GDR citizens did not realize that key positions in the police force were usually held by disguised MfS officers. Because of her father's position, I had myself needed the special permission of the personnel head of the East Berlin regional office before starting the case. At the same time, I was cautioned not to let the father ever know anything about this operation.

My first request was that Petra write down everything she knew about Gewecke. When she mentioned his desire to immigrate to the GDR and marry her, I refrained from revealing the sad truth of the matter. According to the personnel head, an MfS officer was not permitted to have a son-in-law from the West, even if he were a member of the DKP. That meant that Gewecke could never become a GDR citizen and that her marriage had no chance of taking place.

To start my own background check of Gewecke, I went to the Office of Directorate II, a unit specifically designed to monitor relations between the DKP and the GDR. It was certainly no secret that the DKP received important financial and political assistance from their Eastern comrades. That a large network of clandestine party members also existed has been much less publicized. These persons, acting under instructions from both the SED Central Committee and the MfS, have sought to promote communist influence in the FRG. Besides helping to expand the vast numbers of active MfS agents, they stood ready to serve as a "fifth column" in the event of an overt attack on the FRG. Only a few persons within the MfS knew the precise activities of the Office of Directorate II. As a large and relatively autonomous unit, it maintained its own index file of DKP members and known sympathizers. In principle, these persons were strictly off-limits to all other MfS units.

As the check on Gewecke turned out negative, I now had permission to proceed further. Another possibility crossed my mind—that his communist sympathies had been feigned to gain entry into the GDR for subversive purposes—but I preferred to ignore it for the time being.

At my next meeting with Petra, I collected her report on Gewecke. We decided that I should approach him directly upon his return to the GDR and ask him to assist the MfS as a proof of his communist loyalty.

Christian, however, wanted a further check on Gewecke by installing a listening device in Petra's apartment. My initial task was to get a copy of her door key. Pretending that a couple of points in her report needed further clarification, I returned for another visit. As we were talking, the in-house intercom rang, and she was asked to come down for a parcel. When she left the apartment, the key was still in the door, and I had enough time to make an imprint on some special modeling clay. Petra, of course, found no one at the downstairs door, for it was a colleague of mine posing as a mailman who had rung the bell. Returning to her apartment, she simply dismissed the incident as a prank.

From Karla, I next obtained Petra's schedule of classes to find out when her apartment would be unoccupied. I also submitted my plan for Wolf's personal approval, and then consulted with the audio specialists of division 26 to determine the best type of installation. On the arranged day, I went to Karla's apartment accompanied by one of the specialists. The key that had been prepared by the HVA's technical division opened the door without difficulty. Within a matter of minutes, the specialist was able to fasten a harmless-looking, sixteen-inch-long block of wood underneath the wardrobe that stood near the living and sleeping areas. Inside this block of wood—a so-called "stereo bug"—were two sensitive Western-made microphones, a transmitter, and batteries. It had the impressive capacity to filter out all extraneous noise from the sound of human voices.

The receiver had been placed in an MfS office roughly two hundred yards away. To make certain that the equipment functioned properly, I left the technician in Petra's apartment and went immediately to that office. Having seen my signal from the window, the technician began to count aloud in various corners of the apartment. His transmitted voice could hardly have been clearer, even with the television set turned on. To indicate to him that everything was in order, I dialed Petra's telephone number and hung up after three rings.

Since a mail check had been placed on Gewecke's correspondence, I knew that he would be arriving in East Berlin three days later. As if by happenstance, I telephoned Petra, who confirmed his imminent visit. On the day of his arrival, I was sitting in the nearby office wearing a pair of headphones. Possibly Gewecke had already received some communist intelligence training, for upon entering the apartment, he immediately turned on the radio to full volume. But thanks to the stereo bug, I had no difficulty hearing his conversation with Petra.

As soon as she mentioned my visit and desire to meet with him, he became quite irritable. "What do those guys want from me?" he asked.

Attempting to calm him, Petra explained that the inquiry had been prompted by her father's high post in the police department. "Just have a friendly talk with them," she insisted. "If you want to resettle here, then at least you will have made a good impression."

It took a while longer, but he grudgingly agreed. Hearing those words, I took off the headphones and returned to headquarters with the taped conversation.

According to Christian's rigid logic, Gewecke's unflattering comments about the MfS simply showed that even politically progressive and engaged citizens were not immune from the lies of Western propaganda. I wondered, however, whether a meeting was now advisable.

"Of course we'll see him," he replied. "As long as he's not registered at the Office of Directorate II, we needn't think of him as a communist. Besides, if he wants to immigrate to the GDR, let him do something first in return. That he'll never be permitted to resettle here is a wholly different matter."

That evening, Petra confirmed on the telephone what I already knew. As we were discussing arrangements for the meeting, I could hear Gewecke in the background making some derogatory comparisons between the MfS and the West German counterintelligence service.

The next day Petra brought her boyfriend to the Restaurant Budapest where Christian and I were waiting. Since we wanted to talk with Gewecke alone, she left right away.

Following some general remarks, Christian began to apply his pressure tactics on the young student. "As the name implies, our ministry is responsible for the security of the state. Because of his official access to classified information, your girlfriend's father is forbidden to have any direct or indirect connections to the West. Your close relationship with his daughter, however, has produced a very difficult situation. Even though we feel that you have the correct political convictions, there are still rules that must be followed. Anyone close to the DKP must realize how cunning and dangerous the West German imperialists can be. In fact, how can we know for sure that you are not working on their behalf?"

As Christian continued in this vein, I gave Gewecke a more careful scrutiny. Tall and powerfully built, he had an intelligent face with an impressive beard. His casual attire as well as his frequent antiestablishment comments marked him as a typical product of the leftist student movement in the FRG. With his firm allegiance to Marx and Marcuse, he was also many stages removed from the orthodox DKP position. Initially, I had myself admired such people, considering them to be the enlightened vanguard of the West. Yet seeing how their uncontrolled and ill-conceived protests played ultimately into the hands of the SED, I had developed an instinctive dislike of them long ago.

Christian now came to the point. "So you see, Herr Gewecke, if you can give us some evidence that you are indeed the patriot you claim to be, then we would not hesitate to support your request for GDR citizenship."

As a look of dread came over his face, he asked what we had in mind.

"There are numerous possibilities," Christian continued. "You must be acquainted with many progressively minded students like yourself. Detailed information about them would be very helpful, for we need to know for certain who's on the correct political side."

After a few moments of reflection, Gewecke replied, "I couldn't do that.

It would be completely contrary to my basic humanistic convictions. In any case, I have no aptitude whatsoever for those things that strike me as spying."

Although I silently admired his defiant attitude, the possibility of his recruitment seemed more distant than ever. He then added, "I'm perfectly willing to obtain the recommendations of some DKP members as proof of my political convictions."

Christian remained unimpressed. "You don't seem to understand that some concrete task must be accomplished if you expect to settle down here with Fräulein Fehr. Given the magnitude of our security requirements, there is no way of avoiding it."

"Are you then trying to coerce me to work for you?"

"Oh no! Not at all!" Christian replied. "We merely want some definite proof of your political convictions."

"Give me some time to think it over," Gewecke said. "On my next trip to the GDR, I'll have an answer for you. Perhaps I'm mistaken, but the way the state handles matters here is somewhat disappointing. Nevertheless, you have my assurance that I'll keep this conversation to myself."

Although his request was granted, I expected a negative answer in the end. It was hard to feel much disappointment, for even if the recruitment turned out successfully, my own career would not have received much of a boost. Besides, seeing Christian's rough methods come to naught would have given me a certain pleasure.

Since the audio penetration yielded no further information, I assumed that the couple were now having their discussions away from the apartment. After Gewecke's departure, I checked Petra's class schedule and returned to retrieve the stereo bug. Presumably he would be making his next visit in two weeks' time.

A few days later, however, Vogel unexpectedly summoned Christian and me to his office. "I've just come from Comrade Wolf," he said. "It seems that two of my officers are accused of not having sufficiently scrutinized a targeted person before deciding to make a blackmail attempt. That's what happened with Gewecke, isn't it?"

Never before had I seen Christian so completely humbled, and I relished the moment. Although we were both under fire, it was Christian who had initiated the blackmail and who also bore a greater responsibility as my superior.

Vogel next admonished us at length for the severe damage we had inflicted on the sector's reputation. Having already risen rapidly through the HVA ranks, he was currently aiming for a promotion to brigadier general. Clearly this was the sort of setback he had wanted to avoid.

Finally Vogel handed Christian some closely typed sheets of paper from his desk. As Christian began to read them, a stream of profanity could be heard.

"Comrade Streubel," Vogel solemnly asked, "are you trying to criticize the private connections of the deputy minister?" By using Wolf's official title rather than his name, Vogel wanted us to feel the maximum degree of intimidation.

Then suddenly his manner changed. "You were just unlucky. How could you have known that Petra Fehr's mother works with Wolf's wife in the Ministry of Culture?"

When the report was handed to me to read, the chain of events became clear. After Petra had told her mother about the incident, her mother had mentioned it to Wolf's wife, who in turn informed her husband.

The charge that two MfS officers had attempted to blackmail a sincere patriot was accurate enough, but Christian attempted a mild rebuttal. "Horst, if Comrade Wolf wants to believe such politically dubious reports, then I'm quite willing to be criticized."

"Nonsense," Vogel replied. "Comrade Wolf has expressed his own consternation at the report and has yet to give Comrade Fehr an answer. In any event, he told me that it's far preferable to have active staff members rather than those just idling about."

Vogel, in other words, had only intended that we tremble a bit in the face of MfS authority. Christian heaved a sigh of relief, but Vogel continued. "I'll accompany you the next time and tell this pseudo-communist what we officially think of him. I'll also drop a hint to the DKP to be especially wary of him."

When the meeting took place, Vogel proved true to his word and issued such a severe reprimand for an attempted "illegal entry" that Gewecke never returned to the GDR. That also meant the end of our recruitment attempt.

8

A few weeks later we were again summoned to Vogel's office. Although we had expected some further repercussions from the Gewecke case, it turned out that Vogel had another matter to discuss.

"For the last six years, the West German government has been headed by a liberal-social democratic coalition," he began. "From our point of view, there are good reasons to feel satisfied with the results of that period. Particularly through the policy of détente, we have been able to end the FRG's claim to sole legitimacy and gain worldwide diplomatic recognition for the GDR. Admittedly, détente has caused an ideological slackness in certain groups at home as well as a rise in emigration applications, but on the whole, the class struggle has continued to advance in our direction."

This was merely a preamble to his main point. "I wonder," he continued, "whether you have given any thought to next year's general election in the FRG. Even though we prefer that the present coalition remain in office, there is no certainty of that happening. We must therefore be prepared for the advent of a right-wing government. That means taking off the kid gloves and doing everything possible to make life difficult for the conservatives.

Our colleagues in political intelligence have already established some effective positions in conservative ranks without diminishing their presence in the two coalition parties. I now ask you, comrades from the nuclear department, what can we do to help?"

Thinking he knew what Vogel had in mind, Christian said, "Naturally we are giving consideration to future developments. Horst, you belong to our party group and must have heard these discussions."

"Of course, I have," Vogel interrupted, "but some things cannot be discussed in the party group, if you understand what I mean."

A knowing look appeared on Christian's face, but I was still in the dark.

"For some time now," Vogel continued, "we've observed a sizable growth in the anti-nuclear movement. Because its opposition to the policies of the Bonn government benefits us in the long run, we've given the movement a modest degree of support. At the moment, however, its attacks on the liberal-social democratic coalition make us less than enthusiastic. Of course, with a conservative government in power, these environmental nuts could be unleashed to destabilize the entire system. The question is how best to help them."

Christian was ready with an answer. "Horst, we've already done an analysis of that, and our 'active measures' network is poised for deployment. Remember last year's trial run."

In this instance, an MfS agent assigned to the FRG had happened to learn of a reactor malfunction at the Stade nuclear power station. While the management was hesitating to make the news public, a report to a West German newspaper had already been dispatched by division X of the HVA. The object was to determine the effect of such assistance on the anti-nuclear movement.

"That's exactly the sort of thing I mean," Vogel said. "But with a new government, we can mobilize our heaviest artillery. The time is rapidly approaching when the simple procurement of scientific or even political information will not suffice. We must find active ways to weaken the West, not through a full-scale attack but by the slow and systematic capture of individual positions. Just consider how much Western influence is declining in country after country in the so-called developing world. The present-day class struggle demands that economics, politics, diplomacy, and intelligence form a cohesive whole. Think about that a while and work out some new ideas. When fewer tactical considerations need to be shown toward the FRG, I don't want to be caught empty-handed."

Having stated this new strategic concept, Vogel ended the discussion and dismissed us. I began to ponder a number of his points. One of his specific references had aroused my skepticism, and I queried Christian.

"If Comrade Vogel says it was so," he brusquely relied, "then it has to be right. Stop worrying about water under the bridge and start thinking about our new assignment."

In any event, this long-term strategy for communist victory possessed a definite logic. Given its many ways of implementation, it also had a good chance of success. Besides infiltrating the West with even larger numbers of agents and activating the underground network of West European communists, the MfS had begun to provide assistance to fledgling Marxist regimes in Asia and Africa. All these efforts further benefited from the "disinformation" activities of the HVA's division X. Such offensive campaigns, probably better described as psychological warfare, could be undertaken either independently or in conjunction with other operational units. By carefully mixing real facts with "doctored" information, the specialists of division X tried to manipulate public opinion in the East as well as the West. In some instances, it was possible to combine both audiences by staging a heated controversy in the GDR and then letting the sensational-minded Western media report the story.

Of all the MfS campaigns undertaken in the FRG, one of the most durable and influential involved the so-called West German "occupational ban." According to this legislation, persons holding radical political views were automatically excluded from holding civil service positions. Knowing that members and sympathizers of the DKP would probably be subject to this ban, the MfS specifically ordered that they begin applying on a regular basis. In several individual cases of rejection, the media was carefully orchestrated to provide maximum coverage. With charges of fascist behavior in the air, West German security officials then came under strong political pressure to weaken even further what the MfS considered to be an essentially lax system.

Vogel, however, was not requesting some new ideas for another media campaign. Our meeting had made quite clear that he wanted an offensive plan that would threaten the fundamental political stability of the FRG. At the same time, I had become curious as to whether the MfS felt any moral scruples whatsoever in such matters. Drawing on a reliable scientific study, I thus wrote a memorandum proposing that carefully calibrated amounts of radioactive material be placed in areas adjacent to various West German nuclear power stations. It would then take only a few discreet tips to the anti-nuclear groups, which were already penetrated by the MfS, to unleash a storm of public protest. To reinforce this destabilizing operation, I recommended the circulation of reports about near-accidents at the nuclear plants as well as the provocation of real incidents involving the transport of radioactive material. If implemented in a technically "clean" and skillful manner, these measures would be nearly impossible to trace to outside sources. In addition to a list of potential targets, I included a documented breakdown of the damage already inflicted on the West German nuclear industry by the environmental movement.

My memorandum received Christian's approval and was forwarded to Vogel. At the conclusion of the next party meeting, he took me aside for a private conversation. It turned out that my proposal, having greatly exceeded the prerogatives of division X, had been discussed by the top officials of the HVA and approved in principle. No one felt concerned about the possible safety risks that I had also mentioned in the document. Nor, to my utter lack of surprise, had any moral objections been voiced. The only question was one of timing.

Their sheer unscrupulousness was further confirmed by the immediate boost my own career received. Vogel, in a remarkable display of trust, now included me in matters completely removed from the daily departmental routine.

9

Before the year was over, I also managed to strengthen my connections to several MfS regional offices. Since the majority of my domestic agents resided in the cities of Dresden, Karl-Marx-Stadt, Leipzig, and Halle, I usually made an official two-day visit to the area every other week. In each of these cities, my schedule included not only meetings with my agents but a couple of hours in the regional office, either collecting new tips or simply maintaining some of the friendships I had made. Frequently these meetings yielded some valuable information, which I recorded and filed in my safe house.

In addition, I developed a good relationship with the recently established MfS installation authority at the Dresden Technical University. Part of the reason lay in the conflicting areas of jurisdiction with division XV of the regional MfS office. Because of its responsibility for intelligence matters within the region, it insisted, for example, on screening all Western visitors as potential agents and on exclusive control of every university member making a trip to the West. The head of the installation authority, Manfred Hippe, and his colleague, Rolf Schilde, soon resented the arrogant manner of the division XV officials and started to work more closely with the HVA. Because of my earlier acquaintanceship with Hippe, I was all the more welcome at the installation authority.

Our first coordinated effort came as a result of the groundwork laid by my agent Bodo. Since his last reprimand, he had succeeded in obtaining the information that led to an exchange program of GDR and American scientists, and had himself gone to the United States to negotiate the final details. As we had been under pressure to intensify our North American efforts, I next examined the list of GDR scientists selected for the exchange program. The person who struck me as having the greatest potential for intelligence work was a physicist from Dresden, Professor Roland Reif. A check with the records offices then revealed that he had already been "taken" by the installation authority.

When I went to Hippe and suggested a joint endeavor, he quickly agreed. Reif had only recently been recruited by Schilde, and a definite assignment was still pending. The sole caveat voiced by Hippe and Schilde was that the physicist should not be sent on such a long journey without full awareness of his actual mission. Otherwise, I could formulate Reif's instructions and evaluate the results. Hippe, of course, reckoned that his own career would benefit from this cooperative attitude toward the HVA.

Several meetings with Reif followed. "Just take all the documents that look interesting," I told him, "or let them be given to you as a present. We know that the Americans are incredibly naïve in such matters. They allow valuable research results just to lie around on their desks, whereas we would keep them under strict lock and key. Everything that you acquire should be sent by mail, preferably to your institute's address. That way we can avoid any trouble with customs."

Reif was agreeable, and I posed another question. "Do you already know someone over there?"

"Yes," he replied. "There's a professor in New York who's married to a woman from the GDR. When he once came to Dresden, we became well acquainted, and I am planning to see him now in the States."

At our next meeting, Reif told me everything that he knew about the professor, and I submitted his name for a background check. My assumption that a visiting American physicist would automatically spark the interest of the MfS proved correct. Indeed, a very large file had been compiled by division XI, the HVA unit that handled matters pertaining to the United States. According to these documents, two MfS officials posing as members of the "GDR Peace Movement" had approached the professor in 1965. Completely unsuspecting, he believed their contrived story and began to expound on the current American political situation. At this point, however, the two MfS men concluded that the professor was unsuited for political espionage and decided to drop the matter. That a nuclear physicist had the capacity to deliver far more valuable information than an ordinary political informant never occurred to them. He still seemed very interesting to me. There also existed two good avenues of approach, for besides his connection to Reif, his wife had relatives living in Saxony.

From our perspective, Reif's three-month sojourn in the United States proved a decided success. The professor had responded in a most hospitable fashion, allowing Reif to look at various confidential papers and helping him to gain access to several scientific institutes. Large packages of research reports and other important documents continued to arrive long after Reif's return to the GDR. Moreover, the professor had noted his desire to spend a year in Europe quite soon and include the GDR on his itinerary. Hearing this news, I registered him under the codename "Charles" as a promising contact person.

Although we began a written correspondence, his visit to the GDR never materialized. Even the American authorities must have recognized his openhearted nature and warned him of the dangers of traveling in the East bloc. Three years later, another opportunity arose to meet him personally, but too many other matters were commanding my attention. In any event, the professor never became involved in any MfS activity known to me.

A second joint operation with Hippe and Schilde originated in the same period that I took over Reif. In perusing some of the old files that Christian occasionally gave me to read, I had found repeated references to the German Nuclear Forum. Based in Bonn, it sought to coordinate nuclear research activities in the FRG with their industrial application. As this organization ranked high on our list of departmental priorities, I decided to pursue someone whose name had frequently recurred in those files. The person in question was Bernhard Feigenspan, a research scientist at the Institute for Nuclear Physics in Dresden-Rossendorf. It also happened that Feigenspan had been previously recruited by Hippe and given the codename "Max." When I suggested combining our forces, Hippe readily concurred.

"It would be best," I explained, "simply to send Max as a delegate to the next reactor conference in Nuremberg sponsored by the Nuclear Forum. To make his appearance seem more legitimate and less conspicuous, he'll be accompanied by one of my agents."

The person I had in mind was Rudi Rockstroh, another physicist working in the same institute as Max. Although Rockstroh had been reassigned to me early on by Christian, I had only recently established contact with him. A close associate of Klaus Fuchs at the time*, he unfortunately lacked the requisite cleverness and flexibility to function as a good agent. Yet I foresaw no problem in making him the second man on the Nuremberg trip.

By contrast, it took only a ten-minute conversation with Max for me to realize that he had the ideal personality and mental agility for this assignment. Afterward, however, Hippe warned me that his one weak area was discipline. "We can't be sure that Max will always stick to orders. Contrary to what we told him, he's slept with at least two women from the Nuclear Forum."

Believing that an agent should be an adventurous type, I differed with Hippe in this respect. I even thought that one of Max's old relationships might be rekindled to our advantage. Besides, Rockstroh would be with him to act as a restraining influence should the matter get out of hand.

At the Nuremberg conference, Max succeeded in initiating some new contacts as well as renewing several older ones. Despite the interest still shown by one of his women friends, we thought it better to concentrate initially on another earlier acquaintance, Dr. A. Max had already considered him to be a promising candidate for recruitment. When he then

---

* One of the most famous Soviet nuclear spies, Klaus Fuchs returned to the GDR in 1959 and was given new research facilities along with a later position on the SED Central Committee. He died in 1988.

responded in a very friendly manner at Nuremberg, Max utilized the occasion to invite him to the GDR in the late summer. Fully confident of Max's ability to handle the man alone, I decided not to involve myself directly in their relationship.

This meeting resulted in a promise from Dr. A. to send along a number of specified scientific documents. When they arrived in the GDR, we registered our first official delivery and gave him the internal codename "Wagner." A year later, Max met with him again in the FRG, and an actual recruitment now seemed in sight.

Knowing that Dr. A. would soon be coming to Prague with his family and wanted to see Max in particular, I worked out a detailed plan and obtained my superiors' approval. In short, Max was to offer Dr. A. the sum of 5,000 West German marks for a special study made by the FRG Ministry of Research and Technology. To make certain everything functioned properly, I journeyed to Prague myself.

The plan, however, went awry. Despite some intense discussions with Dr. A., Max declined to make any mention of our offer. As I later discovered, he was cleverly pursuing an agenda for his own career advancement. Allegedly his institute—in reality, it was division XVIII of the regional MfS office in Dresden—had proposed that Max serve as the GDR representative to the International Atomic Energy Commission in Vienna. By helping to recruit Dr. A., however, he would become an accessory to the act and therefore would be disqualified to hold any official position abroad. That explained his betrayal of our plan. Yet in the end, I had the final revenge, for my defection two years later effectively eliminated any possibility of a foreign posting for Max.

In the meantime, the department was facing more stringent demands to increase its productivity. One casualty was my calm and friendly colleague, Horst Kessig, whose lackluster performance resulted in a transfer to the teaching staff of the HVA school in Belzig. Upon the arrival of his replacement, a Thuringian named Paul-Rainer Huth, I was no longer the youngest member of the department. Although his rather carefree, boyish manner helped to lighten the daily atmosphere, the basic operational dilemma remained the same. The travel restrictions caused by the Lorenz manhunt had resulted in a significant reduction in the amount of material retrieved in the FRG. On every possible occasion, we were therefore urged to make more recruitments and extract more results from our agents. Inevitably certain safety precautions had to be disregarded, which led in turn to a greater number of arrests. Even more pressure was then applied from above for us to find replacements.

10

In the fall of 1975, Gerhard Jauck, Vogel's successor as divisional head, summoned me to his office. His even-tempered and realistic attitude was a welcome change, and if Christian had not been his deputy, the new working conditions would have been quite agreeable.

In the presence of Christian, Jauck began to praise my individual achievements, including Sperber, Sturm, and Fellow. Moreover, the fact of two Western recruitments placed me well above the divisional average. Regarding me therefore as an experienced staff member, Jauck thought that I had the capacity to take on another case.

It seemed that the Main Division I of the MfS had offered to transfer one of their West agents to us. According to the files, the person was considered well trained and disciplined. Jauck knew no further details, merely that Main Division I had not had much success with the man. My first task was to contact Comrade Barnikol in Hildburghausen and make preparations for the agent to be transferred at his next scheduled meeting.

I knew that Main Division I was responsible for security within the GDR armed forces. Over the years, acting with the concurrence of the SED leadership, Mielke had heavily infiltrated all levels of the NVA with his own agents and informers. This was in fact the main reason why such a strained relationship existed between Mielke and GDR Defense Minister Heinz Hoffmann. Apart from maintaining surveillance over individual army units, Main Division I had also targeted the West German Army and the NATO forces stationed in the FRG. Its key activity in this regard was scouting the so-called "advance battlefield," the thirty-mile-wide strip of West German territory immediately adjacent to the border with the GDR. In order to monitor all enemy activity, these intelligence units were stationed as close to the border as possible.

Something, however, seemed amiss with this case. Why, I thought to myself, would anyone willingly abandon a potentially productive West agent? With considerable skepticism, I telephoned Barnikol and arranged to meet him at his office the following Saturday morning. Since Hildburghausen was located in the southernmost part of the GDR—a 280-mile drive from East Berlin—I left at 3:00 A.M.

Some thick early-morning fog delayed me at the outset, so I decided to floorboard my Wartburg to make up for the lost time. Until the turnoff to Oberhof—the winter vacation retreat of former GDR leader Walter Ulbricht—the autobahn had been superbly constructed. It was yet another reminder of the many perquisites—from well-appointed suburban villas to private hunting lodges and luxury yachts—that the communist hierarchy had allocated for themselves. In any event, I arrived at the border command station precisely on schedule. Upon seeing my official identity card, the guard snapped to attention and lifted the barrier for me to enter.

I proceeded to the Main Division I barracks, where Barnikol and the agent's case officer, First Lieutenant Scharlibbe, were waiting. For the next hour, they gave me a detailed background briefing. Judging from the seven large files that Scharlibbe had placed on the table, it seemed clear that the agent had been fairly active. The file number further indicated that the recruitment had occurred only two years ago. Feeling even more puzzled than before, I asked them bluntly why this agent was being transferred to me.

According to their explanation, Günter Senger, or codename "Koehler," had been assigned to infiltrate the Federal Office of Military Technology and Procurement in Bonn. This attempt, however, came to naught because of his decision to marry and take up residence elsewhere in the FRG. Currently he was residing in Neustadt near Coburg and working as an engineer in the Siemens cable factory. For Main Division I, his usefulness had apparently come to an end, for neither was he in a position to acquire the desired military information nor did his new employer offer anything of particular value.

Since the scheduled meeting with Koehler was rapidly approaching, I had time only to glance at his papers. In the operational reports, he had received high marks for the precise and conscientious execution of various assignments. Although nothing in his biographical data seemed out of the ordinary, I was somewhat troubled by the circumstances surrounding his recent marriage. His new wife, the sister of his brother-in-law, had been divorced by a man who had immigrated to Canada and left her with three children. Quite likely, it was the relatives who had arranged the marriage, indicating a certain naïveté on Koehler's part. Continuing through the files, I noticed that Scharlibbe had meticulously recorded every word that the man ever uttered, made copies of all letters sent to the cover address, and retained every single piece of supplementary information. Why seven large files had been amassed so quickly now seemed understandable.

On our drive to the meeting, Scharlibbe began to talk about his heavy workload.

"How many agents are you handling now?" I asked.

"Well, I've got Koehler, another contact person, the cover addresses for them, and several domestic helpers."

"If that's all," I said, "then being transferred here would be like a vacation for me." He was then amazed to learn that I had the responsibility for forty persons altogether—West agents, domestic agents, and contact persons.

Thus far, this unit had made a distinctly provincial impression, and I feared that Koehler would be no exception. Cautiously I inquired about his motive for working with the MfS.

"As far as we can tell, it stems from his pacifist convictions," Scharlibbe replied. That only increased my curiosity about the man.

We arrived shortly ahead of schedule and waited in the car at the appointed spot.

"This is very close to the border," I said. "Aren't you worried that the man might inadvertently lead an enemy surveillant to the car?"

"According to our information, the other side doesn't do that sort of thing," he replied.

This remark left me aghast. At every departmental conference, we had been drilled never to make contact with a West agent without first ascertaining whether the other side was keeping watch. Obviously no one in this unit had seriously considered such a possibility.

Ten minutes later, a tall, athletic-looking young man came into sight. Correctly dressed and carrying a briefcase, he could well have been a normal white-collar worker on the way to the office. Still, if this visitor to the GDR had escaped the special attention of the Bavarian Border Police, then its high reputation among HVA officials was quite undeserved.

When Koehler got into the car, Scharlibbe mistakenly introduced me by my real name, which should never have been revealed to him in the first place. Knowing that he was about to be transferred to another unit, Koehler greeted me correctly but displayed none of his own feelings.

All of us then drove to a secluded wooded area outside of Hildburghausen. In the immediate distance was a structure resembling a lumberjack's cabin—presumably Main Division I's "safe installation." When Scharlibbe handed me an axe to chop some wood for the potbelly stove, the whole situation took on a quite amusing character. After brewing some coffee and cutting the cake that had been purchased in town, we settled down for a very cozy meeting.

Taking off his belt and pulling some miniature slides from between the two layers of its leather, Koehler explained that this method of transport had been his own idea. Next he unlocked his briefcase and, by inserting a needle in an almost invisible hole, opened a secret compartment that contained several strips of film. Because several agents had previously been arrested carrying such briefcases, headquarters had explicitly warned us not to use them any longer.

"Why," I asked in astonishment, "has this film already been developed? If an enemy search turned up these photographs, there would be solid physical evidence against you."

"That's what I was advised to do," he replied. "It's the best way of being sure of their quality."

When he then reached in his briefcase and pulled out several maps of the GDR-FRG border area, I was even more confounded. In response to my question about meaning of the maps' colored markings, he casually replied, "They indicate where the FRG Border Patrol and the American troops in the region are stationed and exercise control. That was my assignment."

Finally it began to dawn on Scharlibbe how carelessly everything had been handled. To spare him any further embarrassment, I changed the subject. "What's the border control like?" I asked Koehler.

At least some thought had been given to his cover story. Should the border officials have raised any questions, a number of "gifts"—a pound of coffee, some bars of chocolate, and a small bottle of brandy—had been placed in his briefcase to prove that he was visiting friends in the GDR.

For the remainder of the day, Koehler dictated several lengthy reports into a tape recorder. Much of the material came from previously prepared notes and covered such topics as his last two border crossings, his observation of military movements in the Coburg area, his family and work situations, and his many friends and acquaintances. This relaxed provincial style, I thought to myself, seemed far removed from the hectic routine back at headquarters. Our reports had to be kept as short as possible, for there was neither the time nor the personnel available to process such exhaustive documentation. As a result, many small but potentially important details were often omitted.

With Scharlibbe still officially in charge of the agent, I remained in the background until the late afternoon. Because his cable factory job had only limited intelligence value to us, my main concern was to see if Koehler could be persuaded to resettle elsewhere. I decided to ask him directly whether a large financial increase would be reason enough to move.

"Yes," he answered, "why not? My salary certainly doesn't stretch very far for a family of five."

Obviously it had never occurred to Scharlibbe to make a simple monetary offer, and an expression of regret now came over his face. Although the outlines of a plan were already clear in my mind—either attempting again to place him in the Federal Office of Military Technology and Procurement or securing a position with a large electrical power supply firm in Erlangen—it seemed better not to mention anything further in Scharlibbe's presence.

All in all, I felt quite satisfied with my new agent. His steady and practical temperament augured well for our future work together, and I would try to make his resettlement as appealing as possible. As a clear signal to Scharlibbe that he was no longer the case officer, I set the date for the next meeting with Koehler.

As we departed, Scharlibbe pressed Koehler's "gifts" into my hands. "These belong to you now," he said. But hearing a slight tone of regret in his voice, I immediately gave them back to him.

11

My first task was to put Koehler's activity on a more professional footing. Because of the distance restrictions on all border visits, we had to continue meeting in the same area. Nevertheless, he was instructed to follow a particular path so that I could check beforehand for any enemy surveillance. We then held our main meeting at a hotel in the vicinity. Besides renaming him "Hauser," I took away his specially equipped briefcase, trained him in personal security techniques, and devised a reliable plan for making contact with one another. Finally, I told him that the military intelligence maps, however interesting, were useless to me and put him at unnecessary risk.

In the meantime, I had discovered that the feeble GDR cable industry welcomed every scrap of information about Western technology. As a result, it was possible to raise Hauser's salary substantially—1,000 to 1,500 West German marks at each meeting—and he was most pleased.

To increase his motivation for my main plan—infiltrating the Ministry of Defense in Bonn—I had begun to cultivate his political attitudes. From several hints he had dropped, I also knew that his marriage was in serious jeopardy. The final break with his wife seemed only a matter of time, and then Hauser would be at my disposal. A defense position in Bonn, however, automatically entailed security screenings by the West German Military Counterintelligence Service. Even though our own estimation of this unit was fairly low, all of Hauser's trips to the GDR would have to cease immediately. To maintain future contact with him, I had already begun to prepare an instructor.

I also attempted to utilize the case for my own interests. So that Hauser would have an emergency escape route back into the GDR, my colleagues in Main Division I had ascertained a point in the border with West Germany that was unmined and not regularly patrolled. Logic told me that this route could also be used in the opposite direction if necessary. Unfortunately, when I told Christian about wanting to include it as part of Hauser's overall plan, the idea was vetoed and a path of retreat devised that led through Austria.

At one of our next meetings, I introduced Hauser to his future instructor. Codenamed "Film," the person in actuality was Steffen Kind, the public relations director of a Dresden firm that produced high-voltage installations. His credentials for intelligence work were excellent, for besides being quite clever and cunning, he had worked for many years previously with the criminal police department.

Yet before the first scheduled meeting with Film in Coburg took place, a letter of despair arrived from Hauser. Complaining of insurmountable problems in his domestic life, he announced that his work with us had to be terminated. The breakup of his marriage was having an effect that was precisely the opposite of what I had expected. Hauser apparently did not want to add the danger of an espionage assignment to his marital woes. I initiated an investigation that confirmed this assumption.

I felt determined, however, not to let Hauser slip so easily from my hands. After an appropriate interval, I instructed Film to reestablish contact. As a meeting in the Coburg region appeared too risky, Film proceeded to West Berlin and telephoned Hauser at work. Despite his refusal to come to a requested meeting in the GDR, Hauser indicated that one might be possible in several months' time. Nevertheless, each time Film called, the same answer was given.

Not until the late summer of 1978—a momentary jump into the future is necessary—did the operation become reactivated. Under pressure from Christian to bring this stalling to an end, I proposed sending Film to Coburg through one of the secret border channels. After brief reflection, Christian agreed, maintaining that an unexpected development might force a change in our regular routine and that our travel personnel should acquire some experience with this alternate method. I then made arrangements with the Border Work Patrol. At 6 A.M. on the designated day, Film was to be at the post office in Hildburghausen wearing clothes appropriate to a day-hiker. I could collect him in the evening of the same day.

By that time, I had also established direct contact with the BND. Since these channels were used in a highly circumspect manner by the MfS, the interest of the West Germans was all the keener. Naturally the exact location of the border crossing point had been withheld from me, but having set up the meeting with Hauser myself, I conveyed to the BND in advance the details of Film's movements in Coburg. In order not to endanger my own position, we agreed that no action would be taken against Film or Hauser for the time being.

Upon his return, Film gave me a detailed account of his journey. First, a uniformed member of the work group had driven him by jeep to a point near the so-called "death strip." Then, after being warned about the importance of staying in a single file—the NVA had densely mined both sides of the path to compensate for the absence of a regular border patrol—he set out with two "channel specialists." Ten minutes later they came upon a barbed-wire fence. By removing two loosely attached nails, the guides created a hole large enough to allow them to crawl onto West German territory. Since the two men also knew the patrol schedule of the Bavarian Border Police, there was no danger of being apprehended. The infiltration of an agent in this manner could occur even in broad daylight.

Continuing through a driving rain, the three men arrived in Coburg an hour later soaked to the skin. With instructions to rendezvous again at 8:00 P.M., Film proceeded to the restaurant in the railway station to give his clothes a chance to dry out. He then called Hauser at work and arranged a 5:00 P.M. meeting at the "theater," the prearranged codeword for the Union movie house. Although surprised to have received the call, Hauser eagerly responded to the sum of money that Film surreptitiously handed him at their meeting. The large alimony payments resulting from his divorce settlement had left Hauser strapped for cash.

To my great relief, Film mentioned nothing that indicated his awareness of the BND observation team. By that point, having just finalized an escape plan with the BND, I knew that my own days in the GDR were numbered. That meant that Hauser would probably be arrested upon my defection. Despite feeling a certain sympathy for the unlucky fellow, I had no alternative but to proceed with the original infiltration scheme involving the Federal Office of Military Technology and Procurement. Otherwise I would be putting myself in jeopardy.

To further that plan, even though it had no chance of ever being implemented, Hauser and I met in a safe installation belonging to the MfS regional office in Suhl. I requested that Hauser come to East Berlin for three days at the beginning of January. As it turned out, this was to be my very last meeting with a West agent. After my defection later that month, FRG authorities arrested Hauser as a foreign spy. He was just preparing to flee to Brazil. Under questioning, Hauser explained that emigration seemed the best way to escape both the alimony payments and the MfS. His agreement to work again as an agent was a complete pretense, and he had gone to East Berlin simply to obtain the money necessary for his plane ticket. In light of his full confession and the documentation supporting these claims, the West German court gave Hauser lenient treatment. He had clearly wanted to terminate his MfS involvement once and for all.

12

To return again to late 1975, I found myself in a very strong position within the department. Despite the absence of a Western recruitment that year, my domestic network was regarded as stable and reliable, and no one had a better record of information obtained. There were also a number of fruitful prospects for the coming year. My married life, by contrast, had seen a further deterioration. Official business frequently kept me away from home, and I spent most of the free time that remained doing things better withheld from my politically suspicious wife.

The next year began on a very disappointing note. For reasons that I never discovered, the much-anticipated trip to Salzburg for a meeting with Sperber was rescheduled at the last minute for Budapest. Besides losing the opportunity to make contact with the BND, I had to find a way to notify Sperber of this change in plan. At that moment only one trained man was available—"Mark," in actuality Bernhard Theurich. After examining a photo of Sperber, he received from me a forged West Berlin identity card and the Paris metro ticket that served as a recognition signal. Still the possibility remained that Sperber might reject him, a total stranger.

Because all the later flights were already booked, Christian and I had to arrive in Budapest two days early. That evening I took him to the bar of the Hotel Intercontinental where we were staying. Knowing that it required only a few drinks to loosen his tongue, I hoped to discover what personnel changes were scheduled for the department. A comment about his double workload as departmental head and deputy divisional head produced the desired effect. As the HVA had embassy positions to fill, Christian noted, our department would have one less member by mid-year.

"Comrade Werner Heintze has been showing signs of fatigue lately," he said. "A change of scene would do him good."

Since two persons could hardly be removed in quick succession from the same department, my own chances for such a posting now seemed very remote.

Sipping his gin and tonic, Christian continued: "In his place, there's going to be a new deputy departmental head who will assume full responsibility a year later. In my opinion, you're still too young for this job, so Comrade Peter Bertag from department four has been appointed."

Besides being Vogel's personal favorite, Bertag handled the most important spy network in the sector along with some well-placed Austrian sources in the field of microelectronics. Perhaps, I thought to myself, more information about these agents could be gleaned directly from Bertag.

According to the new plan, Sperber was to meet us at the Corvin department store in the Rákószi utca. On the designated day, Christian and I left immediately after breakfast. Since another night at the bar had given Christian a severe hangover, we stopped en route for some Hungarian coffee, which allegedly could bring even a corpse back to life.

At the appointed hour, we positioned ourselves in front of the store, but there was no sign of Sperber. Chilled to the bone, Christian began to curse the "idiotic meeting place." To remind him that this poorly situated location had been his own idea would have only provoked a total denial. After an hour, we went to the alternate site, which had also been indicated in my instructions to Sperber. When he failed to appear there as well, I started to doubt whether the contact with Mark in Salzburg had been successfully made.

My attempts to assuage Christian's foul mood by showing him the sights of Budapest were to no avail. In fact, he blamed me for everything, including not having assigned more alternate locations. That charge forced me to confess a breach of rules, for, owing to the sudden change in plans, I had also revealed the name of our hotel and my travel alias in Sperber's instructions. Admittedly, this had been a conscious violation on my part, but the fury of Christian's reaction bore no relationship to the actual deed. By 9 P.M., unable to bear his company any longer, I angrily retired to my room.

Around 2 A.M., the phone rang beside my bed, and I answered, half-asleep, in Hungarian. Only gradually did I realize that the caller was speaking German. It turned out to be Sperber, who wanted to know how long he would be kept waiting downstairs. I immediately leaped out of bed and woke Christian in the adjoining room.

When we met in the hotel foyer, Sperber relayed a briefcase filled with thirty interesting documents. Christian's mood suddenly shifted, and I received credit for having saved the day. It was as if his harsh words had never been uttered.

In regard to his late arrival, Sperber explained that the Hungarian border officials had initially refused to admit his dilapidated Mercedes into the country. Only by much cajoling was it possible to gain entry. He also complimented Mark for the handling of his Salzburg assignment, even though their first contact did not occur until they got to the alternate location.

To acknowledge this happy outcome, we decided to celebrate in the hotel lounge. Unfortunately Sperber, who was wearing the same shabby corduroy suit and an open-neck checkered shirt, clashed with the elegantly attired members of Budapest society already present. To get Sperber past the doorman, we had to pretend we were all thirsty hotel guests.

Once seated, we became absorbed in discussing our own affairs and took little notice of the performers. Just as I was pushing a billfold containing 5,000 West German marks over the table to Sperber—his payment for the documents—a female singer approached us from behind. With the spotlight following her movements, she picked up the billfold in jest and let the banknotes flutter to the ground. As the audience began to laugh, she picked up the money and returned it to us. Despite her apology, it was a highly embarrassing situation.

The following day, Sperber drove Christian and me to the airport. Although this constituted another violation of the rules, Christian could overlook such technicalities when his mood was right. Riding in Sperber's rickety, rust-corroded automobile made me understand all too well the reaction of the Hungarian border officials. At the same time, it was difficult not to feel a certain sympathy for the miserable, marginal existence that he led.

The airport was enveloped in a thick fog. Despite a delay in his flight from Vienna, Mark arrived as planned. While waiting for the announcement of our flight to East Berlin, he presented his version of the Salzburg meeting with Sperber. Initially unable to recognize him from the photograph, Mark then remembered his quirk of rattling his keys. Yet no verbal contact was initiated at the first location.

"I simply couldn't believe that an East German spy would walk around looking like that," he said.

"That's a disguise," I joked. "In order to avert suspicion, we advise all our people to dress in this manner."

When Sperber was later arrested in Paris as a result of my defection, I learned how true my ironic comment had been. In actuality, he enjoyed a much better life than we ever suspected. The threadbare clothing as well as the ancient Mercedes were specifically calculated to increase our willingness to pay.

In February 1976, as part of the MfS anniversary celebration, I received a promotion to first lieutenant. The substantial salary increase that resulted now put me on a par with the director of a medium-sized GDR firm. Feeling a swelling pride, I decided to buy a brand-new Skoda, a four-cylinder automobile made in Czechoslovakia. I also used my MfS affiliation to shorten the waiting time considerably. As an opponent of the regime, why should I refrain from exploiting its weaknesses to my own advantage?

13

The same month saw the transfer of Peter Bertag to our department. As he took over Werner Hengst's empty desk, we now shared the same office as well. When he began to unpack his files—all his previous agents remained under his supervision—I noticed such codenames as "Prokurist" and "Sander."

Gradually Bertag revealed to me the main outlines of the so-called Vienna residency. In 1971, an Austrian businessman with communist sympathies had been recruited at the Leipzig trade fair by the head of department three. Within a relatively short period, a total of ten agents were involved in this operation. By founding interlocking front companies on behalf of the MfS, they managed to extend their influence beyond their Viennese base into Switzerland and eventually to their most important source—the United States.

Because of the GDR's lagging research capabilities, nearly all information about microelectronics depended upon the operations of the Vienna residency. Besides the constant demands made by the NVA, enormous pressure for this knowledge also came from the KGB. The Soviets required the manufacture of microelectronic parts on a mass basis, notably in the development of new tanks and aircraft, but their own scientists could produce only incomplete "handmade" pieces. In this respect, the contribution of the Vienna residency can hardly be overestimated. Not only was an imposing amount of information obtained, but it invariably received the highest marks for quality.

My aim of learning more about this spy ring met with little initial success. Whenever I brought up the subject, Bertag, who was otherwise quite talkative, remained decidedly reticent. Several months later, however, I arranged a trip with him via automobile to Budapest. Whereas he had to confer with someone connected to the Vienna residency, I was responding to Fellow's request that our next meeting take place in Hungary. Christian had hesitated for a while but finally agreed.

Arriving in Budapest, Bertag and I booked rooms in one of the better downtown hotels. Since his meeting was not scheduled until two days later, he planned an excursion by himself to Margaret Island. Fortunately, I was well acquainted with the area and could follow his movements without difficulty. From a well-concealed position, I spotted him in an outdoor café talking intensely with a bearded young man. Bertag seemed quite dissatisfied, as the other man periodically shook his head. Judging from Bertag's earlier comments, I concluded that the other man must be an Austrian, but nothing more could be discerned from their conversation. I therefore decided to wait until they had finished.

Luckily for me, they parted in different directions. Had Bertag taken him in his car, all my efforts would have been for nothing. Keeping the man in sight, I could tell by his naïve manner that he was no professional. Following a casual shopping tour, he stopped for an espresso, and I took a seat at the table next to him. I wrote down the license-plate number when he finally returned to his car. If my earlier assumptions were correct, this piece of information could well lead to the uncovering of the Vienna residency. That

I would be in direct contact with the BND in only a matter of weeks never crossed my mind.

Back at the hotel, I found Bertag in a disgruntled mood. He then admitted his unsuccessful recruitment attempt.

"He was simply scared," Bertag growled. "Nowadays there are all these radical types professing sympathy for the communist movement. They study Marx far more thoroughly than we would ever do, and they come up with one revolutionary theory after another. But when it comes to the actual deed, they always turn tail."

Despite our plan to meet in the foyer of the Hotel Astoria, I wanted to give Fellow a pleasant surprise. Just prior to his arrival in Budapest, I drove to the airport and waited until he had cleared immigration and customs. As he was standing in front of the terminal signaling for a taxi, I offered him a lift. Later that evening, we went to dinner at the Citadella, a restaurant overlooking the city from high atop the white chalk cliffs of the Gellért Hill.

I hoped this background of baked fish, Hungarian wine, and gypsy music would be conducive to my next request. True, Fellow had brought along a full briefcase of documents, including the annual internal report of the Jülich nuclear research station. What I had in mind, however, was an operation of even greater magnitude. Recently the GDR had lost a court challenge by the West German Afga film company and could no longer use the prestigious name in the marketing of its own film. Sales had declined earlier because of the film's poor quality, but now under a new name, exports were dwindling more than ever.

Based on the "wish list" compiled by those responsible for film research, I enumerated the many ways that Fellow could lend his assistance. The main problem involved the gelatin component, and I gave him a detailed explanation. When I finally mentioned the sizable minimum that would be paid for this information, he responded as usual with great interest.

"Naturally I have the necessary connections, my dear Schilling," he replied. "If this is an urgent problem for the GDR, then I'll see what can be done. Since I have been invited by Kodak to a presentation in the United States, something could easily be put in motion then. Of course, you know that I'm doing this not for the money, but rather to serve the German fatherland. Whether we call ourselves capitalists or socialists, all of us must stick together."

Although his strange political notions corresponded with neither my official nor my personal beliefs, it was easier just to let such remarks pass unnoticed. Having completed the business part of our meeting, we were free to partake in the more pleasurable activities I had arranged for the following day. Fellow wanted to make the most of his trip, and I had always taken great delight in my visits here. For us in the GDR, Hungary had the well-deserved reputation of being the merriest barracks in the socialist camp.

8

Face to Face with the BND

1

Several weeks after returning from Budapest, I finally received my first direct communication from the BND. Ever since my meeting with Küster's friend in Leipzig four years before, I had keenly anticipated this moment. Occasionally situations arose that caused me to dismiss the thought as highly implausible. Still, convinced that this day would eventually come, I had started eighteen months ago to collect information that would benefit the other side.

Beginning a genuine double life, however, raised the possibility of permanent emotional damage. Because of the increased risk of detection and the inevitable death penalty that awaited all turncoats, my daily surroundings took on a quite different appearance. I worried especially that my heightened suspicion would result in acute paranoia. Whereas it was possible to make the necessary adjustments for the time being, I also knew that one day the nervous strain would become simply unbearable.

My fears had a number of sources. While I still carried the totem, the encounter in Leipzig might well have been part of an entrapment scheme cunningly staged by the MfS. Moreover, even if Küster and his friend were completely legitimate, the possibility of a mole within the BND or the West German counterintelligence unit seemed all too real. Indeed, several MfS colleagues mentioned that an inside source had alerted East Berlin prior to

Günter Guillaume's arrest in the FRG. At the same time, until the BND could be certain that I had not undergone a change of heart and become a double agent for the MfS, first priority would naturally be given to the safety of their own people.

There was the further issue of my future in the West. Based on various cases guardedly related by my colleagues, I knew that the MfS could never tolerate a defeat to the communist system and would ruthlessly pursue any renegade who had changed allegiances. At the time of my decision, I therefore realized the impossibility of ever being able to lead the life of a normal citizen. Even so, some difficulties later arose that had been completely overlooked by me and would never be healed by the process of time.

2

The first message that came from Pullach—I have purposely omitted the precise details of how contact was reestablished—was the description of a nearby dead-letter drop that contained all the items that I would initially need. Even though my mind was essentially made up, collecting those items would constitute definite physical proof of my treason. Warily, I began to ponder the possible dangers. Either a member of the BND had prepared the drop in person or, more likely, a GDR co-worker had been given the assignment. Something might easily have gone awry, and the area could be under MfS surveillance. Then, too, the drop could have been discovered through some bizarre coincidence.

While I had become accustomed to taking risks by myself, it was unsettling to realize that my fate now depended upon an unknown third party as well. Still, I had to trust my new partner or drop the relationship entirely. In addition, I was feeling the stirrings of a certain excitement in this double role. My aim was to challenge the hated SED regime and, in my own small way, emerge the victor. By continuing to act according to my training as an MfS officer, I reckoned that my chances were reasonably good. Yet, like all my colleagues, I possessed only fragmentary information about the functioning of counterintelligence within the MfS. Fairly reliable rumors circulated that a division XXI was exclusively charged with this task, but I knew nothing more specific.

The next day, following the instructions of the BND, I went to the Friedrichshain city park. My destination was an artificial hill constructed from the wartime rubble, jokingly known to East Berliners as "Mount Rubbish." At its summit stood a viewing platform, which was surrounded by a stone wall. I carefully looked around again and, finding no one anywhere in sight, removed one of the stones. Quite cleverly, a sealed, watertight packet had been placed in a well-concealed crevice. After repositioning the stone, I proceeded to my safe house to open the packet.

Inside were three items: a number of closely written sheets of plastic film, several innocent-sounding texts for letters to an uncle in Hamburg, and a plain white sheet of paper. I began with the first sheet of the plastic film. Apart from a welcoming greeting, it requested some information from me in order to establish my bona fides. The next two pages were divided into a series of well-formulated questions including a further subdivision that required merely yes-or-no responses. The point was not to determine the extent of my knowledge but rather to confirm a basic familiarity with the HVA's internal procedures. The fourth page explained how to use the blank sheet of paper that had been impregnated with a invisible writing agent. Having employed this method before, I had no difficulty mastering the BND variation, which, incidentally, seemed of a higher quality.

After placing the sheet with the secret writing agent between one of the "uncle" letters and an ordinary sheet of writing paper, I drew a row of crosses and circles to indicate my answers to the yes-or-no questions. It was important that my symbols fell between the lines of the prepared text. I then burned the top sheet and carefully placed the impregnated sheet in my cache above the kitchen ceiling. Finally, after wiping away any possible fingerprints, I inserted the letter in an envelope and wrote out the cover address that had also been enclosed in the packet. For a return address, I selected a name at random from the telephone book, making certain that the street address was not located in a high-security area and thus less liable to routine inspection. As an added precaution, I mailed the letter from the main Prenzlauer Berg post office, which had the advantage of a direct connection with the West.

The MfS operated according to a strictly enforced "need to know" principle. Although my immediate superiors had access to the files of the agents I handled, members of other units as well as departmental colleagues were denied all knowledge whatsoever. Naturally we related some minor incidents and exchanged observations of a less confidential nature, but the larger rule about divulging important information— whether intentionally or accidentally—was taken very seriously by all of us.

Nevertheless, it frequently happened that a colleague or superior would be examining a file when one came by for a word of consultation. Because of my desire to offer as much information to the BND as possible, I started training myself to read documents upside down. Soon enough, aided by my above-average eyesight, I could read papers lying on the desks of other persons as quickly as if they were in a normal position.

To test my newly developed skill, I went to Werner Heintze's office just prior to his departure from the department. Using the pretext of an upcoming party meeting, I began to scrutinize the file that lay open in front of him. As I talked, trying to disguise my actual intent, he kept turning the pages. By the time he had closed the file, I knew the identity of the West agent involved—Reiner Fülle or codename "Klaus"—and the year of his recruitment from the last two digits of the file number, /64. He was also employed at the Karlsruhe nuclear research center, the very installation assigned to me by Christian under the allegation that no HVA agent had been successfully placed.

As his imminent departure was no longer any secret, I asked Werner who would inherit his West agents. To his knowledge, no decision had yet been made. Then, nodding at the closed file, he added, "Since the man's working in your installation, you'll probably get this one here."

Although Werner said nothing more, I was now positive that I had read the file correctly. Regardless of whether the man was reassigned to me, the knowledge of his identity could be used to increase my credibility with the BND. Still, uncertain about the procedures of my new partner, I wanted to convey the name of one agent not directly under my control. In the event that the BND unwisely decided to make an immediate arrest, a person who could not be directly traced back to me would be better. That evening, I placed a note with Fülle's name and file number in the cache at my safe house.

3

In the meantime, my marriage took another turn for the worse. An official trip happened to bring me in the vicinity of Bad Elster, where my wife was taking a four-week health cure. My plan was to surprise her by making an unannounced visit. Yet upon spotting her totally preoccupied with a male companion unknown to me, I was the person caught unawares. As she did not notice my presence, it seemed better simply to let the matter pass. With my own career entering its most critical phase, an emotional confrontation of this sort could only have a detrimental effect. In addition, my superiors normally reacted disapprovingly to news of a marital conflict and scrupulously attempted to ascertain its causes.

My next message from the BND contained the location of a new dead-letter drop. Obviously the West Germans had yet to exclude the possibility of a double game—or merely wanted to protect their courier, who might have been seen at the first locale. Feeling less trepidation than before, I set out for the Plänterwald on the banks of the Spree River. My confidence increased even more when I saw how cleverly the packet had been deposited. I was clearly dealing with professionals who took no unnecessary risks.

Besides confirming the receipt of my letter, the message inside the packet asked me to complete a new series of questions requiring longer answers. I was also requested to convey detailed information about all the West agents known to me. But as long as my own safety was involved, the message continued, no action would be taken against them. Without this stipulation, it would have been impossible for me to proceed any further. As a final precaution, not only should I use the secret writing agent again but my reply was to be encoded. Having already learned the basic method from the MfS, I had no need for the lengthy instruction booklet that accompanied the enclosed coding materials.

After returning to my safe house and making a cup of strong coffee, I pondered the advisability of revealing the names of all my agents. Although the BND's pledge to give my own safety first priority seemed totally credible, I worried about other contingencies. If an illness, for example, caused me to lose contact with Pullach, would the conclusion be drawn that I had been unmasked by the MfS? If so, would all my agents be immediately apprehended, leaving me with the impossible task of providing an explanation to my superiors? Divulging this information, in other words, meant placing myself completely in the hands of the BND. Since this high-stakes game permitted no other choice, I now wanted to demonstrate my absolute trust in order to put our mutual suspicion quickly to rest.

Feeling considerably relieved by this decision, I turned to the technical preparation of the information. In contrast to the standard codebooks of years ago, an agent today works with an individualized set designed to be destroyed after its first use. The BND employed a so-called double enciphering method. Although it demanded much time and absolute precision—one mistake would render the whole text unintelligible—it was impossible to break without prior knowledge of the code groups. With practice, I hoped to develop greater speed in the double-stage process of changing letters into numbers, but that first evening required over three hours.

Then, of course, the message had to be transferred onto another prepared cover letter utilizing the impregnated sheet. In this instance, the addressee was a presumed grandmother in Hanover. As far as the handwriting was concerned, no one could trace the letter back to me, but if subjected to a routine mail check, the text was bound to arouse the suspicion of the MfS's well-trained personnel. A laboratory analysis might then reveal the secret writing. Although the code would remain virtually undecipherable, the MfS would still have positive evidence that clandestine messages were crossing the West German border. At the same time, the failure of the letter to arrive at its destination would create uncertainty at Pullach.

In my reply, I listed the real names of all the West agents under my supervision—Sperber, Sturm, Fellow, and Hauser—and included some background details. I also noted the name of Reiner Fülle, warning, however, that a move against him would lead to a thorough internal investigation and put me at greater risk. If the BND nevertheless felt obliged to verify my information, then I urged that Fülle be the first person chosen. A return address was again selected from the phone book and the letter posted.

In the meantime, my regular duties consumed an ever-increasing amount of time and energy. Besides handling my West agents, I had to tend to the contacts and leads that came from my extensive domestic network. Each month, I also sent a minimum of three people to the West on instructor or surveillance missions. Not only did these trips require detailed preparation and later evaluation, but a host of other bureaucratic responsibilities needed my attention. Finally, as a result of my successful recruitment of Fellow, I was frequently consulted by both Christian and Jauck on matters of basic strategic planning. Naturally, this knowledge would prove most beneficial to the BND, but the time involved was considerable.

At this stage, I also had to take greater precautions for my own personal safety. Even though no one else used my safe house, a superior occasionally attended a meeting between me and one of my agents. I had to be certain, for example, that no footprints had been left after mounting the window sill to reach my cache above the kitchen ceiling. Further, I ceased making brief notations at work and placing them in a secret compartment in my wallet. Outside of my safe house, nothing now should be written down that did not have official legitimacy. In the past, I had sometimes allowed incriminating evidence against GDR citizens simply to disappear instead of forwarding it to counterintelligence. Henceforth this risk would be taken only in the most serious cases.

4

After our trip to Budapest, my relationship with Peter Bertag became quite friendly. Just as he appreciated my help in orienting him in the department, so it was important for my own security to be on good terms with the future departmental head. Although he handled the sector's most important agents—Vogel directly oversaw matters permitting no intervention from Christian—his record contained no actual Western recruitment. As a means of compensation, Bertag took a highly visible political stance, but it could not mask the fact that someone with his aspirations had yet to secure a Western source by himself.

From his high spirits one day in the office, I realized that a Western recruitment was about to be concluded. Confident of success this time, Bertag gradually began to reveal some details about the person. The son of a key member of the Vienna residency, he was currently studying medicine at the University of Vienna. According to Bertag, the parents had done the preparatory work—not only instilling communist sympathies in their son but also encouraging him to explore the lucrative possibilities of working with the MfS. At this point, he had accepted an invitation from Bertag to visit the GDR and learn about its "achievements" in person.

My curiosity was naturally aroused. When Bertag returned from a meeting with Vogel, he placed the recruitment file on his desk and turned away for a moment. With my ability to read papers upside down, I quickly noted the name Wolfgang Wein, codename "Prokop." In all likelihood, there was a Wein père, who might even be the head of the entire Vienna residency. At the time, the latter seemed a reasonable assumption, since I knew that the person in charge was called "Prokurist." After my defection, however, I learned that Udo Proksch was the man behind the codename. Incidentally, that my agents had codenames wholly different from the person's real name was the exception rather than the rule in the MfS. As a result, some inspired guesswork later enabled me to identify several other agents solely on the basis of their codenames.

In any event, I initially kept all my information about the Vienna residency to myself. Because it had such enormous military and economic implications for the West, I worried that the BND would take immediate action and thereby imperil my position. Yet as it turned out, once convinced that I was not acting on behalf of the HVA, the officials in Pullach always gave highest priority to my personal safety.

In the early summer of 1976, one of the very worst fears of the HVA leadership came to pass. Under the name "Operation Registration," the West German counterintelligence office succeeded in uncovering the HVA method of placing agents as returning immigrants. After a couple of individual cases had come to light, the West Germans began to check the credentials of other returnees using a computerized grid system. In the end, more than thirty HVA agents were apprehended, including the two husband-and-wife teams of Lutze and Wiegel working in the Ministry of Defense. Fearing that more arrests would soon follow, the HVA ordered another 120 resettlement agents posthaste back to the GDR. It even adopted the term "Operation Registration" to indicate one of the most severe setbacks ever experienced in its history.

There were other repercussions as well. Whereas the arrest of Günter Guillaume had actually bolstered the morale of HVA agents in the West, this latest incident had precisely the opposite effect. New recruitments that had appeared certain suddenly fell through, while many established agents either stopped working or began to ask embarrassing questions. Within our department, Olaf Junghanns suffered a particular loss, as four of his agents—two married couples—were ordered to retreat immediately. Although one couple had proven more devoted to the pleasures of Western life than to fulfilling their assignments, the other pair—"Armin" and "Beate"—had performed extremely well for many years. He had headed the residency to which Sperber was once attached, and she had worked as a secretary with Olivetti.

Nor did I remain completely immune from the aftereffects. When Fellow came to his next East Berlin meeting, I quickly detected an altered attitude on his part.

"Herr Schilling," he commented, "one of the most important attributes of an intelligence service is an unblemished reputation for prudence. That's something your establishment earlier possessed but now appears to have lost. What negligence must have been permitted that so many people could be captured all at once! Am I to assume my imminent arrest as well?"

I proceeded to explain in detail how his activity differed entirely from that of the resettled agents. He, however, remained unmoved and refused to pursue the Agfa project. Then, seemingly as an afterthought, he inquired whether I knew a certain Dr. Markianov. Not acquainted with anyone by that name, I asked who that person might be.

"Oh, just a Soviet scientist I happen to know," Fellow replied casually. He had actually revealed a very important clue, but not until after my defection did I understand its significance. At the time, it seemed perfectly normal that he would maintain contacts in the Soviet Union.

The material that Fellow had to convey was well below its usual standard. When I hesitated to give him the full sum of 2,500 West German marks, he remarked, "Since you brought along the money, it might as well be given to me." With lightning speed, he then snatched the bills from my hand.

I merely shrugged my shoulders and set the date for our next meeting. Knowing that he enjoyed becoming familiar with other East bloc countries, I arranged for it to take place in Cracow.

Two months later, on a rainy, overcast day, my driver and I left East Berlin to join Fellow as planned. My mood was darkly apprehensive. Riding through the bleak, rundown Polish countryside and then the dreary outskirts of Cracow certainly did nothing to lift my spirits. Not until we reached the renowned historic center of the city were conditions noticeably different. At our hotel—the best in the city—the parking attendant promptly offered us a black-market rate for our money. When I later attempted to exchange money at the official rate, the bank clerk made a similar proposal. Upon finding mostly empty shelves and non-sellers on a shopping tour, I soon went back to my hotel room.

The climax of this miserable trip came the following day. After waiting in vain for Fellow to appear, I decided to telephone the scientist at the university who was serving as his cover. Apparently Fellow had written him several days before to announce the cancellation of his trip. In a foul temper, my driver and I returned to East Berlin.

Nevertheless, I was not prepared to abandon Fellow quite so easily. After all, he represented my most impressive recruitment to date, and my own reputation depended upon keeping him in tow at all costs. In addition, I felt convinced that only his lingering insecurity over the wave of arrests had prevented him from coming to Cracow. Therefore, upon my instructions, "Secretary"—an agent whom I had placed as a private secretary to Rompe—telephoned Fellow at his institute and extended an invitation to a new meeting. He declined the offer, however, and merely sent his greetings to Schilling.

Despite many repeated requests, it was not until the following year that Fellow actually agreed to come. At that meeting, he explained that his fears had finally been surmounted and our project could now be continued. Although this seemed to be a satisfying development, I had the impression at all subsequent meetings that certain material was being deliberately withheld. Indeed, on the last occasion we met, he pointed to his advancing years and the approach of winter and asked that our next meeting be postponed until the spring. But since my own days in the GDR were numbered, I put up no resistance.

Fellow's subsequent arrest and interrogation by West German authorities revealed a number of startling facts. Once I had successfully lured Fellow back into active service, Rompe proceeded to notify KGB officials, who in turn assigned their own case officer. That person turned out to be Markianov, the Soviet scientist whom Fellow had mentioned to me several years before. Presumably he had wanted to ascertain whether I was working secretly in conjunction with the KGB. In any event, since the friends had either offered more money or insisted on their earlier rights of acquisition—one reason does not preclude the other—the information that I received dwindled significantly. Certainly it was not fear of arrest in the FRG but rather orders from the KGB to terminate the MfS relationship that explained his absence in Cracow.

Why Fellow reestablished contact with me in the final phase never became clear. Perhaps it was simply the prospect of earning a double salary again. During our period of working together, he had made occasional trips to Bucharest, presumably to visit a scientist friend named Murgelescu. To suppose that Fellow was also on the payroll of the Romanian secret service would not be stretching the imagination very far.

5

In the early summer of 1976, the BND notified me of a new dead-letter drop. Once again it was located in a park, the Königsheide, which lay in the vicinity of the MfS apartment house where I lived. Concealed under a bush was a normal-looking but quite large chunk of stone. I placed it in a shopping bag as instructed and went directly to my safe house. When I pushed a needle into a tiny hole on the surface, the stone immediately split into two halves, revealing a small transistor radio inside.

Before reading the enclosed instructions, I switched on the radio and played with the dial but heard merely a hissing noise. Had an audio specialist examined the used radio, which was constructed solely from East German parts, he would have simply concluded that the expense involved did not warrant the repair. According to the instructions, only the transmissions of the BND could be received on the radio. Henceforth, after finding a secure locale, I should tune in at specified times and listen to the long lists of numbers being read aloud. The announcement of my code number meant that the following ciphers contained a message for me. To make certain that the message reached me, it would be repeated several times at stated intervals using a different code number and radio frequency.

Along with the set of code numbers and decoding strips was a letter of gratitude for the information I had conveyed about the HVA agents. Although some preliminary checks would be made, the BND assured me that my own safety had top priority and that assistance would be provided in the event of an emergency. Underscoring the dangers involved in our relationship, the BND advised me to exercise utmost caution myself, even at the expense of securing valuable information. Another set of questions, which no longer dealt with my authenticity but rather with the internal structure of the MfS and the HVA, had also been enclosed. After promptly preparing the coded response, I followed the instructions and destroyed the piece of stone and its locking mechanism.

At this stage, I felt very pleased with the direction things were going. Without having checked out my information, the BND now appeared far more trusting than before. Yet I also knew that full confidence would come only after my list had been verified. After all, no secret service organization would ever sacrifice five of its own people just to place one double agent in the enemy camp.

A week later, at the prearranged time, I was at my safe house ready to receive the initial radio transmission. First came the distinctive rise and fall of the Pullach signal—the so-called "Wessel Anthem," named after the second man to head the BND. Then an unemotional voice stated, "I have a message for . . ." Hearing my number, I wrote down the five groups of ciphers that followed. Once decoded, the message contained a word of congratulations on the commencement of radio contact along with some safety precautions to be observed. This first communication was designed simply to test our new linkage. To confirm receipt of this message, I sent an innocent postcard to the cover address in the FRG.

Although the radio had eliminated the need for complicated dead-letter drops, a considerable amount of time would have to be spent listening for my number, deciphering the messages, and sending coded replies. In order to get a head start on the day's workload, I now began to arrive an hour earlier at the office. Because of the number of agents I handled and my reputation as an industrious worker, no one seemed to think twice about this new routine. On the contrary, my superiors found my conspicuous dedication all the more praiseworthy. Then, too, arriving earlier in the morning—rather than staying after hours—aroused less suspicion as a general professional rule and permitted me to be at my safe house to receive the afternoon BND transmissions.

I had yet another plan in mind. Since official files could not be taken from the office, I wanted to request a small, well-disguised camera from the BND. It would allow me to photograph various documents before my colleagues arrived at work. Moreover, having acquired the recently converted bathroom as an office, I could see anyone approaching the entrance to the building from the small window.

Once Werner Heintze's departure became official, my hunch about receiving his West agent was confirmed. In making the presentation, Christian remarked, "Unbeknownst to you, this man is working in your Karlsruhe installation."

Unaware that I had already relayed this fact to the BND over a month ago, Christian continued enthusiastically, "If anyone can keep us abreast of Bonn's nuclear weapons potential, then it's this person. Because he's working in the FRG's only reprocessing plant, the actual amount of radioactive material can be monitored. By profession, he's merely a tax accountant, but never underestimate the espionage value of such positions."

Werner and I were to organize the next trip together. "Incidentally," Christian added, "you'll also be inheriting the very best instructor in the division." As I later discovered, this person's performance fully matched his reputation, and my own tasks were minimal.

As soon as Werner put the file on the desk, I saw that my reading of the name had been correct. For twelve years, Reiner Fülle had worked for the HVA. A native of the Erzgebirge like Sturm, he had gone to the FRG after completing his technical training. Quite clearly, it was a desire for adventure rather than political discontent that had prompted his decision. For the next few years, he took a series of odd jobs and evening courses until a position opened at the newly built Karlsruhe nuclear facility.

The reprocessing plant to which Fülle was assigned had special significance for the SED leadership. Viewed solely from their ideological perspective, the plant provided evidence of Bonn's imperialist aims in the nuclear field. The real explanation—that existing resources could be better utilized by recycling the burned-out fuel rods from nuclear reactors—was ignored. In addition to the periodic anti-nuclear campaigns in the FRG, the penetration of the Karlsruhe facility was given top priority. Any employee who happened to visit the GDR became an immediate target for recruitment. Ultimately, this enormous operation had little to do with ascertaining the FRG's military plans, but sought instead to aid the Soviet Union with the production of its nuclear arsenal. In overseeing this endeavor, our department shared responsibility with another MfS unit—the Wismut Installation Authority (OVW), based in Karl-Marx-Stadt.

6

After 1945, the Soviet Union embarked on a crash project to end the nuclear monopoly of the United States. Besides using the NKGB/MGB to press important German scientists into service—our department unofficially referred to them as the "spoils of war"—the Soviet occupation forces also appropriated the rich uranium deposits found in the Erzgebirge near Aue and Zwickau. A so-called joint-stock corporation called Wismut was established, and all the mined ore began to find its way to the Soviet Union. Indeed, after the successful testing of the first Soviet atomic bomb in 1949, the mining operations increased to a feverish pitch.

Whereas Stalin had never considered making any concessions to the GDR, his immediate successors decided to declare Wismut a joint Soviet-East German venture. Under this farcical arrangement, the Soviets held the "majority shares" and appointed the corporation's chairman. Every ounce of uranium also continued to be sent to the Soviet Union. To compensate the GDR, Soviet troops were stationed in the area to provide the necessary security. As yet another precautionary measure, the MfS had created the Wismut Installation Authority (OVW)*.

When Reiner Fülle requested permission to visit his elderly mother in the Erzgebirge, department XV of the OVW was alerted. Discovering from his application that he was employed at the Karlsruhe nuclear research center, the officials approved his trip without delay and had a recruitment plan ready for his arrival. Because of the enormous intelligence potential involved, it included blackmail threats if necessary. Fülle, however, showed no resistance and eagerly accepted the offer of a "tidy sum" for his first delivery of documents. Moreover, the stack of papers that he brought along on his next visit contained precisely the information desired by the MfS, and an agreement was concluded on the spot. In fact, all standard precautionary measures were blatantly disregarded in order to secure his recruitment as rapidly as possible.

For a long time, the MfS sought an explanation of Fülle's effortless recruitment. To complete the house currently under construction, some extra money was certainly needed, and he also wanted to stay on good terms with the GDR to maintain his family ties. His strongest motive, however, only became clear in the following years. Just as a desire for adventure had prompted his departure from the GDR, so too the lure of espionage had an irresistible appeal to someone seemingly trapped in the monotonous life of a solid, middle-class accountant.

In any event, Fülle, or codename "Klaus," soon dispelled any doubts that the MfS might have had. With a remarkable display of imagination and daring, he proved able to deliver all the documents within his reach. Not long afterward, Klaus was equipped with a special radio and secret coding material to receive messages from his handlers in Karl-Marx-Stadt. In addition, he became skilled in clandestine photography and made copies of certain restricted documents in the "hobby room" of his home. Even

---

* The OVW had the same status as a regional MfS office and was thus directly responsible to East Berlin headquarters.

though the scientific data had little relevance to the GDR and was relayed
to the friends, he acquired useful information about other personnel as well
as the West German counterintelligence agents stationed at the center. He
even uncovered the planned escape of a GDR citizen. Repeatedly amazed
at the amount of information that could be obtained by such a subordinate
worker, the MfS provided Klaus with generous material compensation.

Not surprisingly, Christian viewed this "super spy" with great envy and
set about to wrest control of him from the OVW. First, through a series of
intrigues, our department managed to gain "directional influence" over
Klaus. Then, in the period following the breakup of the Hartmann
residency, the agent himself made a move that played directly into
Christian's hands. When Klaus proposed emptying his superior's safe to
obtain valuable confidential information, Christian agreed on one condition. Because of the high risks entailed, the operation had to be directed by
our department. That effectively brought Klaus under Christian's control.
In the end, however, the suggested operation never took place. Upon
learning later that his permanent return to the GDR was also a stipulation,
Klaus promptly rejected the plan. Besides, from the MfS's perspective, a
long-term agent in place was worth considerably more than a single
spectacular windfall.

At that point, Werner became Klaus's case officer. His new instructor was
Manfred Baschin, a management expert employed by a large East Berlin
combine involved in electrical installations and factory construction.
Codenamed "Hülse," he possessed a magnetic personality and could
handle Klaus with the right blend of firmness and empathy. Meeting either
in the environs of Karlsruhe or at a marina in Zurich, the two men proved to
be a remarkably effective team, and the amount of information continued to
increase. Such was the state of affairs when I took over the agent from
Werner.

The meeting that Werner and I then planned together had a very
unsettling conclusion. According to Hülse's report, Klaus, having frequently seen the same car at various times and in various locales, believed that his
movements were currently under surveillance. Although he wanted simply
to work at a slower pace for several weeks, Werner immediately sent a radio
message ordering the suspension of all activity under further notice. As
stipulated by official regulations, he also sent a report to the HVA leadership
confirming the fact of enemy contact.

Naturally I knew what had happened. Because of my desire to keep
messages to the BND at minimum length, I had omitted mentioning the
possibility that Klaus might be reassigned to me. Obviously the BND had
started its investigation of my list. Returning to my safe house as soon as
possible, I sent a coded letter with the following text: "Fülle noted
surveillance. File given to me. Please no further action." I only hoped that
my letter was not too late.

In the meantime, there was the matter of the license-plate number, which Klaus had also given Hülse. For purposes of identification, it went directly to division IX of the HVA—a counterintelligence unit that had been created two years earlier to keep all the security bodies in the FRG under scrutiny. According to its findings, the automobile in question was definitely an observation vehicle.

A week later, to my great relief, I received a radio message from the BND. The observation of Klaus was now suspended, and I had no cause for alarm. Indeed, he would remain completely undisturbed as long as my safety was at stake. As a result of this episode, my confidence in Pullach increased immeasurably.

Following a three-month interval, Klaus arrived unexpectedly in East Berlin to visit his brother. Although Christian still had strong misgivings about any resumption of activity, it seemed an appropriate time to introduce me as his new case officer.

We met in the breakfast room of the Hotel Unter den Linden. At some distance, he greeted Christian with a wave and then made an immediate effort to include me in the conversation. He was a handsomely tall, athletically built man with an intelligent face.

Apparently Klaus had used the excuse of an urgent inheritance to explain the sudden trip to his superior in Karlsruhe. Christian could not refrain from a word of guarded criticism. "Do you really think it was wise to come here so soon afterward?"

"Don't worry about that," Klaus replied. "Because I now need official clearance to work with classified material, the whole thing was probably just a security check. Naturally, they've no idea that I've had access to those documents for a long time. Anyway, the security head of our section is a good acquaintance of mine. Believe me, the scare is over."

Eventually Christian let himself be persuaded by Klaus's explanations, and I also heaved a sigh of relief.

Clearly preoccupied with other matters, Klaus only half-listened to our warnings to remain especially cautious. It turned out that the main reason for his trip was to restock his film supply. "I've already used up the three reserve reels," he explained.

As he handed me a small packet wrapped in newspaper, a look of shock came over Christian's face. He then admonished Klaus for having disobeyed his orders.

"Relax," Klaus said consolingly. "I did stop for a few weeks, but then such interesting documents landed on my desk that I couldn't resist. In addition, I knew that a friend of mine was negotiating a secret contract with the French nuclear reprocessing plant at La Hague. When he returned from his last trip, I quickly established contact in the hope that the documents were still in his possession. Indeed, he even had a draft of the contract replete with marginal notes and comments. Yet owing to its top-secret nature, he could let me take only a quick look at it. When he further noted that it contained political dynamite, I felt all the more determined to obtain a copy. We then started drinking together, and soon enough he collapsed dead drunk on his bed. I brought the contract home and made a photographic copy. Early the following morning, I went back to his house and replaced the document. Finally, I prepared a big breakfast and waked him up.''

Christian's reaction alternated between admiration and horror. ''What if the whole situation had been just a trap, and you walked right into it?'' he asked.

''All right,'' Klaus said impertinently, ''if you don't want the information, then so be it.'' Turning to me, he added, ''Werner, give me the film back, and I'll destroy it.''

That was obviously not his intention, but it stopped Christian from making any further reproaches. When Christian then started a longwinded lecture about safety procedures, I knew that Klaus's welfare was not his main concern. Following the heavy losses of Operation Registration, Mielke had announced that any further arrests would prompt a thorough investigation of the HVA. As he was renowned for his rough methods, all employees feared for their own positions and refrained from taking any extra risks. Certainly no one would have condoned this sort of daring escapade.

At Christian's request, I went back to headquarters to obtain Klaus's payment—2,500 West German marks seemed a suitable amount—and two replacement reels of film. As might be expected, the film issued by division VIII of the HVA was not the ordinary commercial variety. In order to make enlargements of sufficient clarity, a highly sensitive grade of film had to be used in the normal cine-cameras that most MfS agents employed. To minimize the risk of detection, a camouflage technique known under the codename ''Wega'' had also been developed. Besides being packaged in ordinary commercial containers, the special film was attached to a three-yard length of regular film at the beginning of the reel. When the camera was switched to single frame, one reel sufficed for photographing 3,000 pages of documents.

After I returned to the hotel, Klaus was told that the next meeting with his instructor would be in Zurich and not Karlsruhe.

On the way back to headquarters, Christian began to vent his feelings. ''The man must be out of his mind to have taken such a risk now. Since Mielke has threatened to let heads roll the next time, we simply can't afford another arrest. We also musn't let Vogel know anything about this, or he'd have a heart attack. On the other hand, given the general lull in activity, this contract will certainly work in our favor. Don't forget, if our quota isn't filled by end of the year, we'll also be called on the carpet.''

Until my defection two years later, Klaus continued to operate unmolested. As the aftereffects of the surveillance episode gradually receded, he started to meet Hülse in Zurich on a regular basis and made two trips back to the GDR. Klaus would even provide us with another exciting adventure before his espionage career came to an end.

7

In addition to the "super spy," there were a number of other bequests from Werner's network. In a complete reversal of my former role, I now exercised "sovereignty" over the GDR Physics Society. That meant supervising Linke and all of his files. In addition, Christian wanted the society restaffed entirely with MfS agents in order to exploit Western contacts more systematically. In particular, the foreign scientists attending professional conferences in the GDR could be better evaluated according to their individual intelligence potential.

My strong interest in this plan arose from quite different motives. Any potential damage to the West, in my estimation, seemed minimal. My time remaining with the MfS was too short to make many recruitments, and the society's cover would be blown immediately after my defection. At the same time, I would gain access to a wealth of information, including lists of those physicists actively working for the MfS.

Christian and I agreed that Linke formed the biggest obstacle to this plan. "We must get him out," Christian said. "Because of the Alois affair, the West already knows that he's an MfS man. Besides, he drinks too much and gets involved with too many women."

Despite the extensive power of the MfS, it proved quite difficult to remove Linke from his position as an "officer in special deployment." In addition, I had to find a suitable replacement. The result was a series of delays that prevented the plan from ever getting off the ground.

Another key agent I received from Werner was Heinz Hillmann, the head of the international relations division of the GDR Academy of Sciences. Since all Western trips made by academy members had to receive his formal approval, I could make my influence felt in a variety of ways. Certain scientists might be prevented from traveling abroad, or my own "legally disguised" agents substituted in their place. Above all, however, I was now in a position to know which GDR academics belonged to the so-called "traveling personnel regulars" and which of them stood at the disposal of the MfS. In their trips abroad to various conferences and institutes, nearly all academics carried out some type of MfS assignment. As I then began to compile the long lists of names, the specific MfS unit involved was also noted. That information later allowed the BND to determine the nature of the person's assignment as well.

In the same year, I made an important domestic recruitment of my own. As this official headed the natural sciences division within the Ministry of Higher Education, it was now possible for me to decide which faculty members would receive promotions or be kept waiting. Because of the GDR's highly centralized educational system, my influence ultimately extended to every college and university.

At this point, however, I felt nearly overwhelmed by the possibilities that had been created. Because my normal work could not be neglected in any way, there was hardly sufficient time to devote to my compilation of information for the BND. Then, too, I started to wonder how all of this data could be relayed to the West. Since no possibility had yet presented itself, I might well have to risk bringing everything with me when the time came to defect.

In the meantime, following the success of Operation Registration, West German counterintelligence officials began to arrest larger numbers of MfS personnel and secure many personal confessions. As a result, a new directive—"Regulation 3/75"—was issued. Henceforth all agents and instructors had to sign a declaration to the effect that nothing concerning their activity would be divulged in the event of an arrest. From the case officer's point of view, that meant added time spent training each person before every trip about proper behavior in such circumstances. Indeed, making an instant confession in order to receive a milder sentence had increasingly become the common practice. For the MfS, the rich years of relatively unhindered activity in the FRG seemed at an end.

Fortunately, my own activity was not appreciably affected by these developments. While Klaus used Zürich as his point of contact, Sperber went alternatingly to Lucerne, Innsbruck, and Salzburg for his meetings. Sturm similarly traveled to Austria to deliver material and receive new assignments, and Hauser continued to make regular day trips across the border. Fellow remained inactive for the time being. Whereas my direct contacts with the FRG had been eliminated, anyone looking at the airline passenger lists to Vienna would have frequently spotted the names of my traveling personnel.

9

The People from Pullach

1

Since Sperber was still not allowed to come to the GDR, I tried to persuade Christian to hold the next meeting in Austria. It might then be possible to have my first personal contact with the BND. Our present means of communication had permitted only brief messages, and I felt a growing need to know my partner more fully. The BND could in turn better ascertain what lay within my capacity to acquire.

Unfortunately, Wolf had suspended all Western trips for full-time HVA personnel, and Austria was definitely out of the question. Christian, however, managed to secure permission to go to Yugoslavia as an alternate site. A fall trade fair in Zagreb provided a good cover, and I conveyed the change of plans to Sperber via his instructor. In a secret letter, I also told the BND of the forthcoming trip and my intention of somehow shaking Christian's company for a brief period.

Once my travel plan was approved, I made the final arrangements and wrote a second letter to the BND with these details. Besides describing my selected attire for the day of arrival, I noted that a copy of the GDR magazine *Science and Progress* would be in my hand upon entering the hotel. As my schedule was otherwise dependent upon Christian's movements, any contact would have to be initiated by the BND.

Hoping that a meeting—or an exchange of papers—would indeed take place, I spent the evening before the trip assembling a collection of relevant items. In a long letter about the MfS's internal structure, I provided the names of the persons heading the main divisions and subdivisions along with a breakdown of the regional and district organizations. In the case of the HVA, I supplied even greater detail, including part of the employee list that had been secretly copied during my night on telephone duty. A couple of original documents were appended as examples of the material at my disposal. I also enclosed a number of passport pictures so that the BND could forge some identity papers for my emergency use. Finally, after warning that this trip to Zagreb formed the exception rather than the rule, I advanced a few suggestions regarding future contact. I then sealed the envelope containing these items and placed it in the inside pocket of my suit coat.

Before proceeding to the airport the following morning, I stopped at the office to obtain my official green passport and the 5,000 West German marks for Sperber's payment. Since the airport control authorities had already been advised by Main Division VI about passengers "Schubert" and "Schilling," our papers received merely a perfunctory treatment, and the customs check was entirely eliminated.

Quite by chance, we happened to meet Vogel in the transit lounge and decided to have a beer together. Having just seen a visiting KGB delegation to their plane, he had some important words to impart to us. After first reiterating the need for Sperber to leave France as soon as possible, Vogel noted the KGB's urgent desire to obtain more information in the nuclear field. "I would never have thought the production of a neutron bomb to be so highly valued by the friends. As the Soviet Union lacks the capacity to produce one by itself and thereby maintain a strategic balance with the United States, it will be up to your department to make an even more strenuous effort. Comrades, you both know well enough what has to be done. Have a good trip and give my greetings to the snooper."

When Vogel then took Christian aside for a brief tête-à-tête, I felt a sudden apprehension. Was it possible, I thought, that something suspicious about me had been detected? It was also true that Yugoslavia, an "enemy state" in the eyes of the MfS, would not prevent a visiting GDR citizen from crossing the frontier into Austria. To my relief, once Vogel had gone, Christian remarked, "Horst needs a new water mixer for his dacha and wants me to bring him one." Although 100 West German marks was given to Christian from the operational account, Vogel's high rank squelched any charge of misappropriation of funds.

When the plane was finally aloft, I began to ponder what lay ahead. Because my work for the BND was far from over, I entertained no thought of making an escape. At the same time, the failure of Pullach to respond to my last letter made me wonder whether it had arrived in the first place. If not, then all my efforts would have been in vain. Yet also knowing that no action of mine could now alter the situation, I continued to read my magazine.

The busy air traffic at Zagreb formed a striking contrast to the sluggish East Berlin terminal. After we had deplaned, our baggage received a thorough investigation by Yugoslavian customs officials, but fortunately our clothes pockets were spared. When we then entered a brand-new Mercedes taxi and drove past the neat rows of individual residences into the prosperous-looking center of town, even Christian seemed impressed. Nevertheless, since GDR propaganda officially painted Yugoslavia as a land of poverty and misery, he predictably found a ready explanation. "To build a modest house, the husband had to leave his family and slave away in deplorable conditions as a guest worker in the FRG. Even after every penny had been saved, huge loans were necessary. As for the cars, they're nothing but old jalopies that can be had for peanuts in the West."

As we approached the hotel, I felt a mounting tension and clutched the rolled-up magazine tightly in my hand. Inside the lobby were only a few elderly women and a young couple deeply absorbed in their own conversation. With no one from the BND seemingly in sight, a keen sense of disappointment came over me. Nevertheless, I kept holding the magazine so that its name was clearly visible and went into the men's room. As a precaution, I had told Christian en route about the need to relieve myself. Presumably if someone from Pullach had come, then this would be the opportunity to establish contact.

The door had hardly closed behind me when the male half of the couple in the foyer entered. Smiling, he stretched out his hand and said, "Hello, Herr Stiller, I'm very glad to see you."

Taken totally by surprise, I responded in a similar manner and heaved a sigh of relief. I then reached into my coat pocket and handed him one of the envelopes. "A small present for you," I added. "We'd better hurry in case my boss might need to pay a visit here too."

"Have no fear," the man replied. "If he leaves the reception area, we'll know immediately. What do you think are the chances of a longer meeting in the next few days?"

After telling him that everything would depend upon Christian, I was given a telephone number to memorize.

"You can reach me there at any time," he said, "but be very cautious and take no unnecessary risks. We'll soon find some better ways to make contact." He then handed me a package of GDR "Club" cigarettes. "In case we don't see each other again, there's a message in the front panel for you to read at home. Just be careful opening the package."

As we washed our hands, I answered his questions about the planned meeting with Sperber and the flight back to East Berlin. When an odd bleep sounded, he said, "You must go now. Your departmental head has finished checking in."

Returning to the lobby, I saw the young man's companion aloofly sitting in an armchair sipping a whiskey. Evidently she was equipped with a concealed electronic device and had been watching Christian all the while. I was quite impressed by the technique.

Unfortunately, because of the number of visitors in town for the trade fair, Christian and I had to share a double room. After we finished unpacking our bags, he went to take a shower.

Suddenly I felt a wave of panic. Remembering having placed two identical envelopes in my coat pocket—one containing the items for the BND, the other with Sperber's payment—I quickly checked to see if the correct one had been handed over in the men's room. To my dismay, the BND material was still my pocket, and the money was gone.

Fortunately the water was still running in the bathroom. Since only a short time had elapsed, the couple might still be in the lobby. Realizing the extreme gravity of the situation, I ran downstairs as fast as possible. Luck was on my side. I walked by them in a deliberate manner and reentered the men's room.

Coming in immediately after me, the man asked what had happened. I explained the mix-up, and we exchanged envelopes. Although the sight of the money produced a smile on his face, he warned me not to let such a mistake happen again. Despite my understandable nervousness, he underscored the tremendous risk that I was taking. I repeated the telephone number aloud and left.

Before returning to the room, I bought a copy of a West German newspaper. As we were expected to stay fully informed about events in the West—our instructors were especially encouraged to read the tabloids to learn about any police manhunts currently under way—this was a plausible excuse to give Christian.

After having lunch in the hotel, we set out on a tour of the well-stocked downtown stores.

Our initial contact with Sperber was to occur two days later in front of St. Mark's Church. Seeing a white ecclesiastical structure in the distance, Christian remarked, "That's certain to be the place."

From a posted sign, I knew that it was actually the Zagreb Cathedral. Purposely, however, I let Christian keep thinking it was St. Mark's Church. He then proceeded to explain the special security precautions for the day of the meeting. "After all, we're in an enemy state, and the Yugoslavian secret service can hardly be considered well-disposed to the MfS."

I had hoped that the following day would provide an opportunity to absent myself from his company. Disappointingly, Christian held firm to our cover story, and we trudged endlessly through the stands of the trade fair. Even in the evening there was no possibility of losing him and making contact with the BND people.

The following morning, we went to the cathedral for the presumed meeting with Sperber. With plenty of time to spare, we found a bench in a nearby park and reviewed the operational details. As so often happened on long official trips, the discussion eventually turned to departmental matters. According to Christian, Bertag would become deputy departmental head the following month and relieve him of many responsibilities. "By the way," he added, "you'll be moving up the ladder too. Since a higher political office comes first in your long-term career advancement, we'll be making you second secretary of the divisional party organization next spring."

I was most pleased to hear this news. Not only did it signal continued trust by my superiors, but the position itself would give me greater access to confidential material. Pullach was bound to find some of it most interesting.

Just before the appointed hour, I informed Christian that we were at the wrong location. At first he disputed the fact, contending that the cathedral merely had two different names, but a glance at the street map left no doubt whatsoever. We immediately rushed to St. Mark's Church and found Sperber waiting outside, looking lost. Because of our late arrival, there was no time for Christian's security precautions.

Out of fear that the BND might station its people at the church and thereby arouse Christian's suspicion, I had allowed him to believe in his mistake until the last minute. As it turned out, my concern had been groundless. The head of the assigned BND unit expressly forbade taking any risks and putting my normal MfS operational work in jeopardy. Shortly afterward, however, I was requested not to make any additional Western recruitments if possible. From that time until my defection, none in fact occurred.

Besides having made the journey to Zagreb in his old Mercedes, Sperber was still wearing the same shabby brown corduroy suit. For our meeting, we went to a garden restaurant in the neighborhood. The good news was that Sperber had secured a one-year position in Oxford, England, while his family remained behind in Paris. Since his new company was involved in the so-called JET project—the construction of a West European experimental fusion reactor—the KGB would be particularly interested. As our discussion revealed, Sperber could probably gain access to classified material.

Another idea surfaced at this meeting. For some time, the KGB had been urging the HVA to establish contacts with the People's Republic of China. Apparently the friends' own attempts had not met with much success. Given Sperber's own strong Sinophila, including his recent language study, we suggested that a research trip be undertaken in the near future. The Soviets could certainly make good use of anything he acquired.

In return for an ample supply of material, Sperber gladly received the payment that I had brought along. While once more claiming dire financial difficulties, he also happened to be coming directly from a symposium in Nice. As he noted himself, the opportunity had also been used to spend several days vacationing in the area. We agreed to reconvene in a year's time, preferably again in Yugoslavia. In any event, the announcement that Sperber had temporarily left France would certainly be welcomed by the MfS leadership.

To my considerable frustration, Christian wanted to spend our final evening in Zagreb buying souvenirs. Seeing this as my last opportunity to arrange a meeting with the BND, I exhibited a decided lack of interest in his shopping trip. He, however, persisted, pointing out how much money still remained from our daily expense account and how much my family would appreciate some gifts from abroad. Since a further display of resistance would have only provoked his suspicion, I reluctantly agreed. As we combed several supermarkets, Christian not only found the water mixer for Vogel but bought several items for his own dacha that was currently under construction.

When we finally returned to the hotel, Christian started to pack his suitcase. Having already tended to that task earlier in the day, I now had roughly half an hour to make contact with the BND. I went to a telephone booth some distance from the hotel and dialed the memorized number.

"At last," the man answered instantly. "I was afraid you'd left already."

Unfortunately I had to dash his hopes once again. "I've only got a few minutes, and I just wanted to say good-bye."

Despite the unmistakable disappointment in his voice, he was in firm control of the situation. "There's nothing much we can do about it now," he answered, with a light Bavarian accent. "Your letter is most appreciated. I would have walked all the way here myself for its contents. One other question: what possibilities do you have for some photographic work?"

"It can certainly be arranged," I eagerly replied, "but the camera must be well disguised."

"Well, we'll see what can be devised. If you are agreeable, we also want to establish regular personal contact in the near future."

Although that entailed increased risk to me—an instructor or courier would doubtlessly be used—I felt no aversion to the idea. Writing the secret letters had proven much too time-consuming, and the results were far from satisfactory.

"We've only just begun and must not start rushing things," he cautioned. "For use in an emergency, you'll soon be getting a 'ticket for a free ride.'"

That meant a forged passport. Still, I thought to myself, it could only help me if the danger were known to me in advance.

When I returned to room, Christian had just finished packing and appeared completely unsuspecting.

Once back in East Berlin, I went straight to my safe house to remove the message from the cigarette package. Directly under the first layer of paper was an extremely thin film strip with various groups of numbers. Despite my increased speed in decoding these messages, several hours were required.

What emerged was a detailed list of items deemed most important by the BND authorities. I quickly realized, however, that they harbored a number of basic misconceptions. On the one hand, accustomed to a very strict separation of individual units, they underestimated my overall view of the MfS. On the other hand, they erroneously believed that I had access to military secrets, including information about weapons systems, troop strength, and special military objects. In fact, I had no ties with either the NVA or Main Division I, the relatively autonomous military counterintelligence unit of the MfS. Yet in the end, since my letter in Zagreb had contained a precise account of what could and could not be obtained, their message was superfluous.

2

During the next weeks, I devoted myself to the large backlog of work on my desk. Besides running the most demanding network of West agents in the department, I now had a total of 35 domestic agents of all categories. In addition, I was overseeing the new project involving the Physics Society. At least my achievements did not go unnoticed, for at the next annual celebration of the GDR's founding, I received the Service Medal of the National People's Army.

At the same time, Vogel had decided to dispense with the intermediate step and elevate Bertag to the full position of departmental head. For my purposes, this was all the more advantageous. Whereas Christian tended to notice the slightest discrepancies, Peter was a far more innocent type. Besides, we enjoyed a most amiable relationship, and my leading reputation in the department meant frequent consultation on many matters. In short, this new situation gave me the additional latitude that I so critically needed.

After my return from Zagreb, the first radio message from the BND directed me to a new dead-letter drop in the Friedrichshain Park. Under a pile of leaves at the foot of a tree was a sealed watertight package. Back at my safe house, I discovered that it contained a number of objects. There were two screwdrivers—one with a thick wooden handle bearing the imprint "Made in German Democratic Republic," the other partially broken and covered with rust. I also found a large butane cigarette lighter of the type sporadically available for purchase in the GDR. Finally, there were some additional secret writing materials to replenish my dwindling supply and a coded sheet of instructions.

As I learned, the two screwdrivers provided the means of transport and storage for rolls of film. Through a trick device, the head of each screwdriver could be opened to reveal a secret compartment inside. The screwdriver in good condition contained four exceptionally small rolls of unexposed film and was intended as a storage container to be kept among my car or household tools. The other one was empty. On a designated day each month, I should place my exposed film in its secret compartment and leave it concealed at a prearranged location for a courier to pick up. A week later at the same spot, I would find my screwdriver again with a fresh roll of film inside. As an added precaution, three different locations were to be used on an alternating basis.

By lifting the outside case of the cigarette lighter, I discovered an uncomplicated-looking miniature camera. A roll of film with fifty exposures was simply inserted into a cylindrical hollow and then wound by pressing the sparking mechanism. The shutter release was a tiny button mounted on the inside. Because of the extreme sensitivity of the film, a normal-sized document could be photographed in ordinary light at a distance of roughly 16 inches. Although the gas container had been reduced considerably in size, the lighter still functioned as such. Only with the removal of the case would the camera become operable. Equipped with this ingenious device, I merely needed a safe, undisturbed place to work.

The one note of disappointment was the BND's decision to postpone a system of personal contact and to continue the radio broadcasts and secret letters. But then again, in this situation, I was the agent and not the case officer. While the screwdrivers seemed most safely stored in my safe house, I decided to keep the cigarette lighter on my person. It was a common enough object, and I began putting it to regular use. The only drawback was having to refill its miniscule tank quite frequently.

The following day I set to work with the camera. Arriving as usual before any of my colleagues, I switched on my desk lamp and photographed a list of my agents and contact persons as well as the significant pages of some specially selected files. The next morning the contents of a "highly confidential" report from the HVA training school were committed to film. I also continued this activity at my safe house. Besides photographing the remainder of the HVA employee list, I decided to reserve the last exposures for a general situation report of mine, which ended with the words "greetings to Pullach." With the exception of the invaluable HVA employee list, all my original notations were then placed in the tiled stove and burned. I even took care to poke the ashes into a fine dust. Finally, after inserting all four rolls of film into the secret compartment, I deposited the broken screwdriver at the designated location.

Upon retrieving the screwdriver a week later, I found some replacement film but no message. By photographing my own report, I had hoped to eliminate the laborious coding and decoding procedure—or to rely on it only as a backup measure—and also to give a fuller account of things to the BND. Within a few days, however, I decoded a radio message that took me sharply to task for my foolish behavior. According to the BND, if the film happened to be intercepted by enemy counterintelligence, the inclusion of a personal message would constitute solid evidence against the agent.

My own position was quite different. If the MfS were to develop a roll of my film, the mere sight of documents from my own files would result in a guilty verdict. Whether some personal messages had been appended seemed a wholly irrelevant matter. Nevertheless, since my own fate was now inextricably tied to the BND, I swallowed my strong disagreement and followed its instructions.

3

When the GDR decided to revoke the citizenship of Wolf Biermann in the fall of 1976, I felt no great surprise. For some months, the internal party reports had been underscoring the need for sterner measures in dealing with "that unruly rabble that call themselves writers and artists." Indeed, as the first signs of a civil rights movement began to appear, the MfS instituted a full-scale investigation of anyone who appeared hostile to the regime. Although some lesser-known persons eventually received prison sentences, a far more subtle process of selection and coercion was employed than in previous years. Given the large number of intelligensia—some of whom had even been befriended by certain GDR officials—a loud hue and cry should be avoided if possible. In the case of Biermann, whose fame as a provocative singer and songwriter had also spread to the West, the best solution was simple expulsion while on a concert tour of the FRG.

I decided to utilize this heightened atmosphere to my own advantage. One morning in the office, someone happened to remark, "Surely we can afford to put up with a Biermann. We are a solidly established state, after all, and a little grumbling now and then shouldn't do any harm."

The ensuing discussion revealed several points of view. Some of my colleagues thought the action against Biermann to be merely ill-timed, especially in light of the human rights campaign recently launched by the United States. Others, like Olaf Junghanns, faithfully followed the party line and found the decision completely justified.

My plan, however, was to outdo these complacent party sycophants by presenting a truly combative and dialectical argument. "Imagine someone with a shiny red apple," I began. "Unfortunately, when it is cut open to be eaten, the man finds an ugly, repulsive worm inside. Should that worm be left alone to make its way through the rest of the apple? Of course not. The man simply cuts out the worm, and some of the surrounding apple if necessary. Precisely in this manner, we the MfS—the party's knife—have removed the poisonous worm Biermann from our nation."

However crude my analogy, no one in the room could afford to voice an objection. In fact, Christian gave me a special look of acknowledgment. "Comrades," he continued, "we must assume the offensive and rob the enemy of all arguments. Biermann was an enemy of the state and actually got off quite lightly. That is the only way for you to present the matter to your agents."

Everyone silently returned to their desks. A few minutes later, however, one person entered my office and remarked, "You said that the apple is the nation and the MfS the knife. If I understand you correctly, then the man must be the party. What does he eventually do with the apple?"

We looked penetratingly into each other's eyes. Finally I answered, "He eats it. And you and I are there to help him."

From the expression on both of our faces, it was clear that we shared the same outlook and that I had also gained a potential ally.

On the orders of Mielke, the entire division convened an hour later to hear an official explanation of the Biermann affair. As might be expected, the report branded him a "nasty individual" throughout his life without making any mention of his own strong communist background and commitment. Although normally quite prudish in such matters, the party propaganda machine had uncovered more than ample proof of his moral degeneracy. In this instance, it declared, disgusting sexual excesses and ideological dissent went hand in hand. Even Biermann's songs were deemed to be of dubious artistic merit.

"Comrades, take the opportunity to discuss this case with your agents," our divisional head ordered. "In addition, I want from each of them a report describing the mood at their places of work and leisure activity. Above all, we want the names of everyone uttering criticism of Biermann's expulsion. Then we'll finally know how individuals really stand vis-á-vis the party."

As it turned out, the majority of our domestic agents remained loyal to the party line and provided the names that had been requested for the huge MfS card index. Yet this bureaucratic solution had only limited success. Even though some GDR citizens simply feigned ignorance, contending that Biermann was an unknown figure until the charges against him appeared in the newspaper, many celebrated artists and scientists unexpectedly rallied to his defense and demanded his reinstatement.

The MfS responded in a shrewd manner. First, any agent moving in artistic or intellectual circles was encouraged to write an "anti-Biermann" letter. If a person appeared initially hesitant, the threat of revealing a past misdemeanor usually ensured compliance. Next, the party press published both pro and con letters, making certain that the anti-Biermann letters constituted a clear majority. Besides representing a clear setback for the dissidents, this alleged "open exchange of opinion" enraged a number of persons who had hitherto remained silent. They were then approached by a specially created MfS unit and asked to find a new country for their artistic activities. Simultaneously, some of the best-known sympathizers were subjected to various methods of coercion and began to make public retractions.

In the meantime, knowing that Sturm was no longer allowed in the GDR, I proposed that the next meeting be held in Finland. Although Christian agreed with my suggestion, Vogel insisted instead on Stockholm. Moreover, he wanted to attend himself. Since Wolf would never disregard basic security procedures and approve a trip abroad involving three HVA officers—along with an instructor—I was automatically eliminated.

Nevertheless, as case officer, I had the responsibility of drawing up the travel plans. According to the official responsible for Sweden in HVA division III, the MfS resident in the Stockholm embassy had to be alerted in case emergency help was later required. This HVA official also proceeded to make the hotel reservations and, completely unprompted by me, to recommend a number of porno shops in Stockholm. From his experience, all MfS personnel bound for Sweden wanted to gain a firsthand exposure to "the decadence of Western morals."

For maximum protection, both Vogel and Christian planned to use diplomatic passports on this trip. I knew, however, that some of the personal entries were false and could be grounds for intervention by Swedish counterintelligence. The thought occurred to me of conveying this information to the BND and possibly securing the arrest of two high-ranking HVA officers. After struggling with this decision, however, I concluded that the risk to my own position was simply too great. The inevitable surveillance in Stockholm might well be detected by my superiors and traced back to me. Even though the official in division III and the local MfS resident in Stockholm were also in possession of the travel dates, only Sturm and I knew the actual meeting place and time.

When the approved travel plan was returned from Wolf's office, I happened to notice an additional comment made by Christian. Apparently a so-called "Project Beam" would also be discussed with Sturm at this meeting. Although my curiosity was naturally aroused as to what this entailed, HVA regulations forbade asking questions about topics that lay outside one's own sphere of operation. Still, it seemed only a matter of time before Christian would broach the subject.

The trip went smoothly. Upon their return, however, both men were wearing elegant new fur hats. I immediately surmised the impossibility of having made these purchases with just the surplus travel funds, but not until after my defection—and Sturm's interrogation—did the complete story emerge. Of the 4,000 West German marks that I had given Christian for Sturm's payment, only half that amount was actually handed over to the agent. It was quite likely that I had been purposely excluded from the trip in order to facilitate this large embezzlement. Admittedly, I had never had the highest opinion of either man, but seeing the full extent of their corruption came as a definite surprise.

As I began to prepare Rechner for his next meeting with Sturm, the details of Project Beam could no longer be withheld from me. According to Christian, the KGB had successfully devised a network of special antennae to intercept the electromagnetic waves emitted by computers. By decoding these impulses, a great deal of valuable information could be obtained. With the encouragement of the friends, the HVA had decided to use this method to penetrate two large military research firms in the FRG. As a first step, Sturm's assignment was to learn the details of their computer setup.

At the time, the use of computerized data banks had provoked a heated controversy in the FRG. Despite the existence of explicit legal safeguards, many West Germans felt the possession of personal information by an insurance company or governmental agency to be a basic infringement of their individual rights. I could not help wondering how these same people would react to the systematic eavesdropping on Western defense organizations developed by the East bloc intelligence services. Since electronic surveillance lay outside my own realm of expertise, I cannot attest to the full implementation of the KGB method. That Project Beam received top priority by the HVA goes without question.

4

Although the system of secret photography functioned very well and allowed me to convey much interesting material, I had envisioned a far closer collaborative effort with the BND. Rather than simply copying whatever happened to land on my desk, I wanted to undertake the sort of jointly planned operations that would deal a severe blow to the entire MfS apparatus. In addition, the rather distant, anonymous tone of my instructions as well as the constant admonition to be cautious had only increased my dissatisfaction. As I learned afterward, the BND had intentionally postponed any further moves pending a more precise appraisal of my own security situation.

Finally, in January 1977, a radio message from Pullach solicited my own suggestions for establishing personal contact. Having already reflected upon the various possibilities, I foresaw nothing without a comparatively high risk factor. The least desirable alternative, however, was to arrange meetings in the GDR outside of East Berlin. Besides the long and complex visa procedure that all West Germans faced, I exercised only limited influence over my official trips. Although the biannual Leipzig trade fair seemed a generally predictable occasion, I wanted meetings held on a more frequent basis and also preferred to avoid the swarms of MfS personnel that descended on the city.

East Berlin, by contrast, offered several advantages. Not only could a West German obtain a day visa with relative ease, but his presence would be masked by the many other visitors to the city. Indeed, as a large contingent of West Germans regularly came to East Berlin either to see friends and relatives or to attend cultural and sporting events, devising a cover story posed no problem at all. I knew that surveillance groups belonging to the MfS's Main Division VIII conducted spot checks, but then only a small percentage of visitors was affected, and a plausible excuse never attracted attention.

Far more problematic was finding a secure locale to hold the meetings. Even though popular literature tends to rely on parks, museums, and other public locations, these places are simply too dangerous in the thoroughly controlled environment of a communist state. In light of my sizable network of agents, being seen in a restaurant with another person would hardly have appeared out of the ordinary. In fact, because of the inadvisability of using the same safe house for all one's agents and the limited availability of such locales, official meetings occurred with great regularity in East Berlin's better restaurants. Nevertheless, while I remained unbriefed about the identity of a colleague's contacts, my superiors closely supervised my files and would have instantly spotted a stranger.

Eventually I arrived at two acceptable possibilities, however bizarre their initial impression. One involved contacting the BND man as a routine "West tip." By portraying him as someone with considerable intelligence potential, I could gain official permission to set up regularly scheduled meetings. After a while, the case might even be described as an impending "recruitment success." Naturally my superiors would closely monitor the situation and probably want to attend one of the meetings themselves. That meant that the cover story had to be absolutely airtight and the slightest mistake avoided. This technique, which has been employed quite often in recent times, had much appeal for me.

The second possibility was equally bold but simpler to execute. Following a thorough check against MfS surveillance, the BND man could come directly to my safe house for meetings. The actual danger involved seemed minimal. Ever since I had started to store secret materials there, my colleagues were denied access and my superiors entered its premises only in my presence. To be sure, this safe house gave me a sense of autonomy and safety that the dead-letter drops conspicuously lacked. Despite the alternation of locations, I always pulled the broken screwdriver out of the ground with a strong feeling of apprehension.

After I had briefly sketched these proposals in my next secret letter to Pullach, an answer came via radio two weeks later. It took only a few decoded words for me to see that the BND was less than enthusiastic. Although politely expressed, the message stated that I was essentially crazy to propose sending one of their men into the very heart of MfS territory. If I were unable to devise an alternate scheme, then the BND would come up with a solution. In addition, I was advised that the material to be deposited at the next dead-letter drop would be quite extensive.

Determined that my original suggestions should not be so abruptly dismissed, I decided to break the rule about sending photographed messages and present a fuller account of my reasoning. After preparing the film and loading the screwdriver in the usual manner, I was ready for the dead-letter drop in the Friedrichshain park. Because of my heightened anxiety, some extra precautions were taken to make certain that no one had followed me.

As it was still winter, twilight arrived at an early hour, and very few people were out walking because of the cold. Pretending to be responding to an urgent need, I first approached the designated tree. Stepping aside and bending over as if to retie my shoelace, I pulled a package out of the loosened ground. Should the soil have been frozen solid, my instructions included an alternate site. I quickly slipped the package into the inside pocket of my overcoat and stuck my screwdriver back into the ground. After standing up, I feigned a test of the retied shoelace in order to pack the soil and scatter some dead leaves. The whole process required only a few minutes and would have appeared completely normal to a casual observer. Finally, a special signal indicating a successful transfer was left in a nearby public restroom.

Opening the package back at my safe house, I first found a duplicate of the broken screwdriver. To accelerate the exchange of materials between us, two interchangeable film containers had been introduced some time ago. I also discovered the emergency travel documents that had been promised in Zagreb—a GDR passport, an accompanying visa valid for the remainder of the year, a foreign currency authorization receipt, and the necessary entry-and-exit permit. With the exception of my photograph, all the personal data were completely fabricated. Although I still intended to collect as much information as possible and depart only when absolutely necessary, these skillfully executed papers would doubtlessly fulfill their purpose at the border control point. I placed them along with the new film supply in my cache above the kitchen ceiling.

Besides acknowledging my last delivery of material, the next radio message from Pullach indicated that a serious reappraisal of my proposals was underway. I felt a certain measure of progress. In order to check out the location of my safe house and establish a possible means of approach, the BND understandably needed some additional time. Within four weeks, however, I should have a definite reply. To confirm my receipt of this message, a simple birthday card was sent to the cover address in the FRG.

I now began to intensify my photographic activities, replicating not only my own files but the minutes of departmental meetings and confidential political documents available through the party organization. Yet I also saw the increasing dilemma that this information created for the BND. Since my personal security necessarily demanded first consideration, all this docu-mented evidence against active MfS agents in the FRG had to be held in reserve. Certainly the BND officials must have felt a bitter irony watching several current operations proceed with my own direct involvement. To minimize their frustration, I tried to concentrate on activities completely removed from my operational area.

To that end, Comrade Werner Schlenkrich from the HVA's Division VI/K proved of particular value. Because he was charged with issuing falsified passports and visas, more personal data came across his desk than at any other point in the entire HVA. In particular, he knew the real names and faces of the West agents as well as their dates of travel. A decidedly grumpy chain smoker, he was also well aware of the significant role played by his seemingly subordinate position and therefore maintained a strict, tightlipped attitude in his official dealings.

Our department, however, was treated somewhat differently. Owing to an earlier but unsuccessful attempt to become a case officer in the department, Schlenkrich still felt an attachment to his "old buddies in the corps." To enhance this special relationship, we regularly gave him Western brandy and cigarettes. That meant that our requests normally received top priority, even though he remained outwardly as unfriendly as ever.

Slightly to the side of his desktop lay a strongbox containing day visas and other entry papers for the use of HVA personnel. As a general rule, Schlenkrich kept this box shut when talking with members of other departments, but in our case, it was usually left open. Occasionally I managed to cast a quick glance at the box and memorize the passport number noted on an exposed visa. The number was then written down at my safe house and stored along with the other confidential material. Although it was incomplete information—the passport might have been used either by a West agent coming to a meeting to East Berlin or by an instructor or courier returning from a short-term mission—West German authorities would still have a lead that could be pursued. Moreover, if the person were apprehended, the trail could not be traced back to me. For the moment, however, I decided to withhold this information from the BND until the personal meetings commenced and a fuller explanation could be given.

After the four weeks had elapsed, I learned via a radio message that my second proposal had been accepted. The next step, according to Pullach, was to establish a day and time for the meeting along with a safety signal for the BND man. In order to minimize the possibility of outside interference, I suggested the third Monday of the following month at 7:30 P.M. Unless detained by an urgent operational matter, all my colleagues were required to attend the party group meetings held every Monday at 5:00 P.M. Normally these sessions lasted an hour and a half, and everyone went home immediately thereafter. The additional hour would give me ample time to get to my safe house and make final preparations. Apropos the safety signal, I suggested drawing a simple pencil line on my downstairs mailbox. Should no mark be seen, the BND man would know that something was amiss and could quickly leave the building. A week later I received confirmation of these proposals.

When the day finally came, I left the party group meeting with my colleagues and started to drive slowly in the direction of my apartment. Not until everyone was out of sight did I proceed to my safe house. I parked the car some distance away in the usual manner, and made a careful check of the immediate neighborhood. Shortly after 7:00 P.M., I used the excuse of emptying the garbage bucket to go downstairs and draw the pencil mark on the mailbox. To divert my thoughts—my perspiring hands gave an indication of my own nervousness—I decided to turn on the radio and make some coffee.

Hearing footsteps on the stairs precisely at 7:30, I opened the door immediately. The elderly woman living next door was most inquisitive and would have been alerted by the sound of the doorbell.

The same man I had met in Zagreb had just reached the top of the stairs. "Well, so we meet again after all," he said. "I hope this time we'll have more time together. My name is Günther."

I purposely turned the radio a bit louder and poured some coffee. He was a man in his middle years with a broad, pleasant face and very alert eyes. Although not a member of the BND headquarters staff and unable to make basic decisions himself, he was nevertheless fully briefed about all relevant details. His position corresponded roughly to that of an MfS courier.

After agreeing upon a plan of action if someone should interrupt our meeting, we wasted no time and staked out the main outlines of our joint endeavor. Günther began by summarizing the BND's current assessment of my situation, asking me to correct any mistaken impressions.

Our only point of disagreement concerned my alleged lack of caution. Günther noted that I doubtlessly knew how much the BND valued my information. "What you probably don't realize," he said, "is the enormous responsibility we now have for your safety. Should anything happen to you, we would be rightly accused of a serious strategic miscalculation and a fundamental moral failure. Of course, you're the best judge of your own situation, but if the MfS uncovers our relationship, then there's no way we can help you. Moreover, the risk factors will only continue to increase, and at some point you will have to consider defecting. Whenever that occurs, you'll be welcome in the FRG, and we'll attempt to honor all our obligations."

We then proceeded to review all the security questions that had arisen during the past year. To my relief, I learned that no serious breach had occurred. According to Günther, one of my first secret letters had been opened, but the invisible writing had gone undetected. As a future precaution, I suggested making visible contact at a designated spot downtown before coming to the safe house. That would allow me to spot any MfS surveillance of my new partner.

"That's all right as an all-clear signal from your end," Günther said, "but you shouldn't worry too much about my safety. We've developed some methods too."

As it turned out, his female companion in Zagreb would continue to play the same critical observation role in East Berlin. He told me that she might even attend a meeting in his absence. After we had decided to reconvene in roughly six weeks, I revealed my cache above the kitchen ceiling and gave him a duplicate key to the safe house. Around 9:00 P.M., he left for a local restaurant as part of his cover story.

5

In the meantime, true to Christian's prediction, I was elected deputy secretary of the divisional party organization. In actuality, this exercise in "internal party democracy" merely reflected the wishes of the top SED leadership as well as my MfS superiors. A person chosen by this procedure was certainly not supposed to represent a constituency, but rather to reinforce the decisions already made from above. As this designation normally preceded an official promotion and showed continued trust on the part of my superiors, I felt a certain satisfaction.

Fortunately I was on good terms with the first party secretary, and we more or less shared the large bureaucratic workload. One of my responsibilities happened to include collecting the required party dues from regular divisional employees and from those agents presently stationed in the West. Although the latter group used codenames to conceal their real identity, it was still possible to gain some knowledge of their activities. In particular, I now had a pretext to speak occasionally with their respective case officers and discreetly coax a few off-the-record comments. Over time, these details gradually began to form a composite picture of the persons involved. In fact, after my defection, West German authorities used this information to identify nearly all of the agents maintained by my division.

Because this new party position was directly tied to my own career advancement, I wanted to fulfill all its obligations in the proper manner. Yet I also had no intention of cutting back on my BND work. That left me with no alternative but to start reducing my case officer load. Some of my domestic agents—especially the least promising and productive ones—either got "lost" in the archives or were given to fellow staff members, who incidentally felt a debt of gratitude.

My next "Monday" meeting with Günther took place as arranged. Although visual contact had occurred an hour earlier in front of the downtown post office, I had also drawn the pencil line on the mailbox. Both of us, however, felt decidedly more relaxed than we had the last time. After noting the BND's general satisfaction with the current situation, he then relayed an extensive list of inquiries—how did MfS counterintelligence function; what methods were used by the mail control division; how were border crossings regulated; and which considerations were primary in the placement of MfS surveillance and investigative teams. To his astonishment,

I could neither produce relevant material or give an adequate verbal reply to most of these questions. Military information still remained totally out of my purview, but I could now offer news of the latest internal political developments.

Finally there was one important technical matter to be broached. Unhappy with the time-consuming correspondence procedure, I wanted to start leaving my photographed reports in the dead-letter drops on a routine basis. Should the MfS discover one of these drops, my cover would be blown whatever the contents of the film. While Günther agreed with my logic and said he would convey my request to Pullach, the old method was to remain in effect for the time being.

In this context, I explained that my greatest anxiety arose over matters seemingly beyond my personal control. Whereas I could gauge the dangers posed by the MfS, it was unsettling to think that my information might be freely distributed in the FRG. Günther attempted to reassure me, contending that no one other than those officials directly involved even knew of a fresh MfS source, and that information pointing to certain conclusions was withheld as a matter of principle. Still feeling somewhat skeptical, I became completely convinced only when the BND's evaluation reports were shown to me after my defection.

During the following summer, I made the personal acquaintance of one of the most remarkable agents in the department, if not the entire MfS. The man had been transferred to me after Werner Hengst's departure, and however incomplete the documentation, his file had aroused my strong curiosity. Egicio di Luca, codename "Faust," had counted among the first businessmen who came after the war to the newly formed Soviet Occupation Zone of Germany. His first endeavor involved the sale of Thuringian-made "Erika" typewriters throughout the Middle East. A frequent visitor to the Leipzig trade fairs, he soon came to the attention of the MfS and was recruited in the 1950s.

Through his involvement in some shady Middle Eastern arms deals, Faust was able to provide the MfS with occasional political and technological information. As in the instance of Sperber's resettlement in Paris—Faust was the person who had sent the monthly "study grant" payments from Switzerland—there were also periodic short-term assignments. At one point, upon the advice of the MfS, he had opened a West Berlin office to provide a better cover for his various activities. Although long suspected to have been employed by other, highly diverse intelligence organizations, he was never a double or multiple agent in the strictest sense. Doubtlessly aware of the old adage that a person who plays one service against another will end up the loser, he always took pains to keep his various contracts wholly separate from one another.

For the MfS, Faust's most valuable contributions resulted from his close relationship with former Egyptian leader Gamal Abdel Nasser. Especially in the period when Nasser established closer ties to the Soviet bloc, it appeared that Faust had acted as an agent of influence. Certainly he played a key role in laying the groundwork for Walter Ulbricht's dramatic trip to Egypt in 1965—a pivotal event that helped to end the GDR's diplomatic isolation. As Werner once told me, Faust was considered at the time to be "a brilliant star in the Eastern secret service constellation."

With Nasser's sudden death in 1970, however, Faust's importance soon waned. He got into difficulties with Anwar Sadat, the new Egyptian head of state, and was thus excluded from top-level political participation. His regular meetings with Werner also came to an end. Although the HVA had ceased to consider him for any important assignment, the man simply knew too much and had to be monitored.

One day Christian informed me of Faust's impending visit to East Berlin. Even though Werner now headed another group within the division, Christian thought him better qualified to handle the arrangements. When I conveyed the news, Werner exclaimed, "Good heavens! I had no idea that the old fellow is still knocking about. But if he's coming here, then I know just what he wants."

It seemed that Faust was drawn to sexual activities of a quite rare and perverse sort. To indulge his fantasies, he had found a similarly inclined young East German girl, who might well have passed for his granddaughter. During the past years, the MfS had given her an extended visa to make regular trips to the West and keep the old epicure content. Now that the girl's visa had expired without the possibility of an extension, he was coming to East Berlin himself.

Following his arrival, Werner and I paid a visit to his hotel. Greeting us in his pajamas, Faust showed no reaction to the announcement that I was his new case officer. One more new face meant little in his long history of such encounters.

"Things have been difficult ever since the death of my friend," Faust remarked, apparently referring to Nasser. "I fell into the hands of certain individuals who wanted to settle some old scores."

Judging from several other oblique comments, these persons were probably Palestinians who had objected to his earlier business practices. Then, with no hint of embarrassment, he showed us the extensive scars on his naked posterior.

After continuing to lament the end of his productive years, he eventually turned the discussion to Paris. "By the way, is that young man whom I helped financially still there?" he asked with a pert look on his face.

Having insinuated his knowledge of the Sperber affair, he then wasted no time in proposing his silence over the matter in exchange for a renewal of his girlfriend's visa. Christian, however, had completely ruled out any such possibility. Should the young woman have decided to remain in West, then the MfS would have lost all its leverage over the man.

Werner chose his words carefully. "But Herr Doctor, such a demanding young friend would cause a grave strain on someone your age. We simply can't allow you to be placed at such risk. As much as we value your past favors, the young woman must regrettably remain in the GDR."

Faust's disappointment was unmistakable. To make absolutely certain of his continued silence, Werner then displayed his keen professional marksmanship. "What the Palestinians inflicted on you is quite appalling. Yet don't forget, since we now enjoy excellent relations with them, they would probably be even less restrained the next time. I would advise staying away from any risky endeavors."

Even though this threat had been simply contrived by Werner, Faust swallowed hard and said nothing more about the visa or his old activities. As it turned out, Werner had succeeded in disarming him permanently, and he never again returned to the GDR.

Fortunately, my operational activities were proving rather uneventful, and I could devote more time to my BND work. Since the last meeting with Günther, I had received permission to use the dead-letter drops for my own filmed reports. As a result, some new material—my own minutes of departmental meetings, my private notes regarding party matters, and my reports about the HVA training school—could now be photographed.

Above all, however, I tried to avoid the danger of falling into a fixed routine. Knowing that so many espionage failures are the product of a mechanical attitude toward daily chores, I deliberately kept changing my route to the dead-letter drops and took extra precautions against possible surveillance. Periodically I stopped my photographic activity for several days and even refrained from acquiring certain valuable documents. Yet at the same time, it was possible for me to become habituated to the steady, permanent danger of the situation. Whereas my initial period of BND involvement had been plagued by periodic nightmares, I now found satisfaction in conceiving new ways to strike a blow at the MfS.

When official approval came for my next meeting with Sperber in Zagreb, I was greatly pleased to note the absence of any traveling companion. In fact, I had purposely chosen a period when both Christian and Peter would be abroad on assignments themselves. Although Vogel had disliked the idea of having three officers simultaneously in the West—the MfS classified Yugoslavia as a Western country—I stressed the urgency of the meeting with Sperber. Not only was the plan for penetrating the People's Republic of China on the agenda, but he would have answers regarding the feasibility of using a high-energy laser beam to detonate a hydrogen bomb.

Given the auspicious outlook for the meeting in Zagreb, I urged Günther to persuade one of his BND superiors to attend as well. Yet he evaded a clear response, indicating only that I could count on his definite participation.

Before leaving for Yugoslavia, I made a brief trip to Budapest with

Christian. The occasion was Sturm's annual meeting. Besides having been allotted a role in Project Beam, he had now recommenced his valuable IBM deliveries. In the aftermath of Operation Registration, his competitor from division XIV had been pulled from duty as a security precaution.

6

Arriving in Zagreb, I found all of the hotel rooms booked because of the trade fair. At our prearranged meeting at the indoor marketplace, I then learned that Günther was similarly without accommodations. As rooms were available in Ljubljana, we agreed on this alternate site and decided to take the express train together. Two hours later—after Günther had attended to some unspecified matter—we met again on board the train.

Immediately before departure, I noticed a slim, conspicuously well-dressed young man take the seat directly opposite us. Günther and I ordered a beer and began to talk quietly. Although showing no signs of understanding our conversation, the man kept giving me an occasional inquisitive look. Not only was his behavior irritating to me, but I felt disappointed not to see any headquarters representative accompanying Günther.

Just as the train was leaving the outskirts of the city, the man suddenly confronted me and said, "Herr Stiller, it's a great pleasure to meet you finally in person. My name is Karl-Heinz."

To Günther's noticeable amusement, I had had no inkling of the man's real identity. For a while, we simply conversed in general terms without bringing up the subject of our work together. Obviously Karl-Heinz wanted first to gain an overall impression of me.

That evening Günther took charge of security, and I had my first conversation alone with Karl-Heinz. After coming quickly and decisively to the point, he began to pose a seemingly endless series of questions. As this detailed review of every phase of my life and work bore all the marks of a police interrogation, I made my displeasure known.

While fully understanding my reaction, he underscored the importance of this procedure. "If we are to undertake some new projects together, then nothing can be left out of the picture. From now on, anything that happens is the responsibility of the BND."

So accustomed to asking the questions myself, I still felt ill at ease, but there was no choice other than to endure this ordeal. Taking breaks only to change locations, we continued these discussions well into the night and throughout the following day. My official travel plans had been purposely arranged to allow this extra time.

In spite of all these questions, I was surprised at how much the BND already knew about East German operations. At the end of these sessions, I remarked how extensive and up-to-date their information seemed to be.

Karl-Heinz, conceding the existence of other inside sources, emphasized the contributions of one person in particular. "After working successfully for us for many years, he disregarded our advice and took one risk too many." He paused slightly before continuing. "We know that he was discovered and then executed."

Pullach's extreme concern about my security now seemed all too understandable, and I felt rather queasy. Still, my professional curiosity had been piqued. Knowing that my colleagues had dismissed the possibility of any recent Western penetration of their ranks, I pressed Karl-Heinz for a specific name. Although he declined to answer, I later discovered that the person in question had belonged to the MfS regional office in Cottbus. According to the official version, the man had committed suicide because of family problems.

Reluctantly I agreed to observe the security guidelines laid down by Karl-Heinz. Although he found merit in my earlier suggestions of having my BND contact pose as a potential recruit, the attendant risks were simply too great. I then made some additional proposals, but all decisions were deferred until a more opportune time.

"You are a highly valuable source of information for us," he said, "and our aim is to learn everything we can from you. So please, do us both a favor by staying alive."

Our last topic concerned the question of escape. After we had reviewed all the possibilities in detail, Karl-Heinz insisted that the slightest sign of trouble should prompt my immediate departure. Yet as I later found out, making such a calculation was easier said than done. Before parting the next evening, we planned a second meeting for the following year. Somehow, I felt convinced, the pretext for another trip abroad would be found.

Returning to Zagreb the next morning, I proceeded to St. Mark's Church for my appointment with Sperber. I then re-directed him to Ljubljana for our meeting. According to his report, he had unfortunately left his job in Oxford and returned to Paris. While my superiors were bound to be upset with me as a result, at least Sperber expressed his willingness to start working on the China project.

That evening in a local nightclub, our discussion eventually turned to politics. In his usual manner, Sperber launched into a diatribe against the Soviet Union, and I attempted a mild rebuttal. Then, however, I found myself unable to sustain the standard SED line and actually ended up agreeing with his main criticisms. Possibly it was owing to the wine—or the distance separating me from the GDR. In any event, even Sperber appeared taken back by my seeming "crisis of faith." The next morning, recalling the warning words of Karl-Heinz, I gave myself a severe reprimand for this display of sheer carelessness. By the time I had breakfast with Sperber, my "convictions" were once again fully under control.

Shortly after my arrival back in East Berlin, Peter returned from his latest mission. This time the Vienna residency had provided him with an enormous amount of information about new weapons technology. Using an embassy car and traveling under diplomatic immunity, Peter had first transported this material across the Czechoslovakian border to Bratislava. Then an MfS delivery truck was dispatched to bring him and the assorted suitcases, cartons, and packages the remainder of the distance. For the West, this haul meant no less than the loss of a major military battle.

Indeed, in the struggle between communism and democracy, the role played by espionage activity can hardly be overstressed. Seeing the reams of documents that Peter had secured made me feel a particular outrage. Despite my own deep estrangement from the GDR, my greatest anger was directed at those gullible Western politicians who accepted the concepts of détente and peaceful coexistence at face value. From my unique vantage point, the communist strategy was unmistakably clear—breaking the barriers of resistance to acquire Western technology and then continuing its own massive arms buildup and expansion of power.

Nevertheless, I managed to find some measure of consolation regarding the Vienna residency. While I had already conveyed to Pullach all the information gleaned earlier from Peter—notably that the tightly organized group could be uncovered by the positive identification of one person—a new opportunity now presented itself. While gleefully unpacking the various documents a few days later, Peter inadvertently left one of the papers on his desk. A quick glance sufficed to see the name of Dr. Sacher, who, working under the codename "Sander," turned out be another key figure in the operation.

10

On the Powder Keg

1

Apart from a few minor hitches, everything was moving according to plan. Besides tending to all my responsibilities as deputy party secretary, I was able to give my BND work ever-increasing attention. Even a couple of my proposals made at the Ljubljana meeting had received approval and could now be implemented.

In mid-January 1978, I had to return to Oberhof for a meeting with Hauser. Having succumbed again to total apathy because of his family situation, he had been persuaded by his instructor to make the quick trip over the border and have a session with me. En route, however, my service car—an institutional yellow Wartburg—almost became stuck in the deep snow. Still I managed to get to the Interhotel Panorama in Oberhof. Dubbed "Panodrama" by the local residents, it had been the scene of many previous meetings with Hauser.

Following a good dinner, I went to the bar for a nightcap and a bit of conversation. Soon enough a quite attractive young woman from the hotel staff sat down next to me, and we started to talk. I identified myself as an engineer on the way to Suhl to inspect an industrial firm the next day. The conversation turned to politics, and she made no secret of her views. In her opinion, the GDR was still "the zone," the Soviets "the occupying force," and the SED "a bunch of big shots." She also felt a particular antipathy toward the MfS. When attempting to attend her brother's wedding in the

FRG, she had been turned down by the regional office in Suhl, even though such trips were permitted in principle.

Although I knew that this area—the so-called "autonomous mountain republic"—was known for its hard line, it seemed better to remain silent. That she had expressed such criminally libelous views to a complete stranger already made me suspicious. In fact, the MfS regularly employed such undercover personnel to check out targeted hotel guests.

On a trip to the men's room, I realized midway that my specially equipped lighter had been left with my cigarettes on the bar. Returning at a normal gait, I saw—to my dismay—that the lighter had disappeared. Noticing a strange look on the woman's face, I reached for a cigarette and pretended to become aware of the lighter's absence for the first time. After I casually asked about its whereabouts, she reached into her purse and handed me the two separated elements of the lighter.

"I'm very sorry," she said calmly. "It was completely unintentional. I was just playing with the thing, and it fell apart."

Silently I reconnected the two elements into my pocket and then lit my cigarette. As a thousand thoughts ran through my mind, it was impossible to control my trembling fingers. When I resumed our conversation, acting as if nothing had happened, the woman tactfully played along. That gave me a certain reassurance, but then I could not risk letting the matter drop so simply. I had to know more about her—and her opinion of me.

"Come on," I said, abruptly interrupting her, "let me take you home. We have things to talk about." She had already mentioned being a widow and living alone with her son in a new apartment complex.

Despite her rather startled expression, she agreed, and we left the hotel. Outside, my car was buried in snow. After completing the rather messy job of shoveling the snow away and placing pine branches under the wheels for traction, I drove the short distance to her apartment. Tastefully decorated, it also showed no sign of her son's presence.

After asking me to take a seat, she brought something to drink and told me to take off my dirty shirt. "Surely your problems can wait until I've cleaned this up a bit."

Welcoming the delay, I now had a few moments to weigh my options. Despite my growing respect for her skillful handling of the situation—she had no doubt sensed my inner conflict—I decided on a "preemptive strike."

When she returned and sat down, I took out my official identity card and announced, "I am a member of the Ministry of State Security. Through no fault of your own, you have become privy to a state secret. That does not alter the consequences. I must know whether you have any connection yourself to the MfS. If so, then all can be forgotten. If not, a lengthy security check will be necessary, and you will be obligated to maintain complete silence. You realize that our laws are very strict."

Her face darkened. The earlier, slightly bemused quality in her expression now gave way to hostility, even repugnance.

"You are to answer me," I continued sternly. "If you have an MfS commitment, then get in contact with your superior. Otherwise we'll go now to the regional office and take care of the necessary business."

However awkward my method, I had to know for certain whether she belonged to the multitude of MfS informers. I doubted, however, that she had been assigned specifically to me.

With an icy look on her face, she finally replied, "I don't know your name and would rather not find out. I've never had any connection with your organization and never will. You already know my opinion of the Stasi, and your behavior only confirms it. If you want to take me in, then go ahead, but you'll have some explaining to do yourself. You should go back where you came from, and I'll forget what I've seen. What I can't understand is how people like you can pretend to be so nice and then turn out to be so nasty. But then deceit is part of the stock and trade of any good communist. You should leave my house now!"

I had no doubt that her outburst was genuine and not drawn from some prepared MfS script. But what to do now? If I accepted her offer to ignore the whole matter and returned to my normal routine, there was still the danger that she might later have some second thoughts. Obviously the safest course was to defect immediately. On the other hand, it seemed a shame to give up everything just because of such a stupid coincidence.

Realizing that it was impossible to remain in the GDR and leave my relationship with her on this basis, I boldly decided to make an honest confession. Should it fail to convince her, I still had sufficient time to return to East Berlin and—with my falsified papers—take the next train to the FRG.

My first task was to calm her inflamed emotions. "I hope that you'll listen to a story that will probably sound like a fairy tale except for the fact that it's true. Afterward, you still can throw me out of your house. Perhaps, though, you'll see me in a different light, and we can part on friendlier terms."

"Why I'm wasting my time with you is a mystery to me," she replied, "but go ahead if you want to unburden your conscience." I had gained no more than a temporary lull in hostilities.

After listening to my account in utter silence, she finally remarked, "Do you expect me to believe all that?"

I put up no defense. "Whether you believe me or not is beside the point. Just imagine the consequences to me should you decide to tell anyone else my story."

My logic was instantly clear to her. In lieu of a direct answer, however, she began to recount the tale of her own similarly unsettled life. Presumably my trust in Helga, as she was called, had not been mistakenly placed.

When I left her apartment, dawn was breaking. A snowplow rumbled by, leaving narrow lanes in the deep white blanket. Back at the hotel, I paused only briefly in my hotel room before going downstairs to breakfast.

Unfortunately, the harsh light of day caused the full force of my doubts to return, and I was ready to depart for the FRG that evening. In spite of my inner turmoil, I went to keep my appointment with Hauser, but there was no sign of him at either of the two prearranged spots. All that remained now was to return to East Berlin and make my final preparations for escape.

Preferring, however, not to be seen back at headquarters, I planned to delay my trip until the normal working day had ended. With plenty of time to kill, I decided to visit the MfS regional office in Suhl. As no rational calculation can explain this move, perhaps it was my subconsciousness simply refusing to admit defeat.

After finding the official responsible for the hotel's surveillance and thanking him for his cooperation, I happened to mention my unfavorable impression of the staff's ideological standards. In particular, I noted one of the waitresses who had talked at length with me anonymously and openly stated her antipathy to the regime.

With a resigned shrug of the shoulders, the man acknowledged the situation at the hotel. "Even the party members are no exception. We've tried installing reliable ones, but they quickly become just as corrupted. In fact, more gets siphoned off in that kitchen than ever ends up being served to the guests. We also know that the manager hires out rooms for his own profit and that most of the waiters are involved in the foreign currency black market. By the way, who was the woman who tried to enlighten you about conditions in our 'workers' paradise'?"

When I gave Helga's name, he replied, "By no means is she the worst of the lot. Of course, you can submit an official report about the conversation, but there's no way that could secure her recruitment. To force anyone up there to work for us would require something on a quite different scale."

I continued my probe. "Why didn't you let her attend her brother's wedding? With her son still here, she was bound to return."

"As far as I was concerned, she could have gone," he explained, "but we'd received orders from headquarters to restrict the number of permits."

Having learned enough at this point—she obviously had no MfS connections, nor was she in turn an object of local scrutiny—I expressed my gratitude and left. Still, no clear solution presented itself. More reluctant than ever to leave the GDR, I also knew that an incalculable danger would henceforth surround my continued presence.

In order to reach a final decision, I decided to return to Helga. According to my reckoning, if she could be enlisted as an accomplice, her silence would be further guaranteed. That was the measure of security I now required.

Most surprised at my reappearance, she nevertheless invited me inside her apartment. Once again her calm and composed manner inspired a feeling of trust, and I candidly revealed my visit to the MfS regional office. I further mentioned the consequences that an indiscreet remark on her part would have for me.

"I can't really add to what I've said already," she replied. "In your position, I'd leave for the West as quickly as possible. But if you insist on staying, then I can only pledge again that the whole matter will be completely forgotten."

I now put my plan before her. "Would you be prepared to take a further step and actively support me?"

After some reflection, she replied, "I'd rather not give you an answer now. I have my son to consider first. Besides, as much as I would like to send a message to the regime, it's hard to see what kind of assistance I could provide."

Although I too could not conceive of a potential role for her, my main objective was to secure her tentative agreement. Taking advantage of a trip that she had already planned, we agreed to meet again in Leipzig the following month.

On the drive back to East Berlin, I reflected on my predicament. While sufficient time remained to defect that same evening, my stronger impulse was to postpone a final decision until my next meeting with Helga.

Nevertheless, the next weeks proved to be highly stressful, and I telephoned Helga several times for reassurance. In her tactful and knowing way, she expressed the words that I needed to hear.

2

As my next meeting with Günther approached, I debated whether to mention the incident in Oberhof. Knowing that the news was bound to provoke great alarm in Pullach and result in my immediate recall, I decided to say nothing for the time being. Arriving at my own decision had been difficult enough, and I felt no desire to be overruled, not even by the BND. On the other hand, I could not withhold the announcement of my other recent setback. According to an official directive, my colleague Olaf now had permission to meet one of his agents in my safe house, albeit with prior notification to me.

Günther, as it turned out, had his own problems as well. Concerned about the number of Western agents recently unmasked in the GDR, he asked whether I might make some cautious inquiries at the office. Accounts of dramatic arrests involving military espionage had already appeared in our own press, but then the highly polemical and exaggerated style of reporting always prevented the reader from knowing anything for certain. In this instance, as Günther made clear, the stories actually had a strong foundation in fact and were a matter of grave concern.

Although uncertain as to how to proceed, I promised my assistance. By feigning an overbooked schedule, I also succeeded in delaying my next meeting with Günther for several months. My hope was to secure Helga's complete cooperation in the interim. In this way, when finally breaking the news to Pullach, I could simultaneously report a successful "repair" of my misadventure.

For the next two weeks—while professing an admiration for MfS counterintelligence techniques—I tried fishing for information about the arrests. None of my colleagues, however, had any precise knowledge. Then someone happened to mention to me what a friend from Main Division II had divulged to him in strictest confidence. By erecting observation posts along all the streets leading to military installations, it was possible to note the license plates of those vehicles not from the local area. When this data reached MfS headquarters, a computer then compiled a shorter list of recurring numbers. At that stage, the agents could be identified with relative ease. According to the same source, this system functioned only in the northern half of the GDR, where the volume of traffic was much lighter. Needless to say, I wasted no time relaying this leak in a secret letter to Pullach.

Using the pretext of an urgent official matter, I drove to Leipzig to meet Helga as planned. In an ironic twist, upon learning of my trip, Christian had asked me to continue on to Suhl and arrange a new meeting with Hauser, but it was too late to inform Helga of the change in itinerary. After I had fetched her at the train station, we went to the Café am Ring.

"I've thought it over," she said right away, "and I'm willing to help. You must be living under a horrible strain, and mostly because of me. At least I can eliminate your doubts about my trustworthiness."

Although still undecided about her future role, I was again struck by her remarkable capacity for understanding and thanked her sincerely. The following day, after I had tended to a quick matter in Karl-Marx-Stadt, we drove back to Oberhof together. To my knowledge, none of my colleagues were traveling in the area, and the risk seemed negligible.

Proceeding to Suhl, I attempted my telephone call to Hauser, but had no success. Afterward I discovered that the alternator in my car was defective. Normally the repair could have been made at the nearest MfS garage in Halle, but with a heavy snowstorm predicted, I decided to stay overnight in the area. As all the hotels were fully booked, my remaining choice was Helga's apartment. By that point, it should also be noted, our relationship had taken on a romantic dimension. Since my wife had been pursuing her own affairs for a long time, I felt no moral compunctions in this regard. What troubled me, however, was the absence of any official certification for the evening's lodging. Indeed, as a standard procedure, the MfS required that all individual travel plans be subsequently checked against the relevant hotel registration books, although the bureaucracy entailed normally meant a certain delay.

On the next payday, I had to make my usual divisional rounds collecting the party dues. Arriving at Vogel's office, I wanted simply to pick up the sum from his secretary in the normal manner. Unfortunately, he and Ovsyannikov had just finished a working lunch and entered the office together.

The KGB liaison officer gave me a friendly nod of recognition. Vogel, however, prodded me in the chest with his finger and asked in an inquisitorial tone, "Who was the woman?"

I was filled with alarm. Uncertain as to what had been discovered, I could only hope that a serious matter would never have been left to such a chance encounter. In any event, anything I said had to correspond exactly to what my superiors knew. Otherwise my whole situation would begin to unravel.

Attempting to take the offensive, I replied with a look of astonishment, "Which woman?"

"The woman in your car in Oberhof," he said.

Despite his reputation for fast, tough, and precise thinking, Vogel had just committed a major tactical error. Had he continued his line of questioning and not revealed his actual knowledge of the matter, I could hardly have avoided an eventual contradiction. Now, aware that MfS regulations forbade picking up hitchhikers in a service car, I needed merely to confess to this misdemeanor.

"She's someone from Oberhof," I answered. "It was bitter cold, and I gave her a lift from Arnstadt."

"And . . . ?" Vogel said, pressing further.

"That was it," I insisted. "I was simply in Suhl on official business."

Vogel silently turned and went into his inner office.

I knew that the issue had not been resolved. Moreover, I had just made a careless mistake myself. Rather than describing Helga as a person on vacation in the area, I had identified her as a resident of Oberhof. That would enable the MfS to locate her with much greater ease.

The next day, Jauck came to my office and inquired about the Oberhof matter.

I forced a smile. "Oh yes, I happened to pick up a hitchhiker. The poor woman was standing in the freezing cold, and I felt sorry for her."

Jauck continued his probe. "Are you sure that was all? Perhaps a one-night stand? That would be bad but not all that serious. You'd better come out with the truth, for if we discover that you're deceiving us, there will be big trouble."

After I had vouched again for the correctness of my version, Jauck requested a detailed written report of the trip from me. It would then be thoroughly investigated.

My position seemed doomed. I constructed a more or less accurate account except for one major point. Since the most vulnerable part of my story was having spent the night with Helga, I substituted my sister in Halle. Naturally this falsehood would eventually be uncovered, but at least I had gained a day's postponement. In any event, I had no choice but to defect that same evening.

At the close of work, I placed a few important files in my briefcase and started driving in the direction of my safe house. With my wife away on a trip, there was no need to return to our apartment. Then, however, I suddenly realized that Olaf had been given the use of my safe house that evening. To compound matters, the agent he was training would be spending the next two nights there so that their sessions could continue all of the following day. That meant that my BND cache would be inaccessible for the next thirty-six hours, and by then, the whole truth would have emerged.

Feeling increasingly helpless in this situation, I decided to call Helga. Fortunately it happened to be a free day for her, and she promptly agreed to take the next train to East Berlin. In the meantime, I returned the files to my office.

It was late in the night when she arrived at the Lichtenberg station. We spent the next hours wandering from one tavern or public waiting room to the next. For the first time in my career, my optimism had completely deserted me. Helga, however, drew upon her own vast resources and lifted me out of my despair.

Before she left on the first morning train to Oberhof, we had managed to formulate a contingency plan. Should the lie about spending the night in Halle be detected, I would reveal her identity and plead guilty to a brief affair. When examined herself, it was imperative that she hold to this story at all costs. Under these circumstances, I might even be able to return to my safe house and empty my cache.

Back at my office, I waited expectantly to be called by my superiors, but nothing happened. When the summons finally came the following day, I went with leaden feet up the stairs to Jauck's office. Christian was also present, and both men looked quite grim.

Holding my report in his hand, Jauck asked whether I had any additional comments to make.

A bold tack still seemed best. "Not that I'm aware of," I replied. "My offense was taking a freezing hitchhiker in my service car."

They both gave me a sharp look, and I waited to hear the official accusation of perjury.

Then I could hardly believe my ears. "Various details of your report have been checked out, and they all seem correct," Jauck began. "Although picking up a hitchhiker is a violation of the rules, given those circumstances we would probably have done the same thing ourselves. So we'll forget it this time. But in the future, just make sure that nothing is ever withheld from us. Incidentally, as a really good intelligence man, you should have known that the head of the sector was on vacation in Oberhof at the time."

Relieved beyond measure, I quickly left headquarters to telephone Helga with the good news. Still, great caution had to be exercised. Because of my own deeply ingrained mistrust, I began to consider the possibility that my pardon had been a deliberate sham designed to engender a false sense of security. Fearing that the investigation might still be under way, I started to redouble all my safety measures regarding off-duty activities. Yet in the following days, nothing unusual came to light that would indicate even a minor inquiry.

Once the immediate tension had subsided, I also asked Helga to return to East Berlin. As our discussion revealed, she had no illusions about my decision to defect. Although I wanted to take some precautionary steps to prevent her implication in the inevitable MfS investigation—the description of her in my report had been left as vague as possible—her own clear preference was to accompany me. Pullach, however, had still not learned of her existence, and I had no idea what the official reaction would be.

3

My next test of nerves was not long in coming. In the usual manner, I had arrived early at the office to work on my BND information collection. Just as I had finished writing my report and was poised to take out the camera, Christian suddenly opened the office door. Normally he was the last person to be expected at work in the morning, and I had not heard his approach. I barely managed to turn over the document on my desk.

Nevertheless, it was evident from his expression that he had noticed my abrupt movement. To conceal my agitation—and also explain the lighter in my hand—I reached for a cigarette. As the tank had not been refilled since Oberhof, I knew that the lighter was inoperable. After pressing the striking mechanism several times in vain, I casually expressed my annoyance at its malfunction.

Despite my attempt to defuse the situation, I could almost feel Christian's desperate desire to see the document on my desk. My office—the former bathroom of the one-time apartment—was exceedingly narrow. Although only two steps away, Christian would have had to push me aside in order to reach the side of the desk where the paper lay. As a result, while we pretended to talk about some minor office matter, an intense war of wits was taking place between us.

Christian seemed to be saying just one thing: "Get out of the way, so I can see that paper."

He was bound to have sensed my reply: "If you must see it, then you'll have to push me out the way first. If you do that—and the paper turns out to be harmless—you will have insulted me and made a fool of yourself."

He in turn was answering: "You had better move voluntarily, since I have the right to see what's there."

As this silent antagonism steadily escalated, our spoken conversation grew louder and louder, even though the topic could hardly have mattered less.

In the end, Christian finally gave up and abruptly left the room. A few minutes later, I tore the paper in tiny shreds and flushed them down the toilet. Afterward, I sat for a long while motionless at my desk.

In spite of these near disasters, the prospect of finding additional ways to inflict damage on the MfS gave me a feeling of renewed vigor. One such possibility involved the new thirteen-story HVA building that was nearing completion. For a long time, we had been working in cramped quarters, and this imposing high-rise—with its bright rooms and ribbed glass partitions —had been conceived as a solution. Although my sector was not scheduled to move until later that spring, we had begun to install some of the furniture.

One morning, seeing that three new filing cabinets were to be taken upstairs, I quickly volunteered for service. I also arranged to assist with the one designated for Jauck's luxuriously appointed future office. Of a light metal construction, the filing cabinet had a simple lock with the key still inserted. As we were maneuvering the cabinet into its special place in the expensive wooden wall unit, I unobtrusively dropped my pack of cigarettes. Once outside, after the door had been relocked, I asked the officer for permission to reenter and retrieve my missing cigarettes.

As I had hoped, he was too lazy to return himself and gave me the door key instead. I now had a few moments alone in the office. Having placed some modeling clay in my pocket beforehand, I managed to make a quick impression of the key to the filing cabinet. As it would later contain much confidential material—including records of the agents maintained by the division—I knew that a major success had been scored. The next step was to give the clay impression to Günther so that Pullach could prepare a copy of the key.

When our next meeting occurred a few days later, I realized that the Oberhof story could no longer be withheld from the BND. Because of the long two-month interval, Günther gave me an especially warm greeting. But as I began to relate the details of the unlucky accident and all its repercussions, he became conspicuously uneasy. To reassure him that my own safety had not been recklessly disregarded, I pointed to my willingness to defect when danger had appeared imminent. Now, however, I felt quite secure and saw no reason to leave so soon.

While refraining from any comment, Günther clearly wanted to return to West Berlin and submit a report as quickly as possible. So that he would also have something positive to include, I handed him the clay impression and explained my new objective.

His self-control pushed beyond its limits, he exclaimed, "Are you really contemplating another daring exploit in your situation?"

After handing me a new updated passport and an entry-and-exit permit, he nevertheless placed the clay impression in his traveling container. "If I were you," he said, "I wouldn't push my luck too far."

With the next BND radio message came the urgent command to suspend all my activities forthwith and to keep quiet for the time being. As I later discovered, Günther's report had hit Pullach like a bombshell. Not only was my enlistment of Helga considered to be an insane move, but officials thought that my cover would be blown in a matter of days. In fact, the next radio message merely requested a sign of life from me in a secret letter. By contrast, I remained convinced of my own secure position and, in a rather impudent manner, asked that operations be resumed. Pullach made no immediate response.

In the meantime, I had to grapple with another hapless incident. To minimize my own exposure, I had given Helga my BND radio and decoding material to keep hidden in Oberhof. Instructed in the procedure, she also collected my messages and then utilized our telephone conversations to convey their contents in a disguised form. One day, however, just as she was taking down a new message, the doorbell unexpectedly rang. Although the caller had only come to collect the church tax, she had momentarily panicked and dropped the radio. As a result, it ceased to function.

Upon learning of the accident at our next East Berlin meeting, I felt a keen setback. Moreover, in light of my complicated relationship with Pullach, it seemed wiser not to ask for a replacement unit. In all likelihood, the BND—suspecting that I had been arrested and that this request was just a ploy to capture the courier bringing the radio—would reject my story out of hand.

There remained one other slender possibility. By searching the Intershops in the area, I thought it conceivable that a radio capable of receiving the unusual shortwave frequency could be found. As my participation in this quest had to be ruled out, Helga would have to comb these stores alone and keep all the technical specifications in her head. In addition, since every person purchasing radio equipment had to be officially registered and was subject to a later inquiry, she was putting herself at considerable risk. As it turned out, after a very extensive search, she found the equivalent unit and used the name of an acquaintance for the registration form. To me, given the odds involved, it seemed like a miracle.

In following weeks, I patiently listened at the specified times but failed to hear my number called. When the next message finally came, Helga happened to be with me at the safe house. I was informed of a new transmission time and given a different code number. Shortly afterward, the next message told me that my activities could resume again and that a meeting with Günther should be arranged. Helga and I hugged each other in delight.

Now that everything seemed back to normal, I felt the need to do something nice for Helga. Indeed, she had shown exceptional courage and resolve in the trying circumstances of the past weeks. With my family away visiting relatives in Hungary, we decided to make a trip to the country the following Sunday. While the results of our last excursion together had not been forgotten, I could not imagine that such an unusual coincidence would ever occur twice.

4

After heading north from the city for about an hour, we found an idyllic lake surrounded by a thick forest. With not a soul in sight, it seemed the perfect spot to spend a warm summer day, and I parked the car in a lane next to the main road. After several hours, however, the unnatural stillness had begun to make me feel uncomfortable, and I suggested that we leave. Just at that moment, an automobile happened to stop on the main road. Hardly had we packed our swimming gear when two uniformed members of the People's Police came into sight. Before they reached us, I quickly whispered to Helga how to behave.

"Good afternoon, is that your car parked on the road?" one of them inquired.

Hearing my affirmative response, he next asked whether I had seen the "no parking" sign. Sticking to the truth—and silently cursing my carelessness—I meekly acknowledged having overlooked such a marker.

Then came the alarming question, "Do you realize that this is a restricted zone?"

Again answering negatively, I knew instantly what was in store for us. Any unauthorized persons found in a restricted zone had to undergo a thorough police investigation. I had also noticed that the keener of the officers held the higher rank.

We all returned to my car to fetch the identification papers. Since I had not brought along the driver's license issued to "Schilling," I had to present the one with my real name. That at least prevented them from immediately knowing my MfS connection and reporting back to East Berlin.

Having previously memorized the necessary personal details, Helga claimed to be my wife. Yet she also had no choice but to state that her identity papers had been accidentally left at home. That admission provoked a sharp reprimand from the senior policeman.

Despite their meticulous efforts copying down the details of my personal papers, the two officers fortunately forgot to ask for the automobile registration. As it happened, that document declared in bold print that the owner of the car was the "Ministry of State Security." On the other hand, the fact that they departed in silence was a bad omen. To have received a citation on the spot would have meant the end of the matter. Obviously it was now going to be investigated further.

As we started to leave, I found the two signs in question, but they were so poorly placed as to be nearly invisible. Putting her hand on my arm in a gesture of reassurance, Helga had yet to grasp the sheer hopelessness of our predicament. According to standard procedure, the policemen would submit their report to the appropriate MfS district office. The personal data included would then be checked against the central MfS registration files. As MfS officers were indexed separately in the personnel division, verification of my identity would not be immediate. My license-plate number, however, could produce quicker results. If it were sent either to my local police precinct or to the MfS district office in Berlin-Treptow, my own department would soon be alerted. At that point, I could foresee no possible means of defending myself against the inevitable charges.

Whereas nothing now prevented me from leaving the GDR posthaste, I knew that my defection would have serious consequences for Helga. To be sure, the MfS would leave no stone unturned to find the mysterious woman last seen with me in the restricted zone. Moreover, my report about the hitchhiking incident had linked her with Oberhof. However vague, that lead alone would enable the investigating officers to locate her within twenty-four hours. Then, relying on its own special methods, the MfS could extract the full truth from her.

Back in East Berlin, feeling a measure of composure, I explained to Helga the dangers that confronted both of us. I also asked her to find a place in Oberhof to bury the radio and coding material. On the rare chance that events might develop differently, these items would be required again. As I had already arranged a meeting with Günther for the end of the following month, some means of notifying him in an emergency had to be established as well. Each day I was to call Helga briefly from a public telephone. Should the daily call not occur, then she should cancel the meeting by sending a telegram with several prearranged phrases to the cover address in the FRG.

Finally, I promised Helga to attempt my own escape if faced with the worst eventuality. Henceforth my BND-forged passport was always to remain on my person, and to avoid being captured alive, I also started carrying my loaded service pistol. In retrospect, however, it seems questionable whether I could have actually abandoned Helga in this manner. In any event, when we parted on that "black Sunday," there appeared to be no possibility whatsoever of seeing her again.

During the following days, I stayed glued to my desk, but nothing happened. At first ascribing this lack of action to general bureaucratic procedures, after two weeks I began to feel a glimmer of hope. At the same time, with our next meeting rapidly approaching, I had to assess the potential dangers confronting Günther. Were Helga and I to be apprehended on the eve of his arrival, he would be walking into a fatal trap. Nevertheless, realizing that a cancellation would also signify my total resignation to the situation, I let the scheduled meeting stand.

A few days later, I happened to see the head of the personnel department entering Jauck's office with a file. Such an unprecedented event, I thought to myself, had to presage my own demise. A number of possible alternatives raced through my mind, but I still kept delaying a decision to defect immediately. To try to steady my nerves, I returned to my work.

The tension, however, continued to mount. After a while, I invented a pretext and went to Jauck's secretary. Known to us as "dumb Iris," she gave me a serious look and confirmed that the personnel head was still inside.

"Now Iris," I jokingly asked, "what have you been up to? Have they finally found out about your secret Intershop visits?"

In reality, a strange sense of detachment had now come over me, almost as if I were no longer an active participant in my own future.

When the personnel head emerged from the office, I gave him a polite greeting. Then Jauck, instead of summoning me inside, proceeded to nod in a friendly manner and leave as well. The last act, it seemed, had merely been postponed.

As I managed to discover, the personnel head had actually come to endorse my promotion to first divisional party secretary. I was further heartened by Christian's approval of my next meeting with Sturm. The site of Helsinki was put forward by Christian and me, and easily received official confirmation.

By the end of the month, nothing concerning the incident on "black Sunday" had come to light. Even to this day, I cannot explain what stroke of good fortune prevented the worst from coming to pass. Was it, as Helga believed, that the policemen had merely succumbed to the summer heat and failed to write their report? Or perhaps the assigned officer in the district MfS office had considered the incident too trivial to warrant a full-scale investigation? Luck thus far had remained on my side, but I now vowed never to take such risks again.

5

The meeting with Günther proved to be a happy reunion for both of us. Not wanting to cause Pullach any further worry, I deliberately omitted any mention of the "black Sunday" incident. In the meantime, aware of my upcoming Helsinki trip, the BND was anxious to talk to me about replacing our old methods of communication with some "new arrangements." Although puzzled as to what this meant, I should have known from Günther's detailed questions about Helga—and his request for a passport photo of her—that something was afoot. In any event, my travel plans had been specifically arranged to allow some undisturbed time away from Christian. Yet, still unsure of the precise hours, I told Günther that we should make initial contact at the Helsinki airport using the men's room trick again.

In preparing for the trip, I had also requested GDR diplomatic passports for both Christian and me. Not only were these documents regarded as more secure protection in a Western country, but I would not have to take along my own BND-forged passport. The HVA officer in division three charged with Finland had further notified the MfS resident in Helsinki to book hotel rooms and meet us at the airport. For me, this would represent the first visit to a Western country since the world championship soccer games in Gelsenkirchen four years ago. Moreover, I had Günther's assurance that the BND would directly intervene in the event of an emergency.

Upon landing, I immediately saw Günther and Karl-Heinz standing behind a glass partition in the arrivals building. Our eyes briefly met to acknowledge one another. The disembarkation procedures—as well as the baggage retrieval—seemed remarkably fast in comparison to East bloc standards. As my suitcase arrived first on the conveyor belt, I was able to leave the transit area ahead of Christian. Nevertheless, with an unknown MfS resident somewhere in the arrivals hall, it was much too risky to make a BND contact. Günther and Karl-Heinz similarly refrained from showing any sign of recognition.

When Christian appeared, I was taken over to a corpulent young man with prematurely graying hair. After introducing himself by his real name, Klaus, he began to escort us to his car. I stopped several paces later, however, and inquired about the travel time into the city. Learning that it was a half-hour ride, I then excused myself and went to the men's room. Because of the heavy traffic inside, there was only the opportunity to whisper to Karl-Heinz the name of the hotel and my round-the-clock telephone number. Both Christian and Klaus appeared unsuspecting upon my return a few minutes later.

Of a lower rank than Christian, Klaus was especially keen to show his professional gusto. Wheeling his Lada through the city as if on a slalom course, he commented at one point, "You never know when someone might be hanging on your tail."

After some brief sightseeing and a stop at the hotel, we went to Klaus's apartment. Presumably in Helsinki for a conference at the GDR embassy, Christian and I had actually been barred from the building. Yet a visit to Klaus, who was attached to the embassy as a cultural attaché, would lend sufficient credence to our cover story. Naturally Klaus's own MfS affiliation had been kept absolutely secret from the other embassy personnel.

My astonished reaction to his opulently furnished apartment prompted a simple explanation. When Erich Honecker had come to participate in the ratification of the Helsinki Final Act in 1975, accommodations befitting his status as GDR head of state needed to be found. Despite the expenditure of nearly two million West German marks, an unfavorable resale market had forced the government to retain the apartment for the use of embassy members.

After several rounds of cognac had loosened Klaus's tongue, we began to hear a series of strictly off-the-record stories. One of them, in fact, involved Markus Wolf himself. It seemed that the past summer, en route to meet one of his top agents in Sweden, he had made a stopover in Helsinki with his new wife. Having been charged with their care, Klaus was now anxious to vent his pent-up emotions.

"It really was disgusting," he grumbled. "The way they bought every-thing in sight made you think that nothing was available back home! Apparently Mischa needed a complete change of furniture for his new wife—Finnish wood, Finnish design, only the best quality. And then it was left to me to have the whole lot packed and shipped back to the GDR."

Familiar enough with the uninhibited behavior of our elite when abroad, I was still very surprised to hear these remarks about Wolf. Yet they did not remain an isolated instance. Following my defection—thanks to West German authorities—I was permitted to see some photographs taken during the remainder of Wolf's trip by a Swedish counterintelligence team. Besides showing the deputy HVA chief Werner Grossmann, these pictures captured Wolf visiting some porno shops as well as meeting with a Bavarian Social Democrat. Needless to say, that politician's career came to a quick end.

As it turned out, our bottle of cognac was merely a prelude to a long and expensive tour of various Helsinki bars. Then, early the next morning, we drove out of the city in a northwesterly direction toward Somero. After passing through the beautiful fall landscape, we arrived at a spacious lakeside log cabin that Klaus had rented for our meeting with Sturm. The cabin also had a sauna and was generously stocked with alcohol.

Yet Sturm's premature arrival in Helsinki forced Christian and me to return to the hotel the same day. Indeed, our security plans rapidly fell into utter disarray. While Sturm's instructor was waiting in the hotel lobby unbeknownst to us—he was to have met Sturm and brought him to the cabin—we accidentally ran into Sturm outside. When the three of us then returned to the cabin, the instructor was left to continue his vigil in vain. Günther and Karl-Heinz had donned disguises and likewise planned to be at the hotel, but the mix-up caused them to arrive too late for the full show.

After the next drinking session got underway, Sturm brought up a matter of urgent concern. Admittedly, the recent defection of a top Romanian secret service officer had produced some anxiety among our West agents, but Sturm seemed truly frightened.

"What would happen if one of your people did that?" he exclaimed. "I take all these safety precautions only to be blown sky-high with everybody else."

Promptly ruling out such a possibility, Christian confidently pointed to the MfS's perfected system of internal security and to the maintenance of high ideological standards. "Don't worry, my dear Gerhard, our officers are all completely and enthusiastically committed to the party."

Despite having told the BND about Sturm long ago, I unhesitatingly endorsed Christian's assertion. Yet on such a beautiful autumnal evening in the picturesque Finnish countryside, my thoughts did not dwell very long on either my own or Sturm's eventual fate.

The following morning, as Sturm and Christian sat down to a "vodka breakfast," I drove to Somero to replenish the low stock of food. Upon my return, both of them were quite inebriated and wanted me to pretend to be their "servant." Since Sturm was easily provoked when drunk, it seemed better to go ahead and scratch his feet and row Christian across the lake. At the same time, I fulfilled a longstanding wish of my own and prepared the suckling pig that had been purchased in town.

As the eating and drinking persisted well into the night, I hoped that the two men would be sufficiently incapacitated the following afternoon not to notice my absence for several hours. To my frustration, they appeared livelier than ever when we returned to Helsinki around noon the next day. A final session to discuss some important new plans with Sturm was to take place that evening. In the interim, they wanted to take a walk and do some shopping. With the return flight booked for the following day, I knew that no other opportunity would be available to meet with the BND.

Fortunately, the alcohol had dulled Christian's normal suspiciousness, and my excuse of an upset stomach and headache was not even necessary. Maintaining a discreet distance, I followed them for a while and then called the telephone number given to me by Karl-Heinz. Ten minutes later, I had joined him in a room of another downtown hotel. Outside the building, Günther again assumed the role of watchman.

A tall, middle-aged man then entered and sat down. Turning to me, he said, "Herr Stiller, it's indeed a pleasure to see you alive and looking so well. Since these circumstances don't permit much time together, we had better get down to business."

From his direct and purposeful manner, I took him to be a high-ranking BND official.

"During the past year, we've experienced a number of mostly unpleasant surprises," he continued. "You must know yourself how often luck has come to your rescue. Our conscience, however, can no longer permit us to keep tempting fate in this way."

I now heard the words calling for my imminent departure. My first reaction was shock. Although prepared for all sorts of reproaches followed by the announcement of new safety procedures, I had not anticipated anything so abrupt and conclusive. To be sure, my desire had been to continue this double game a while longer. I momentarily considered making an objection and refusing to leave. Reason, however, then prevailed, and I saw myself that the risks had become too great. I could only imagine how the BND would react to the "black Sunday" incident.

According to the senior BND official, an immediate defection in Helsinki would have been preferable, but arrangements for Helga and her son had not yet been completed. "Day X" was therefore set for the end of the year, roughly three months hence. He then reversed my question about the technical details involved and asked for my thoughts about various alternatives. Above all, I insisted on being put in the driver's seat. Were something to go wrong, then the fault should be entirely mine. While we found agreement on this point, the BND assessed the situation with Helga and her son in a quite different light and wanted to rely on a so-called "exfiltration maneuver."

I could not help feeling a strong sadness regarding my own family situation. Clearly my marriage had been troubled for many years now, and my actions had often taken little account of both my wife and daughter. Still, I had never completely abandoned the relationship, nor had my wife. In fact, her political transformation was largely my own doing. Because of these circumstances, I was promised assistance for my family in the improbable event that my wife's attitude suddenly changed.

We utilized the remainder of this short meeting to discuss possible operations for the immediate period ahead. Nevertheless, I was forbidden to send photographed messages and had to return to the original method of radio broadcasts and secret letters. Shortly prior to "Day X," Günther would make his last trip and bring me a newly forged GDR passport and my final instructions.

11

The Final Escape

1

After my return from Helsinki, the strain of anticipation began to cause many sleepless nights. At my request, Helga came to East Berlin, and I informed her of the latest developments. Just as before, she accepted everything trustingly and proved to be of great help to me. Then, too, my normal MfS duties demanded as much energy and concentration as ever and helped the days pass quickly. When officially informed of my upcoming election as first divisional party secretary, I tried to show the proper blend of modesty and pride. My regret, of course, was that too little time remained to exploit this new opportunity to its fullest.

Upon learning that this election would also signal my future appointment as departmental head, I felt even greater consternation. The only other requirement was a six-month advanced course in Marxist theory at the HVA school in Belzig. In this instance, the announcement of my late January departure had been made many months ago and then conveyed by me to Günther. That meant that my impending isolation was known to the BND before our Helsinki meeting, and would therefore have been all the more reason to hasten the date of my defection.

As "Day X" grew nearer, I increasingly focused my attention on collecting as many important documents as possible. Since my new party position necessitated a move to different quarters, I now had the excuse to go carefully through my files looking for any references to West agents and

218

any significant internal papers not previously photographed. Although my plan still included obtaining a complete list of West agents from Jauck's file cabinet—Günther was to bring the duplicated key to our last meeting—it seemed a wise precaution to compile whatever names I could. This material was then stored in my cache at the safe house.

In the meantime, the BND had worked out the details of the exfiltration maneuver for Helga and her son. On "Day X" they were to travel from Oberhof to East Berlin and meet me at the safe house. I would then deliver them at a prearranged point no later than 6:00 P.M. and let the West Germans handle the rest. But the BND also emphasized that if they arrived more than fifteen minutes late, the maneuver would have to be canceled. Her son would not be informed until the day itself.

In order to obtain the documents from Jauck's file cabinet, I wanted to remain after work that day and wait for all my colleagues to leave. Once the papers had been removed, I would then return to the safe house and pack everything in a single briefcase to avoid attracting attention. Should the GDR diplomatic passport still be in my possession, I would proceed to the Friedrichstrasse station and take a train to West Berlin. If not, I would have to hide the briefcase somewhere and use the forged passport to cross the border as a normal GDR citizen. Instead of leaving directly from East Berlin, it seemed less dangerous to drive to Magdeburg and board the Halle-Hanover train.

A week before "Day X," Günther arrived with all the necessary items, and we carefully reviewed our plans. After packing those objects I no longer needed and giving me a few words of encouragement, he tried to say good-bye in the normal manner, as if to convey his final reassurance that all would go well. Even so, I began to experience the sort of acute apprehension that had previously been held in check. As it steadily mounted during the following days, I had to exert exceptional effort to maintain my normal outward appearance.

On the day itself, feeling more fear than anticipation, I first telephoned Helga to confirm our plans. She intended to drive to Erfurt and take an express train to East Berlin. As she and her son had to be at the safe house no later than 3:00 P.M. and deep snow still lay in the Oberhof area, I urged her to allow some extra time. In contrast to my nearly paralyzed mental condition, she appeared to be in good spirits.

Around noon, I went to the safe house and started packing the documents. At that point, I committed a grievous error. Confident that the escape plan would succeed, I decided to burn the remaining sheet of paper with the secret writing agent. Yet as the hours passed and Helga and her son did not appear, it became increasingly clear that something had gone awry.

At 5:00 P.M., I telephoned Oberhof directly from the safe house, but there was no answer. Experiencing an almost unbearable tension, I continued to wait another hour. By then, since a half hour was needed for the drive from the safe house, it would have been impossible to reach the appointed spot in time. The exfiltration maneuver had failed.

I considered going to the spot alone and requesting a postponement, but realized that the persons involved had been briefed only about Helga and her son. My appearance was certain to arouse further suspicion and close down the operation entirely.

I decided to call Oberhof one more time. To my considerable shock, it was Helga who answered the phone. She proceeded to explain that her Trabant had broken down just outside of Arnstadt. Although she eventually found a mechanic who then repaired the car—charging an exorbitant amount in West German marks—her arrival in Erfurt was too late to catch the last train to East Berlin. An attempt to drive the remaining distance at full throttle proved beyond the capacity of the two-stroke engine, and her automobile collapsed after a few miles. A helpful truck driver had towed her back to Oberhof.

From the tone of her voice, I knew that her nerves were stretched to the breaking point. Desperately she implored me to leave by myself and not give her another thought.

Such a move, however, would have assuredly sealed her fate. In the aftermath of my departure, the hitchhiking incident was bound to be reexamined and her identity established. My inquisitive next-door neighbor, who had seen Helga several times at the safe house, could provide eyewitness testimony. On the other hand, having done nothing yet that was not irreversible, I might easily remain in the GDR, and both of us would be safe for the immediate future. Despite her protests at my refusal to escape, I detected a great fear of being left to fend for herself.

I then went to the post office and sent a telegram to the cover address in the FRG. The message read: "Aunt Helga missed the train. Don't bother waiting at the station. Regards, Uncle Paul."

Now unable to explain to Pullach the details of what had happened, I realized the full seriousness of having destroyed the sheet of paper with the invisible writing agent. As the swirling snow outside seemed merely to reflect my own bewildered state of mind, I needed a moment to rest and collect my thoughts.

2

As I began to assess the situation the following day, two main obstacles presented themselves. First, the BND now had grounds to suspect not only my apprehension by the MfS but also my forced participation as a double agent in setting up some elaborate traps. That meant that Pullach would have to be fully convinced of my legitimacy before requesting another meeting with Günther or a new escape operation for Helga and her son. Second, having foolishly entered the date of "Day X"—December 15—on the required entry-and-exit permit, I could no longer use the forged GDR passport and would have to rely on the diplomatic one.

Faced with these circumstances, I concluded that my best alternative was a "normal" letter sent to the BND cover address. Pretending to be a grandmother affectionately writing to her grandchildren in the West, I attempted to summarize the new situation that had developed. Since it was imperative that the letter make sense only to someone acquainted with my particular case, the task of finding the right phrases proved to be very tricky and time-consuming indeed.

The letter also contained a revised plan of escape. On the assumption that four weeks would be sufficient time for making new preparations, I asked the BND to arrange for Helga and her son to be taken over the border on January 19. As my intention was to leave the preceding day—the precise means would be determined by the options available at the time—the BND could therefore be assured that no traps had been laid for their people. Nevertheless, since the MfS would immediately start searching for Helga, the operation had to commence as quickly after my defection as possible.

In drawing up this plan, I had made certain that January 18 fell on a Thursday. Because this was the day of the week normally devoted to visiting my domestic network, my absence from the office would not appear at all unusual. Moreover, there was a period for sports activities scheduled every Friday morning and attended by most of my colleagues. According to my calculations, the first alarm would be sounded by the discovery of the missing files from Jauck's office. Yet to reassemble the entire staff in order to ascertain who was missing would require some extra time. My hope was to gain a few precious hours, not only for Helga and her son but for the West German counterintelligence officials. The longer it took the HVA to notify their agents, the greater the chances of their arrest in the FRG.

Before I had received a reply from Pullach, two new setbacks occurred. One was the loss of my diplomatic passport, which had been discovered missing in the meantime and had to be returned. Although I felt lucky that the incident had had no further repercussions, there was now the problem of obtaining a new entry-and-exit permit. Still uncertain as to how to accomplish this task, I was worried that a later notification would not reach Pullach in time. Thus, during an official trip to Halle, I mailed the following message to the cover address: "Uncle Paul will arrive by train from Halle."

The other matter involved the return of my service pistol. On January 1 we received an order that all individual firearms had to be handed in at the armory. Whereas the written decree merely mentioned the phrase "centralized safekeeping," it was common knowledge among us that a number of MfS officers had recently used their service pistols to commit suicide.

To add to my nervous tension, I noticed a car with GDR license plates following me part of the way to work one morning. Having been rushing about quite hectically of late, I initially imagined that the MfS had placed me under surveillance. Fortunately, upon returning to the safe house that evening, I discovered that my other supposition was the correct one. In the first radio broadcast since the disaster of "Day X," Pullach announced, "We're very pleased to see that all is well with you."

I was further relieved to learn that the BND agreed with my plan and had set up a new exfiltration maneuver for Helga and her son. Although the possibility of a trap was no longer a point of concern, the message continued, I would not be permitted to postpone my defection another time.

In the meanwhile, owing to a new problem that had developed, I too was convinced of the necessity of leaving forthwith. At our last meeting, Günther had mentioned that some careful preparatory steps were being taken to watch my agent Klaus in anticipation of my defection. Apparently, however, an overzealous official misinterpreted the instructions and demanded a full surveillance. Even though the order was quickly rescinded, Klaus had caught sight of the observation team and failed to show at the next meeting in Zurich with his instructor. In a coded message back to East Berlin, Klaus had confirmed the fact of his surveillance.

To make matters worse, the person at the cover address happened to inform Bertag of this message as well. When he then confronted me about the situation, I fabricated a story alleging that Klaus's jealous wife had probably engaged a detective agency to catch him in an extramarital affair. Although his message had been phrased in a way that permitted this interpretation, Klaus himself would soon be coming to a meeting in East Berlin. At that time, my story was bound to collapse and suspicion would automatically fall upon me.

As the new "Day X" grew even closer, I saw an opportunity to regain possession of my service pistol. Every January during the ceremony commemorating the murders of Karl Liebknecht and Rosa Luxemburg, the top party leadership, guarded by a special MfS contingent, made a procession to Friedrichsfelde Cemetery. As divisional party secretary, I could easily have gained an exemption from this extra duty, but the fact that our weapons would be reissued for the occasion prompted me to participate. At its conclusion, I deliberately left my pistol in the snow for a while. When I attempted to return it the next working day, the official at the armory saw the fresh rust and demanded a thorough cleaning. I knew that some excuses could be contrived to keep the pistol for a couple of extra days. In addition, I had slipped some ammunition into my pocket during our regular shooting practices and then stored it in the safe house.

Having just participated in compiling the previous year's annual report— my position as party secretary had elevated me to membership in the "leadership collective"—I possessed definite confirmation that our division maintained about 140 West agents and 500 domestic support personnel. Because of a series of recent conferences in Jauck's office, I was also able to ascertain which file contained the names of those persons. Certainly if these lists could be passed to the BND, not only would a large number of West agents be eliminated in one fell swoop but the panic engendered among the others should cause a host of so-called "self-terminations."

Two days prior to "Day X," I decided to test the duplicate key that had been made by the BND. I remained after work for a while and then went to obtain the key to the office of Jauck's secretary. As a matter of standard procedure, all the office keys were kept in a box directly outside his office and returned at day's end to the duty officer by the last person to leave. Just as I was about to open the secretary's door, Christian suddenly appeared in the corridor. Unbeknownst to me, he had been in a late conference with the head of the sector and wanted to return briefly to his office, which was located directly opposite Jauck's. One minute later, he surely would have caught me.

On further reflection, it seemed better to abandon this trial run altogether. Besides the possibility of another untimely coincidence, the duplicate key might become stuck in the lock and impossible to remove. Indeed, precisely that had happened with some of the original keys. In any event, should the duplicate key not function on "Day X," I also planned to have a hammer and chisel with me. As a final resort—employing a technique that had been successfully developed with my own file cabinet—the door could be sprung open by slightly lifting and then tilting the cabinet forward.

On the last day before my departure, I attended the elections of the HVA's party organization. Held in the staff officers' mess, this gathering of the top leadership included not only the farcical voting ritual but also important speeches and reports. Once again, my new party position had made me privy to discussions of the rarest sort, and I tried to record all that was said. That my work for Pullach as a double agent now had to end seemed more regrettable than ever.

In the afternoon, I was especially eager to copy down a remarkable speech delivered by Markus Wolf. Departing from his usual format, he talked at considerable length about the GDR's internal security requirements. "And don't forget, comrades," he remarked at one point, "an enemy penetration of our ranks would be the worst thing that could happen to us."

A chill went down my spine, and I momentarily thought that Wolf would next point to me in a dramatic gesture and proclaim my guilt. As it turned out, however, this assembly chose to make me its delegate to the March elections of the SED district leadership of the MfS. But I knew—regardless of what happened tomorrow—that it would be impossible to attend. As this session came to a close, I politely said good-bye to the other participants.

3

At 6:00 P.M. on "Day X," I was about to leave the safe house to make my final moves. The missing entry-and-exit permit had been secured in Halle that same day, and a telephone call placed to Helga the day before. Here in the safe house, I had destroyed everything that could provide evidence of my double identity. With its dial setting changed, only the radio was left on the table. As I took a last look around, the codename "fortress" seemed well deserved indeed.

I briefly reviewed my plan again. After the thirty-minute drive to headquarters, I would spend no more than an hour removing the documents from Jauck's filing cabinet. Another thirty minutes had been allotted to get to the prearranged hiding spot. That meant that by 8:00 P.M. I could start the two-and-a-half-hour drive to Magdeburg. Since the train bound for Halle left at 10:49 P.M., there was practically no margin for error. On the other hand, having registered for an official trip to Dresden today, I could not afford to be seen back at headquarters before quitting time. Whereas I could always take a later train from Magdeburg, the delay would cause anxiety for the BND people waiting in Hanover, and also endanger the escape operation for Helga and her son.

I drove very cautiously on the icy streets. Oddly, my fear of the last several days had disappeared, and I wanted to remain as calm and steady as possible for the next hours. As a precaution, my loaded pistol was concealed in a pocket of my overcoat. Although I had agonized for weeks over the question of ever using the weapon—either to defend myself or to take my own life—the present circumstances made it seem the natural thing to do.

Arriving at the headquarters complex, I first parked the car in a side street and then checked for any lights still burning in the HVA building. Fortunately, everything was dark on the two floors occupied by my division. The guard at the entrance—accustomed to our arrival at all hours of the day and night—merely gave my official identification card a bored glance. With my briefcase in hand, I proceeded at a purposeful but unrushed gait.

Upon passing by the internal security checkpoint, I was startled to run into a colleague from my division. The assigned duty officer that evening, he luckily knew nothing about my official trip to Dresden.

After removing the box of keys for the divisional offices, I remarked, "Keep a good lookout. You know very well that the enemy never sleeps."

He stiffly came to attention and said in an overly correct manner, "Yes sir, Comrade Party Secretary!" Then he grinned at me like a normal colleague.

I took the elevator to my recently acquired sixth-floor office. Quickly surveying its contents—a brand-new set of office furniture, a small carpet, and a conference table with armchairs—I realized that my career had been very successful by GDR standards.

For some time, I had kept the briefcase intended for the BND in my office. Of a fairly compact size, it was the type of routine object needed by our travel personnel and thus not liable to attract undue attention. Within minutes I had packed it with the documents brought from the safe house and also some papers from my own filing cabinet. I then gathered the objects that would be needed for Jauck's office—the duplicate key, a small chisel and hammer, a flashlight, and my pistol. Finally, after finding the key to the secretary's office, I turned off the lights. My former colleague Werner Hengst lived directly across the street, and might notice a light burning for an abnormal length of time.

The outside corridor was empty. The night watchman made his first rounds at 9:00 P.M., but by then I hoped to be well on my way to Magdeburg. Quickly I slipped into the secretary's office and locked the door behind me. Since the windows faced the inner courtyard, none of the lights could be switched on. After closing the blackout drapes, I used my flashlight to locate the filing cabinet that was installed in the wall unit in Jauck's inner quarters. The specially padded door leading from his secretary's office provided me with a welcome measure of soundproofing.

Once inserted in the lock, however, the duplicate key refused to turn. Even some vigorous twisting and pushing was to no avail. Concluding that my clay impression had probably been too imprecise, I suddenly felt a bit nervous and paused for a moment. Then came the realization that my alternate method of tilting the file cabinet would not work either. As it was so firmly lodged into the wall unit, the assistance of another person would have been required. That left only the hammer and chisel, but one blow to the cabinet made such a fearsome noise that I promptly ceased.

However tempting the information in the file, I knew that to persist in this endeavor would place everything else in severe jeopardy. Noting how much time had elapsed now made me feel the first pangs of fear. Still, I felt that the fact of my bold intention should not go unnoticed, so the chisel was left neatly on the top of Jauck's desk.

When I went back into the secretary's office, all remained silent in the outside corridor, and my fear began to subside. Reluctant as ever to forgo this unique opportunity, I glanced around the room until my eyes landed on the secretary's filing cabinet. Not only was it free-standing and easily tilted, but its contents turned out to be a true gift from heaven.

As I had suspected, I first found all the material used for the baggage transfers in the Friedrichstrasse station, including my own glued-together passport in the name of "Brückner." That meant that the train trip from Magdeburg to Hanover could be eliminated and a direct entry into West Berlin attempted. Besides being familiar with the complex layout of the Friedrichstrasse station, I could now appear as an MfS officer and take along the BND briefcase.

My other, even more valuable discovery was subject matter lists based on the information obtained by our West agents. Immediately I realized that these documents could provide enough clues to localize, if not identify, all of the division's West agents. In addition, there were several other classified documents that seemed worth removing. In sum, my failure with Jauck's cabinet had been quite generously compensated.

Although dripping with perspiration, I had managed to regain my composure. After first checking the corridor, I returned to my office to fetch my overcoat. Downstairs everything went smoothly. I returned the divisional key box to the duty officer—wishing him the last collegial "good-night" of my life—and passed by both the internal checkpoint and the outside entrance without incident. It was also MfS policy that soldiers on guard duty could not inspect any baggage carried by an operational officer. For a moment, I tried to visualize the sort of panic that would break out tomorrow.

Since this new escape plan required some additional preparation, I returned to the safe house. Specifically, the special duty order had to be filled out and signed. For this purpose, I had taken from the secretary's cabinet a number of blank forms as well as some used ones to serve as a guide. In the space marked "purpose," I wrote the phrase "personal operational business." Because the form further required an authorized signature by either the divisional head or one of his deputies, I selected the person whose handwriting most resembled my own. In this case, it was the second deputy head and chief officer of department three. Without using a model, I mastered his signature after several tries and then signed the form.

At 8:30 P.M. I left the safe house for the last time. After the short drive to the Friedrichstrasse station, I parked the car nearby at the Metropol, a recently opened "foreign currency" hotel. In reality, it mattered little when and where the automobile was later found, but the possibility of a mishap inside the station convinced me to take along the key and registration papers. Due to the bitter cold, the normally busy area was totally deserted. Proceeding briskly to the service entrance of the station, I had in one hand the diplomatic case that was often used for short trips, in the other the BND briefcase that ironically would serve as my cover in this situation. My desire was to put this episode behind me as quickly as possible.

4

I now had to be prepared for all eventualities. One was the possibility that an alarm had been sounded and all the border crossings alerted. Should that have occurred, my arrest was a foregone conclusion. On the other hand, barely an hour had elapsed since leaving headquarters, and all appeared quiet along the platforms.

The second danger involved a possible change in procedures. Although the last departmental conference had confirmed the normal operation of the baggage channel, one of my papers might contain a minor discrepancy unknown to me but detectable to a control point officer. From past experience, I had seen how the MfS occasionally inserted a special security mark—a dot in a particular place, for example, or a distinctive way of indicating the date—that was known only to a handful of people. In this event, with enough armed security personnel in the station to overpower me, I also had little chance of avoiding capture.

The next stage actually presented the greatest element of uncertainty. Television cameras had been placed throughout the "Western section" of the station, and at least six monitors were to be found in the main control room. Whereas my cover story would allow me to move freely on the train platform, I was not permitted to board either a regular or an express subway bound for West Berlin. If I were seen doing so on the television screen, a red signal would stop the car almost instantly. In reality, this means of crossing the border was as problematic as taking the train to Hanover. Nevertheless, I would be spared the interrogation while confined on the train, and would also have my pistol with me.

Before me was the red and white barrier that read: "Stop! Border area. Entry only for service personnel and those leaving the country." This was the point where East Berliners normally waited for relatives arriving from the FRG. About a hundred yards away stood a security control building—known to local residents as "Circus Mielke"—where these visitors underwent an inspection of their papers.

I passed through the narrow gateway and continued to the door marked service entrance. After taking a deep breath, I went inside. Fortunately, the procedure was familiar to me from many previous visits. I also knew that my next obstacle was the MfS officer on duty that night. As the door from the outside vestibule locked behind me, it would now be up to him whether to let me proceed to the "Western section" of the station. A stout man with a quite pleasant face, he gave me an inquisitive look.

"Lousy weather out there," I said, attempting to strike up a normal conversation. "I sure wouldn't mind getting transferred to your outfit and sit in a nice warm room all day."

He grinned. "If you work hard and get to my age, then you can certainly apply for a reassignment."

As I began to show him all my papers, only the "special duty order" proved of interest. After looking at the form for a while, he asked in an official tone of voice, "Do you consider this to be filled out properly?"

For an instant, my heart stopped, but then my calm returned.

"How should I know?" I replied. "The secretary filled it out, and my boss signed it. It's bound to be okay."

"But it isn't," the man insisted. "As of the first of the year, there's been a new regulation requiring that the specific purpose be included. Since you apparently want to deposit a briefcase, the phrase 'baggage exfiltration' must be written in parentheses next to 'personal operational business.'"

Despite having clearly heard him before, I asked, "Since when has this rule been in effect?"

"As of January first, nineteen seventy-nine," he answered.

"Do you realize our secretary is so dumb that it won't register with her until next January first?"

The officer made a noncommittal grunt. Knowing that a telephone call to the HVA duty officer would spell my demise, I reached for the pistol in my overcoat pocket. Yet in the end, like most deskbound MfS bureaucrats, he preferred the path of least effort.

"All right," he said, "I'll let it go this time, but be sure to tell your division about it. Where would we be if the rules were not followed? Incidentally, the number of pieces of baggage to be deposited doesn't have to be indicated." He stamped the paper with the "exit trip" seal and then pressed the buzzer to release the door.

After following several corridors, I reached the main floor of the "Western section." Because the express trains to West Berlin left from the same area upstairs as the trains bound for points in the FRG, an airtight video surveillance had to be assumed. I therefore decided to go downstairs to the subway line that operated under West Berlin authority. Since my presumed task involved the deposit of a briefcase in a baggage locker— acting as if I were simply arriving from West Berlin—it would have been standard procedure for me anyway.

To reach the subway line, I first had to cross the platform of the so-called "cellar-train," which also connected the two halves of the city. Despite being on the platform when a train happened to arrive, I resisted the strong temptation to get on board. In all likelihood, the television cameras had me in full view, for not only had I just entered the "Western section" but the sparsity of passengers on the cold winter night made my movements all the easier to follow. At the same time, I realized that waiting too long on the platform would seem suspicious as well.

After next walking through a long tunnel, I came to the subway entrance. A glance at the ticket booth reminded me of having brought along West German bills but no coins. As there was no barrier—and not a minute to spare—I decided to dispense with a ticket and go directly to the platform. To my keen disappointment, a southbound train was just pulling away when I arrived.

According to the posted timetable, a northbound train was not due for another six minutes. To minimize my exposure to the television camera, I tried to conceal myself behind one of the supporting columns. As this agonizingly long wait continued, my thoughts raced ahead to the next stages of my plan. The most pressing task was to contact the BND people so as not to delay the operations involving Helga and her son and the capture of the West agents. Since my arrival in Hanover was still expected and no one in

West Berlin knew about this situation, I would have to deliver the news in person. At least the northbound train headed in the direction of Tegel Airport, where I could take a regular flight to Munich and then a taxi to Pullach. Of course, this was mere fantasizing on my part until the border had been safely crossed.

To my relief, the train arrived on time. Only a few people got off and on. One of the last to enter, I positioned myself in the first car directly behind the driver. After putting down the briefcase and reaching for the pistol inside my coat, I remained standing in the nearly empty car. Yet no alarm sounded, and the train pulled away from the station. Unfortunately, with a large section of East Berlin left to traverse, the danger was far from over.

After a short distance, the train suddenly slowed to a bare creep. Knowing that we had not yet entered West Berlin, I was now prepared to hijack the train if necessary. Yet once the empty, sealed-up Reinhardstrasse station had passed by, the train began to resume its speed. Two other deserted stations caused the same deceleration, and each time my heart skipped a beat. The train's final return to normal speed, however, meant that my victory over the MfS had been cinched.

At that moment, I felt neither relief at ending this period of long-term stress and recent fear nor anticipation of starting a new life in the West. My only thought concerned the sheer implausibility of outwitting one of the world's tightest security organizations for more than two and a half years. Indeed, what mattered now was simply the fact that I had won a very difficult war.

The first station in West Berlin, just a few yards from the Wall, was marked "Reinickendorfer Strasse." Uncertain as to whether the subway continued to Tegel Airport, I decided to get off and try to find a taxi. The sight of the busy thoroughfare and the bright neon signs gave me my final assurance that the GDR—typified by its dreary street lighting—had been left behind.

A taxi drove up, and I got inside. "Take me to Tegel Airport," I told the driver.

Once we were under way, he inquired about the destination of my flight. Reluctant to say "Munich" and hear from him that no more flights left that night, I hesitantly replied, "I don't know yet. I just need to take the first plane to the FRG."

The man gave me a surprised look. "Surely you must know your destination."

I was still a bit confused but managed to say, "I must get to Frankfurt. If the last plane has already departed, then I'll fly to any point in the FRG and take a train from there."

Despite his doubts about the availability of any more flights that night, he followed my instructions, and we speedily arrived at the airport. I then politely declined his offer to wait until a flight had been confirmed and gave him a West German fifty-mark bill for all his efforts. That he probably considered me a lunatic seemed beside the point.

Inside the terminal, I saw the last shift of workers putting away their papers. When informed that the next flight was not until the following morning, I knew that such a delay was out of the question. My absence at the Friedrichstrasse station must have been discovered in the meantime and a red alert sounded. Most likely, my identity would also have been ascertained. In that case, the MfS was certain to launch a thorough search in West Berlin, intending either to capture or to eliminate me.

I therefore proceeded to the airport police station, hoping that a signal could also be sent to the BND to start the operation for Helga and her son. Upon finding three policemen sitting in a cozy, warm room, I asked to speak to their commanding officer right away.

"What do you want?" one of them asked. "We're all equal in rank here."

That left me with no choice but to identify myself. "I am an officer of the GDR Ministry of State Security and have just defected from East Berlin. Please contact the Federal Intelligence Service in Pullach. They're expecting me." To confirm my statement, I placed my official identity card on the table.

They showed not a flicker of emotion at my revelation. "Sit down and have a cup of coffee with us," one of them said. "There's also some cake that my wife just baked."

In the meantime, following a careful inspection of my identity card, they decided to notify their superior. As one of them remarked, "We've got to go by the rules."

Some time later, the policeman who was to place the phone call emerged from a back office. "Because of their jurisdiction over the airport, my boss will have to contact the French officials. That could take a while, so have another piece of cake."

Another half hour passed, and then a French military policeman appeared. As he understood not a word of German, there was no point in trying to explain the situation. These delays were driving me to despair.

Within an hour, the room was packed with people, all looking at me like a sideshow curiosity. One person, however, conveyed the impression of being involved in intelligence work. Taking me aside, he whispered, "Pullach has been informed. Welcome to the West!"

At last everything began to move quickly, and I felt safely out of the MfS's reach.

The following morning, as my plane started its descent into Munich, I saw the glittering snow-capped peaks of the Bavarian Alps in the distance.

A group of BND headquarters officials were waiting for me. I recognized two of them from our Helsinki meeting. "Good morning," the leader of the group said. "Well, it finally came off. We're very happy to have you with us."

He then escorted me to his car. As we started to drive to a BND safe house, he asked, "Is there anything that should be taken care of immediately?"

On the plane, I had drawn up a list of twenty-two top-priority agents. Since the BND already had received detailed information from me about these individuals, only a few minor points needed clarification. He assured me that the necessary preparations for their arrests had been made.

I next posed the question of great personal concern to me. "How did the operation go with Helga and her son?"

"We're still working on it," he answered. Presumably there had been some technical complications because of the weather.

At the safe house, I started unpacking my briefcase, attempting to arrange the assorted original files and microfilms according to subject matter and degree of urgency. In the meantime, we were joined by other officials from the BND, the federal prosecutor's office, and the counterintelligence authority. In fact, there were numerous persons sitting on the floor amidst these documents trying to make their initial appraisal. Slowly, however, a general order came to prevail.

A stenographer arrived with a typewriter to record my verbal testimony. Quite soon—seeing my ability to formulate the topics and then establish a logical explanatory sequence—the BND officials dispensed with their own questions and needed only to mention an occasional key phrase. Indeed, a compliment about my systematic approach to matters was my first sign of recognition from them.

For three days and nights, we worked in this concentrated fashion, breaking only for coffee, quick snacks, and an occasional beer or cognac. Still, in the back of my mind was my worry about Helga and her son. When the news of their successful departure from the GDR finally reached me, I experienced a boundless relief and joy.

One other incident during this period made a strong impression. While examining some of these documents, an elderly BND man—himself a mixture of scientist and intelligence professional—suddenly exclaimed, "What, Jansen's been promoted to major!" A number of similar remarks about other "old acquaintances" followed.

When this BND man and I fell into conversation, it was soon apparent that his familiarity with certain HVA personnel nearly exceeded my own knowledge. It seemed as if I were back in the MfS canteen talking with a departmental colleague. Yet this moment soon vanished, and the door closed permanently on that part of my life. It was better that way.

12

Epilogue

The immediate repercussions of my defection proved quite gratifying. Within a matter of days, seventeen agents working primarily in the field of nuclear research were arrested by West German authorities, while another fifteen, fearing their own apprehension, made a hasty retreat back to the GDR. It should also be noted that two of them—Reiner Fülle and Erich Ziegenhain—became so disillusioned afterward that they decided to return to the FRG and face trial. Attempting a similar escape, a third agent was caught at the Austrian-Hungarian border and sentenced to life imprisonment by an East Berlin military court. Clearly a severe psychological blow had been dealt to the MfS, for nothing held higher priority than the maintenance of strict internal security. It is little wonder that I later received a death sentence in absentia.

Of even greater value to the BND were the 20,000 pages of internal documents that I had secretly collected. From these papers it was possible to gain a clearer knowledge of the MfS's actual hierarchy as well as the lines of communication between individual units. Some of this information also shed light on certain key areas of cooperation with the KGB. A number of these documents—notably Mielke's speech to the MfS in October 1978 stressing the need for increased military espionage against the West—were subsequently made public. Although my defection was headline news in the West German press, I preferred to remain personally anonymous and work behind the scenes with both counterintelligence and foreign intelligence officials.

Whatever damage I was able to inflict, the MfS nevertheless remained a highly resilient and resourceful organization. Numerous cases surfaced during the next decade showing that its penetration of nearly all aspects of the FRG continued unabated. In the governmental sphere, for instance, information was still being gathered by various secretaries who had been either seduced by a disguised East German officer or directly placed by the HVA itself. Not even the Federal Office for the Protection of the Constitution, the agency charged with domestic counterintelligence, could be considered immune, for in 1985 a senior official and MfS mole, Hansjoachim Tiedge, made a dramatic defection to the GDR. What baffled me, however, was the public's complacent reaction to such revelations and the almost complete indifference to matters of basic security. Was the reason, I often asked myself, merely that the everyday reality of espionage lacked the kind of excitement found in most spy novels?

The events that began in the summer of 1989 and led to the eventual dissolution of the GDR made a profound impression on me. I could well understand the desire for a freer existence by thousands of young persons and their families fleeing the GDR. When mounting protests targeted the Honecker regime and the Stasi in particular, a predictable effort at damage control was made. Within days after the resignation of Erich Mielke came the announcement that the MfS was being replaced by a so-called "Office of National Security." Although the new communist government promised massive dismissals and "fresh thinking in questions of public order," the institution simply lacked the capacity for genuine reform. As most GDR citizens knew, the "Nasis," as they were quickly dubbed, would continue to serve their masters in the same old manner. There was no alternative short of total abolition.

The enormous legacy of the MfS will be felt for many years to come. While some former officers immediately sought employment either with the KGB or with certain Third World intelligence organizations, the majority remained in Germany. Finding suitable occupations for these persons in an economy suffering from serious unemployment has proven to be a daunting and controversial task. There is the further problem of determining which officials should be liable to criminal prosecution. Despite the proposal of a general amnesty, there remains an intense residue of hatred for the Stasi as well as a desire that top-ranking officials be held accountable for their past actions. In this regard, it is worth noting that three of my superior officers—Horst Vogel, Gerhard Jauck, and Christian Streubel (all real names)—continued to hold top HVA positions until the very end.

The greatest concern of former GDR citizens, however, revolves around the question of access to their individual files. As someone who worked very intensively with these dossiers, I find the matter not easily resolvable. Not only did an average person's file contain roughly forty other names, but the information included might have been erroneously gathered or deliberately altered. Given the sheer number of persons involved—approximately six million East Germans and two and a half million West Germans—there have been suggestions that all the files should be destroyed immediately. Such a move, flying so blatantly in the face of public opinion, seems ill-conceived. On the other hand, allowing unrestricted inspection would have a profoundly disruptive effect on the entire society.

I should also not forget where my own Stasi career had begun. The physics department of the University of Leipzig continued to maintain its reputation as a prime MfS recruiting ground long after my departure. Yet, as academic institutions now undergo the process of "de-Stasification," there is an all too common tendency to overlook such instances and concentrate instead on members of the humanities and social science faculties. As my own activities testify, the MfS embraced the scientific community as firmly and enthusiastically as any other group at its disposal.

One final thought bears stressing. The larger struggle reflected in my own experiences is far from over. Recently we have witnessed how the KGB sought to thwart the democratic movement in the former Soviet Union in order to retain ultimate control, while in North Korea and the People's Republic of China—as in many Third World countries—totalitarian security forces continue to hold the upper hand. Only with greater knowledge and awareness can an effective democratic opposition be mounted. Toward that end, I hope that I have made a modest contribution.

Index

Academy of Sciences, East
    German, 28, 35, 37, 102,
    106, 136, 175
Agfa film company, 159, 167
Agriculture, Ministry of, East
    German, 124
Arafat, Yasir, 73
Arndt, Holm, 68, 69
Arnold, Gerhard ("Sturm"),
    123–26, 128–30, 149, 164,
    170, 176, 186–88, 197,
    213, 215

Barnikol, 149
Basic Treaty (1972), 70
Becker, Major, 93
Bellman, Lieutenant Klaus, 63
Berlin, Free University of, 97
Berlin Wall, 51, 65, 77
Berndt, Klaus, 94
Bertag, Peter, 3, 62, 157–59, 165,
    181, 183, 196, 198–99,
    222
Biermann, Wolf, 185–86
Brandt, Willy, 99n
Brodehl, Sergeant Sigrid, 48

Buchenwald, 68
Büchner, Alfred ("Günther"),
    59–61, 66
Bunke, Tamara, 18, 19

California, University of, at
    Berkeley, 76
Castro, Fidel, 18
Central Institute of Electron
    Physics, East German, 102,
    108
Central Institute for Nuclear
    Research, East Germany, 55
Central Office of Statistics, East
    German, 26
Cheka, 46n
Chief Intelligence Directorate
    (HVA), East German,
    44–46, 48, 66, 68–73,
    101, 116, 117, 121–22,
    145, 146, 151, 166, 177,
    214, 215, 221, 228, 233
    Arnold and, 124–26, 128, 130,
    187, 188
    China and, 181
    Division X of, 143–45

embassy positions of, 155
falsified documents issued by,
    191
Fülle and, 162, 163, 170, 173,
    174
Gärtner and, 50–53
Hauffe and, 103–15
internal structure of, 169, 178
and Lorenz kidnapping, 126–27
Luca and, 195
party organization elections in,
    223
Singer and, 82
Sperber and, 76–78, 133
technical division of, 139
Teichner and, 84, 87
training school of, 56, 58, 61,
    63–65, 134, 148, 184, 196,
    218
Western assignments in, 97–99
Chief Section for Personal
    Security, East German, 46
China, People's Republic of, 181,
    196, 198, 234
split with Soviet Union, 95
Combat Groups of the Working
    Class, 37
Commercial Organization (HO), 6
Cuba, 18–19
Culture, Ministry of, East German,
    142
Czechoslovakia, Soviet invasion of,
    15, 22, 25, 96

Defense, Ministry of, West
    German, 153, 166
Dobbertin, Rolf ("Sperber"),
    75–80, 103, 130–33, 149,
    155–57, 164, 166, 176–82,
    194–96, 198
Doerge, Hans-Ullrich, 73–74
Dresden Technical University, 18,
    66, 81, 82, 85, 87, 94, 96,
    145

Egypt, 194–95
Ehrhardt, Elke, 86–92
Engels, Friedrich, 10
Eschberger, Sergeant Iris, 45
Eurocommunism, 84

Federal Intelligence Service

(BND), West German, 1–4,
    6, 7, 67, 101, 118, 122,
    133, 154, 155, 159–65,
    168–70, 173, 175–76, 187,
    200, 212
and defection, 207, 216–26,
    228, 230–32
first contact with, 38–39
personal contact with, 177–85,
    188–94, 196–98, 204–5,
    209, 210, 213, 214
Federal Office of Military
    Technology and
    Procurement, West German,
    150, 152, 154
Fehr, Petra, 137–42
Feigenspan, Berhnard ("Max"),
    147–48
Feliks-Dzerzhinskii Guard
    Regiment, 46, 72
Felke, Heinz, 55
Foreign Affairs, Ministry of, East
    German, 84
Frederick the Great, 111
Free German Youth (FDJ), 7,
    10–12, 14, 17, 19, 21, 25,
    48, 62, 69, 72, 75
Friedrich, Herbert ("Bodo"),
    102–3, 105–11, 145
Friedrich-Engels Prize Award
    First Class, 69, 123, 130
Fruck, General, 58
Fuchs, Klaus, 147
Fülle, Reiner ("Klaus"), 162–64,
    170–76, 232

German Communist Party (DKP),
    137, 138, 140–42, 144
German Nuclear Forum, 147
Gewecke, Heinrick, 137–41
Gey, Lieutenant Klaus, 63
Gottfried, Harald ("Gärtner"),
    48–55, 57, 64, 66, 88
Göttingen, University of, 105
Greek Communist Party, 81
Greifswald, University of, 103
Grosse, Lieutenant Peter, 43–44,
    57–59, 64, 88, 89
Grossmann, Werner, 215
Guevara, Che, 18–19
Guillaume, Günther, 99, 114–15,
    161, 166

Haering, Captain Günther, 47
Halle University, 66, 68, 73, 97
Hauffe, Karl ("Fellow"), 103–15,
    117, 120, 149, 158, 159,
    164, 166–68, 176
Heinrich, Major Günther, 52, 54
Heintze, Werner, 59, 155,
    162–63, 170, 175
Helsinki Final Act (1975), 214
Hengst, Major Werner, 60, 94, 98,
    103–4, 121, 157, 194–96,
    225
Herrmann, Rudolf, 120–21, 123–24
Hertz, Gustav, 36
Hiess, Heinz ("Rechner"),
    125–26, 129, 187
Higher Education, Ministry of,
    East German, 104, 175
Hillmann, Heinz, 175
Hippe, Manfred, 145–47
Hitler, Adolf, 15
Hoffmann, Heinz, 149
Honecker, Erich, 74, 214, 233
Honecker, Margot, 119
Hübner, Klaus, 25–26
Huether, Lieutenant Axel, 44, 46,
    75, 77, 80–87, 94, 95, 122,
    123
Humbolt University, 66, 86, 115,
    120
Hungary, 1956 uprising in, 47
Huth, Paul-Rainer, 148

IBM, 124–26, 129, 130, 197
Institute for Nuclear Physics, 147
Interatom, 97
Interior, Ministry of, East German,
    36, 81
International Atomic Energy
    Commission, 148

Jaenicke, General Horst, 65
Jauck, Captain Gerhard, 47, 126,
    148–49, 165, 206, 207,
    213, 219, 221–26, 233
JET project, 181
Jülich nuclear research station,
    159
Junghanns, Lieutenant Olaf, 44,
    59, 60, 116, 166, 185, 207

Kapitsa, Peter, 104

Karl-Marx University, 11–12, 66,
    68
Karlsruhe nuclear research center,
    50, 163, 170, 173
Karlsruhe Technical University, 49
KGB, 16, 72, 80, 103–5, 108,
    131–35, 158, 168, 178,
    181, 187, 188, 232–34
Kiessig, Lieutenant Horst, 44, 148
Kind, Steffen ("Film"), 153–54
Klein, Hilde, 50, 88
Kodak, 159
Kontos, Alexander and Marie, 81
Kremp, Walter ("Farmer"), 124
Kulka, Herbert, 130

Lawrence Livermore Laboratory,
    76
Leipzig, University of, 100, 234
Leipzig trade fair, 27–28, 44, 52,
    56–61, 123, 158, 194
Lenin, V. I., 10, 101, 104
Leuna Works, 8, 9
Liebknecht, Karl, 222
Linder, Hermann, 116
Linke, Reinhard, 33–36, 38, 42,
    52–55, 98, 102, 103, 106,
    175
Lorenz, Peter, 126–27, 129, 148
Luca, Egicio di ("Faust"), 194–96
Lutze husband-and-wife team,
    166
Luxemburg, Rosa, 222

Magnus, Gustav, 34
Mao Zedong, 132
Marcuse, Herbert, 140
Markianov, Dr., 167, 168
Martin-Luther University, 69
Marx, Karl, 10, 75, 140, 159
Marxism-Leninism, 63–64, 83
Max-Planck Library, 36
Merseburg Polytechnic High
    School, 10
Mielke, Erich, 53, 58, 69, 113,
    149, 174, 186, 232, 233
Military Counterintelligence
    Service, West German, 153
Mössbauer spectronomy, 35
Murgelescu (scientist), 168

Nasser, Gamal Abdel, 194–95

National Committee of Physics, 102
National People's Army (NVA), 41–42, 62, 128–29, 149, 154, 158, 183
  Border Guards of, 79
  Service Medal of, 183
NATO, 149
Nazis, 55, 68, 83
Neumann, Colonel Willi, 48, 49, 52–54, 66, 89, 104, 107, 108, 131, 132
NKGB/MGB, 170
Noetzoldt, Peter, 68, 69
North Korea, 234

October Revolution, 104
Olivetti, 166
Olympic Games (1972), 63
Operation Registration, 166, 174, 176, 197
Ovsyannikov, Captain Igor, 132, 206

Palestine Liberation Organization (PLO), 73
Patzelt, Herbert, 55, 80–81
Peace Council, 59
People's Police, 86, 128–29
Petras, Ehrenfried, 55
Physics Society, 32–35, 37, 40, 42, 55, 70, 102, 103, 106, 175, 183
Poland, unrest in, 96
Prague Spring, 14–15
Princeton University, 76
Project Beam, 187–88, 197
Proksch, Udo, 166

Red Army, 134
Red Army Faction, 126
Reif, Roland, 145–47
Research and Technology, Ministry of, East German, 97, 148
Riesa Steelworks, 15, 27
Ritter, Hartmut, 100
Robotron, 126
Rockstroh, Rudi, 55, 147
Rome University, 83
Rompe, Robert, 35, 76, 103–5, 107–10, 112, 167, 168

Rostock, University of, 75, 76
Roth, Klaus, 26, 34
Rutherford, Ernest, 104

Sacher, Dr. ("Sander"), 199
Sadat, Anwar, 195
Scharlibbe, Lieutenant, 149–52
Schilde, Rolf, 96, 145, 147
Schlenkrich, Werner, 191
Schmidt, Arthur, 10
Schmidt, Helmut, 115
Science and Technology, Ministry of, East German, 60, 108, 109
Second World War, 96, 134
Senger, Günther ("Hauser"), 150–56, 164, 176, 200, 203, 205
Siemens, 150
Sino-Soviet split, 77
Social Democratic Party, West German, 99n, 114
Socialist Unity Party (SED), East German, 10n, 11–13, 17, 18, 33, 37–39, 44, 49, 50, 55, 59, 66, 74–76, 94, 118, 128, 140, 149, 161, 170, 193, 198, 200
  Central Committee of, 35, 103, 104, 138, 147
  district leadership elections of, 223
  hypocrisy of, 96
  PLO and, 73
Society for Sport and Technology (GST), 13
  Central School of, 62–65
Sorge, Richard, 134
Soviet Union, 70, 77, 96, 103, 104, 112, 133–37, 158, 167, 198
  Cuba and, 18–19
  democratic movement in, 234
  economy of, 105
  Hungarian uprising against, 47
  identity cards in, 37
  invasion of Czechoslovakia by, 14–15, 22, 25
  June 17, 1953, uprising against, 9
  Nasser and, 195
  nuclear arsenal of, 170–71, 178

split with China, 77
See also KGB
Spiegle, Der, 13
Sporting Facilities Authority, 117
Sputnik, 9
Stalin, Josef, 77
Stasi, *see* State Security, Ministry
    of
State Security, Ministry of (MfS),
    East German, 1–7, 12, 13,
    23–26, 29, 30, 39, 41, 59,
    60, 95, 106, 118, 134, 143,
    144, 146–47, 160–62, 164,
    168, 174, 180, 181, 189,
    190, 192, 199–200, 206,
    208, 209, 211–13
  apartment building for
    employees of, 47, 116, 168
  Arnold and, 123–26, 128–29
  Biermann and, 185–86
  Border Work Patrol of, 63, 154
  commissary of, 45
  contract with, 43
  counterintelligence section of,
    62, 161, 193–94
  and defection, 218, 220–23,
    225–33
  establishment of, 103
  Fehr and, 138–42
  Gärtner and, 48–55
  and Guillaume affair, 99,
    114–15
  headquarters staff of, 58
  Helsinki representative of, 214
  internal security system of, 215
  internal structure of, 169, 178
  interrogation prison of, 54
  Luca and, 194–96
  Main Division I, 149–51, 153,
    183
  Main Division II, 205
  Main Division VI, 70, 71, 79,
    91, 93, 94, 98, 178
  Main Division VIII, 188
  Main Division for Personal
    Protection, 73
  Physics Society and, 33–36, 40,
    175
  promotions in, 102, 113, 121,
    157
  questionnaire for personnel of,
    32

  recruitment by, 16–21, 57, 61,
    66–68, 72–73, 81,
    120–21, 158, 165–66, 234
  regional offices of, 145, 148,
    154, 198, 201, 203
  Senger and, 149–55
  specialized divisions of, 43
  Sperber and, 75–80, 133, 182
  Teichner and, 81–94
  training school of, 62–65
  twenty-fifth birthday of, 101,
    121
  VSH card index of, 96
  West German arrests of
    personnel of, 176
  Wismut Installation Authority
    and, 170–72
  See also Chief Intelligence
    Directorate
Stiller, Gerd ("Singer"), 82–85,
    87, 88, 136–37
Stiller, Heinz, 82
Streubel, Lieutenant Christian, 3,
    43–45, 47, 54, 56–59, 61,
    65, 67–69, 75, 78–79, 82,
    84, 87, 88, 91–93, 95–96,
    102, 105–10, 112–16,
    122–23, 125, 127–33, 137,
    138, 140–44, 147, 149,
    153, 155–58, 163, 165,
    170, 173–75, 177–83,
    185–87, 193, 195–97, 205,
    207–9, 213–16, 233
Sumpf, Gertraude ("Karla"), 72,
    137, 139

Teichner, Richard ("Ernesto"),
    81–94
Terber, Manfred, 53–54
Theurich, Bernhard ("Mark"),
    155–57
Tiedge, Hansjoachim, 233
Tietz, Lieutenant Klaus, 5–6

Ulbricht, Walter, 11, 12, 26, 149,
    195
Ullrich, "Didi," 134
Unesco, 106
United States
  human rights campaign of,
    185
  nuclear arsenal of, 178

Vienna, University of, 165
Vogel, Colonel Horst, 45–46, 57,
    60, 62, 70, 93, 97–98, 113,
    116–17, 121, 130, 132,
    134, 135, 141–45, 148,
    165, 174, 178, 182, 183,
    187, 196, 206, 233

Warsaw Pact United Strike Force,
    15
Wehrmacht, 134
Weiberg, General Heinrich, 46,
    53, 121
Weiczorek, Heinz, 55
Weigel husband-and-wife team,
    166
Wein, Wolfgang ("Prokop"), 265
Wendel, Colonel Otto, 62

West Berlin Christian Democratic
    Union, 126
West German Army, 149
Wismut Installation Authority
    (OVW), 95, 170–72
Wolf, Lieutenant-General Markus,
    46, 50, 53, 87, 133, 139,
    141–42, 177, 187, 215,
    223
World Youth and Student Festival,
    72, 75

Young Pioneers, 9

Zagreb trade fair, 177, 180,
    197
Ziegenhaun, Erich, 232
Zeisler, Werner, 134–36